LEARNING TO LIBERATE

Few problems in education are as pressing as the crisis in urban schools. Though educators have tried a wide range of remedies, dismal results persist. This is especially true for low-income youth of color, who drop out of school—and into incarceration—at extremely high rates. The dual calamity of underachievement in schools and violence in many communities across the country is often met with blame and cynicism, and with a host of hurtful and unproductive quick fixes: blaming educators, pitting schools against each other, turning solely to the private sector, and ratcheting up the pressure on teachers and students. But real change will not be possible until we shift our focus from finding fault to developing partnerships, from documenting problems to discovering solutions. *Learning to Liberate* does just that by presenting true and compelling community-based approaches to school reform.

Drawing on over three years of ethnographic research, Vajra Watson explores the complicated process of reaching and teaching today's students. She reveals how four nontraditional educators successfully empower young people who have repeatedly been left behind. Using portraiture, a methodology rooted in vivid storytelling, Watson analyzes each educator's specific teaching tactics. Uncovering four distinct pedagogies—of communication, community, compassion, and commitment—she then pulls together their key strategies to create a theoretically grounded framework that is both useful and effective. A poignant, insightful, and practical analysis, *Learning to Liberate* is a timely resource for all educators and youth-serving practitioners who are committed to transforming "at-risk" youth into "at-promise" individuals who put their agency and potential into action in their schools and neighborhoods.

Vajra Watson is Director of Research and Policy for Equity in the School of Education at the University of California, Davis.

The Critical Social Thought Series

Edited by Michael W. Apple
University of Wisconsin—Madison

Public Schools that Work
Creating Community
Gregory A. Smith, editor

Power and Method
Political Activism and Educational Research
Andrew Gitlin, editor

Critical Ethnography in Educational Research
A Theoretical and Practical Guide
Phil Francis Carspecken

The Uses of Culture
Education and the Limits of Ethnic Affiliation
Cameron McCarthy

Education, Power, and Personal Biography
Dialogues with Critical Educators
Carlos Alberto Torres, editor

Contradictions of School Reform
Educational Costs of Standardized Testing
Linda M. McNeil

Act Your Age!
A Cultural Construction of Adolescence
Nancy Lesko

Tough Fronts
The Impact of Street Culture on Schooling
L. Janelle Dance

Political Spectacle and the Fate of American Schools
Mary Lee Smith with Walter Heinecke, Linda Miller-Kahn, and Patricia F. Jarvis

Rethinking Scientific Literacy
Wolff-Michael Roth and Angela Calabrese Barton

High Stakes Education
Inequality, Globalization, and Urban School Reform
Pauline Lipman

Learning to Labor in New Times
Nadine Dolby and Greg Dimitriadis, editors

Working Method
Research and Social Justice
Lois Weis and Michelle Fine

Class Reunion
The Remaking of the American White Working Class
Lois Weis

Race, Identity, and Representation in Education, Second Edition
Cameron McCarthy, Warren Crichlow, Greg Dimitriadis, and Nadine Dolby

Radical Possibilities
Public Policy, Urban Education, and a New Social Movement
Jean Anyon

Could It Be Otherwise?
Parents and the Inequities of Public School Choice
Lois André-Bechely

Reading and Writing the World with Mathematics
Eric Gustein

Market Movements
African American Involvement in School Voucher Reform
Thomas C. Pedroni

Rightist Multiculturalism
Core Lessons on Neoconservative School Reform
Kristen L. Buras

Unequal by Design
High-Stakes Testing and the Standardization of Inequality
Wayne Au

Black Literate Lives
Historical and Contemporary Perspectives
Maisha T. Fisher

Hidden Markets
The New Education Privatization
Patricia Burch

Critical Perspectives on bell hooks
Maria del Guadalupe Davidson and George Yancy, editors

Advocacy Leadership
Toward a Post-Reform Agenda in Education
Gary L. Anderson

Race, Whiteness, and Education
Zeus Leonardo

Controversy in the Classroom
The Democratic Power of Discussion
Diana E. Hess

The New Political Economy of Urban Education
Neoliberalism, Race, and the Right to the City
Pauline Lipman

Critical Curriculum Studies
Education, Consciousness, and the Politics of Knowing
Wayne Au

Learning to Liberate
Community-Based Solutions to the Crisis in Urban Education
Vajra Watson

LEARNING TO LIBERATE

Community-Based Solutions to the Crisis in Urban Education

Vajra Watson

Routledge
Taylor & Francis Group

NEW YORK AND LONDON

First published 2012
by Routledge
711 Third Avenue, New York, NY 10017

Simultaneously published in the UK
by Routledge
2 Park Square, Milton Park, Abingdon, Oxon OX14 4RN

Routledge is an imprint of the Taylor & Francis Group, an informa business

Library of Congress Cataloging in Publication Data
Watson, Vajra.
Learning to liberate : community-based solutions to the crisis in urban education / Vajra Watson.
p. cm. — (The critical social thought series ; 37)
Includes bibliographical references and index.
1. Education, Urban—United States. 2. Community and school—United States. I. Title.
LC5131.W38 2011
370.9173′20973—dc23
2011020518

ISBN: 978-0-415-89836-2 (hbk)
ISBN: 978-0-415-89837-9 (pbk)
ISBN: 978-0-203-19740-0 (ebk)

Typeset in Bembo
by Prepress Projects Ltd, Perth, UK

Printed and bound in the United States of America on acid-free paper by IBT Global

2: JAYDA BOSS, B-TOWN FINEST
who convinced me this story
had to be told and published.
I thank you and love you all wayz and 4ever.

CONTENTS

SERIES EDITOR'S INTRODUCTION

There are moments when books are published at exactly the right time. This is certainly true of *Learning to Liberate*. It provides a powerful statement about what does and does not work in educating youth in some of our most troubled areas. Vajra Watson asks us to think across institutions, to connect what does and does not happen in schools to not only the wider society, but also to educational practices and agents who succeed where so many others have failed. The questions she asks seem simple enough. What can we learn from community-based education and the people who engage in it? What do these deeply committed programs and people do that makes such a powerful difference in the lives of youth of color?

The answers she provides are central to any serious struggle to build an education worthy of its name. It resonates with those of us who agree with the perspectives of Paulo Freire, Myles Horton, Carter G. Woodson, and the many others who have devoted their lives and work to challenging the taken for granted policies and practices that now dominate education. It also will resonate with those of us who actively seek respectful and culturally responsive pedagogies that provide dispossessed youth with critical identities and a sense of possibility. And finally, it will speak directly to those who yearn for hope, for those who say that a continuation of the policies that fail, demonize, and blame urban youth is not and must not be an acceptable answer.

Throughout the country, education is seen as being in crisis. No matter what one's political affiliations, there is justifiable concern about things such as "the achievement gap," about whether schools are meeting the needs of students and communities, about the ends and means of education. Major national policies such as No Child Left Behind and more recently Race to the Top have been proposed, often with a good deal of supporting rhetoric. Yet, looked at from below, from what is actually happening economically and educationally in local communities, these are deeply misguided policies. Educational policies that centralize control, that somehow think that the symbolic violence of a reductive common curriculum that is enforced by an ever increasing regime of testing, and that are deeply disrespectful of the complex and difficult labor of teachers and other educators are not the answer. Nor are policies that assume that privatization and competition will somehow be the engine of thoughtful educational transformation (Apple, 2006; Ravitch, 2010).

What if we trusted communities and the resources that they bring? What if we were more respectful of the intellectual and emotional strengths of youth in these communities? What if we directed out attention to those activist educators who have built programs and relations that have profound and lasting effects on the youth that this society seems to basically throw away in its mad rush to cut budgets and destroy hope?

Watson wants to change what is seen as "what works." She argues for the crucial significance of an answer that goes well beyond our almost religious fascination with test scores and their reduction of knowledge to that which can be easily measured and their resultant marginalization and alienation of identifiable youth. She challenges us to create an educational environment that focuses much more both on critical understandings of the world and one's place in it and on the utter importance of deeply caring relationships. Only by linking the intellectual, the political, and the affective together, and basing these relationships within caring communities, can a powerful education be created and sustained.

With its focus on issues involving "care, love, and solidarity," in many ways *Learning to Liberate* can also be seen as a major contribution to the debates over what Nancy Fraser (1997) has called the politics of redistribution (e.g., economic justice) and the politics of recognition (e.g., cultural and personal respect). It is not "just" that the affective system concerns the politics of recognition, although it does. But it also goes beyond this. The affective system is just as foundational as other structured and structuring systems that serve as the building blocks of society (Lynch, Baker, & Lyons, 2009). For Watson, a society and its major institutions that do not reorganize themselves around the norms and rationality of love, care, and solidarity and do not engage in successful struggles over these forms cannot be considered truly serious about equality.

As I have argued in other places (Apple, 2006), this is especially important given what is currently happening in education. Increasingly, under the growing power of neoliberal ideological forms, education is being commodified. Its institutions are being turned into "products" that are to be subjected to the logic of markets. Students' worth is only to be judged by their test scores. And both the students and the people who work in educational institutions at all levels are to be valued only by their contributions to an increasingly unequal economy. Not only is this amoral (if not immoral) set of assumptions destructive of an education worthy of its name but it devalues and is deeply disrespectful of the labor of love, care, and solidarity that underpins so much of educational activities inside and outside formal institutions of education.

Learning to Liberate goes beyond the general arguments concerning these claims. It provides refreshing portraits of the people and the institutions involved in doing all of this. Unlike many critical educators who give formulaic or rhetorical answers to the questions of what we should do, Watson demonstrates the actual details of what is so necessary if we are to make a difference in the lives of disenfranchised youth in urban settings. These community-based educators foster a culture of social resistance through four pedagogic approaches—pedagogies of communication, community, compassion, and commitment. As Vajra Watson shows, through these approaches they "redirect the trajectory of *at-risk* youth into *at-promise* individuals."

In her book *Tough Fronts* (Dance, 2002), L. Janelle Dance gets beneath the mask that many seemingly alienated youth of color wear in public. The pictures that emerge of so many of these youth do not look like the stereotypes that are so prevalent in the literature on urban education. Real human beings who are sensitive and intelligent emerge. These are youth who have dreams of a better life and who are worried about their futures. But they must constantly deal with an uncaring and quite abusive economy, with the daily experiences of a marginalizing and racializing society and school system, and with the vast array of barriers that stand in their way (see also Dillabough & Kennelly, 2010). Watson is at her very best when she documents how very accurate this more positive assessment of these youth actually is and how they respond to teachers and community educators who demonstrate through their daily actions that these youth are worthy of respect and personhood.

In the process of portraying these powerful educational programs and the people who dedicate their lives to building and defending them, she illuminates a number of major implications for teaching in general as well. In her words: "Although teachers are often trained in content expertise (the science of our profession), we are rarely equipped with tools in *communication, community building, compassion,* and *commitment,* yet these are some of the characteristics that define the art of our craft. And these are not merely tools for the classroom teacher, but are cornerstones of change for us all. Nourished by personal awareness and collective consciousness, we can each participate in the solution."

However, it is not "only" the implications for teaching that come to the fore in her rich accounts of community-based answers to the dilemmas we face in our cities. The policy implications of her arguments are crucial as well. In the current zeal to treat everything that is public as simply a tax burden, not a social responsibility, we are defunding community-based organizations at exactly the same time as Watson shows that they are more necessary than ever. Rightist ideological attacks on public funding also have an almost religious quality (Apple, 2006) and seem to be immune to counter-evidence about what actually does work. Yet it is not only an issue of evidence. Many of the proponents of such policies have little or no understanding of the realities of the actual people living in our inner cities and impoverished rural areas.

The slash and burn tactics of the Right are having effects that are all too predictable. This is conservatism without any compassion. Privatize even when there is little evidence that this is effective, recreate a situation in which those who are "below" pay for the greed of those who are "above," blame those who are below for making "irrational" decisions for their socially caused predicaments, and the list could and does go on and on. Oh, and in case you may have forgotten, defund public institutions and destroy the gains that dispossessed people have made in them. The lives that are lost in this ideologically driven attack on poor communities and on public sector workers will soon be forgotten—or so the Right believes.

In response to this, here once again Watson is articulate. As she says, "Firing teachers and closing schools is not the answer—but teaching for social justice might be." Her sensitive documentation of what it means to actually do teaching for social justice is a significant contribution.

Learning to Liberate is an exceptional example of what can be done when someone honestly and with evident deep social and educational commitment takes up the tasks of what I have called the *critical scholar/activist* in education (see Apple, 2010; Apple, Au, & Gandin, 2009). This is a book in which not only is Vajra Watson fully present as a deeply committed critical educator, but so are the critical educators who have much to teach us about a kind of education that makes a profound difference in the lives of our youth.

Michael W. Apple
John Bascom Professor
of Curriculum and Instruction and Educational Policy Studies
University of Wisconsin, Madison

References

Apple, M. W. (2006). *Educating the "right" way: Markets, standards, God, and inequality,* 2nd edition. New York: Routledge.

Apple, M. W. (Ed.). (2010). *Global crises, social justice, and education.* New York: Routledge.

Apple, M. W., Au, W., & Gandin, L. A. (Eds.). (2009). *The Routledge international handbook of critical education.* New York: Routledge.

Dance, L. J. (2002). *Tough fronts: The impacts of street culture on schooling.* New York: Routledge.

Dillabough, J. & Kennelly, J. (2010). *Lost youth in the global city: Class, culture and the urban imaginary.* New York: Routledge.

Fraser, N. (1997). *Justice interruptus.* New York: Routledge.

Lynch, K., Baker, J., & Lyons, M. (2009). *Affective equality: Love, care and injustice.* New York: Palgrave Macmillan.

Ravitch, D. (2010). *The death and life of the great American school system.* New York: Basic Books.

PREFACE

Gems in the Gutter

I just got the news that another of my students has been shot. Six bullets in his
back. He is in ICU. Another weeping family. In this case, another wheelchair.
More weapons and more retaliation. Less hope.
> —Personal Journal Entry, September 2010

As I witnessed once again only too recently, many youth experience a cycle
of violence on the streets that annihilates their innocence, truncates their
opportunities, and nurtures their rage. These are not "bad" kids; often, these
teenagers are savvy, resilient, and smart. But many of them cannot envision a
world beyond their next hustle—so school seems irrelevant.

When I was teaching high school in the late 1990s, I often felt ill equipped
to address, let alone stop, the spread of violence in my students' lives. Even
with my good intentions and comparative skill, I continued to lose—to prison
and/or death—more students than I won to college and/or formal employment. Over the past two decades, I have been to more funerals than graduation
ceremonies and baby showers combined. I know my experience is not unique.
This is a national crisis.

The calamity of underachievement in our schools and urban warfare in
our communities often elicits blame and cynicism on all sides. But when we
focus exclusively on what is not working, we go nowhere. Real change cannot
occur until we shift our focus to the solution. This realization launched me on
a quest for best practices. I wanted to know how we teachers can work more
effectively so that schools become institutions of equity that serve as catalysts
for social change. It is with these ideals that my journey unfolds. But the story
really starts with one of my students.

When Kenny was in ninth grade, he challenged and expanded my beliefs. I was working as an assistant teacher in his Ethnic Studies class at Berkeley High School. Although the topic was multi-cultural and relevant, Kenny was often preoccupied with flirting with the girls in his class. I was always hard on him and demanded that he focus and pay attention. He seemed to appreciate my high expectations and began coming by with his friends at lunch to talk about assignments and his general struggles with school. When lunchtime started to feel too brief for the help he wanted, I said he could stop by my apartment for additional tutoring. A few weeks later, early on a Saturday morning, I heard a knock at the door. Kenny and his friends were the last people I was expecting to see, but there they stood. I can still remember the shy looks on their faces, their shiny grills of gold teeth, and the way their backpacks hung off their shoulders. I swung the door wide open to let them in. At the time I did not suspect that this small act would not only let them into my home, but also deepen and alter our relationship. Kenny, and his entire family, are now an integral part of my life.

I recently found the naïve personal statement I wrote for my application to the Harvard Graduate School of Education (HGSE). I described how Kenny showed up on my doorstep for help with his homework and that that single incident somehow turned my apartment in South Berkeley into an ongoing study hall and safe haven for various youth. I wrote about what seemed to work in our setting and emphasized the community aspect of community education. It seemed so simple and I earnestly believed that the youth I worked with, especially Kenny, were headed straight to college and beyond. What I did not know at the time is that, when I left for HGSE, I left Kenny unprepared and isolated in a sea of chaos, drama, and strife.

Although I was well intentioned and supportive of Kenny's academic achievements, I assumed he could do it without a support network. One moment vividly stands out that solidified Kenny's work ethic for me. One morning I heard Kenny's knock and he asked if he could come in and study. "No problem," I said, "but I gotta go." When I left the house he was sitting on the living room couch surrounded by books; when I came back nearly 6 hours later he was still sitting crouched over studying, writing, and reading. He had never moved—not once the entire day. He had not even noticed it was dark outside. Although I knew a bit about the deep problems in his home life, I was confident that he could and would follow through with his dreams.

One day I asked him to write down 10 goals. Once he created his list we talked about each goal and what he would need to do to achieve it, realistically. Week after week I repeated this: I would hold him accountable to the goals he set for himself. Since his brother Emmett had dropped out in the ninth grade, his primary goal at the time was to graduate from high school. He always wanted to—and continues to want to, despite getting caught up himself—show his brother a different way of life. Kenny wanted to be his older brother's role model. His aspirations were clear and a bit simplistic: go to college, get a good job, have a nice house, a wonderful wife, and a few kids (in that order). When I left for Massachusetts everything seemed in place. His grades were up and he was focused. What else could he need? I have since learned that grades and determination are not enough.

When I was in school back east I would sometimes receive a distressed letter from Kenny but I would write back or call his house and, as I saw it, "set him straight." I rejoiced when he sent me an invitation to his high school graduation. I made it a point to fly back home to California (with my 1-month-old son) so that I could be at the ceremony, cheering him on. Later we went back to his house for photographs. I vividly remember how dazed he looked, like a deer in the road gazing at oncoming headlights. Kenny did not know which direction his life was headed in. He had just accomplished his major goal: graduation. Now what?

I left for Massachusetts during Kenny's senior year. I did not think to show him how to sign up for the SAT. Though Berkeley High has the resources for such tasks, he generally distrusts adults, especially those at school (and he has many horror stories to back up his perception), unless they make an effort to reach out to him. When Kenny missed every SAT test day his senior year, his college aspirations began to fade. When I suggested it was not too late to take them, he explained to me that he was going to be part of a biotech program with Bayer Pharmacies and Laney Community College in Oakland. Although I was glad that he would have a job while going to school, I was concerned that he would remain on the same block he had so long talked about leaving.

Not even a semester after Kenny began the biotech program, he felt lured into the so-called big money of various street hustles. Things really began to fall apart. After he dropped out of school, he seemed to meander and get caught up around every corner. This was his story for the last couple of years. Recently he got a position working on the graveyard shift for a freight company. The hours seemed ideal; he would be safe and off the street. After 6 months of work—he never missed one night—he was fired because his cell phone rang twice during a staff meeting. He is now looking for another job and has a beautiful 2-year-old son he is trying to support by any means necessary.

Despite Kenny's agency and ambition, barriers continue to stymie him. The intersection of structural racism and devastating poverty is crippling and enraging. And this unmitigated rage is real, often erupting in the form of street violence that further ignites despair and consumes hope. Given this urban terrain, what does it take to succeed? Kenny taught me that simply having an excellent teacher and/or mentor with good intentions will not suffice. So what is the solution?

Learning to Liberate examines answers from the vantage point of four highly effective community-based educators who run youth-serving non-profit organizations in Oakland and San Francisco, California. After 3 years of participating in their programs and conducting in-depth interviews, my analysis of both the plight and promise of public education has shifted. These non-traditional teachers have fundamentally challenged my understanding about how to reach and teach this generation, and specifically students like Kenny who are often deemed "high-risk." Although their programs vary and their philosophies differ, these four educators nurture the development of young people in a way that is lifelong, empowering, and inspiring. They demonstrate how teaching is sacred communal work. I am indebted to them for allowing me to experience social justice as their student, comrade, cheerleader, and critic.

Though social justice is a catchphrase with multiple interpretations, I found that inside these grassroots learning environments a liberatory praxis is functioning, one that disrupts subjugation. This is significant. Since schooling is often used as a tool to validate our own oppression, as both haves and have-nots internalize our status, these community-based educators exemplify a way to realign our priorities, shift our paradigm, and redefine education. There are gems in the gutter, brilliance behind the prison wall, and lessons in the streets. School can embrace the hood in a way that is for the common good.

I invite you to join the struggle and partake in a movement that brings the lives of marginalized youth to the center of school reform. The time is now. For many of us, the crisis in education has a name: it is the names of our students who are failing, dropping out, even dying. But we can, and will, respond. With hope and urgency I share my on-the-ground tools with anyone interested in changing our students' lives—and revitalizing our shared future.

ACKNOWLEDGMENTS

Bismillah ir-Rahman ir-Rahim

A wonderful Ethiopian proverb states: *in unity, a million threads can trap a lion*. Although I have not been trying to trap a lion per se, this journey has been marked by great challenges. Yet every step of the way, I have been surrounded by a community of people who formed a unified bond that pulled me together—literally and figuratively—so that I could write. The gratitude owed to each and every one of them could fill every page of this book, but since we are limited by both space and time, I can only mention a few people here and now.

Dara has the *heart* of an activist and demonstrates love and compassion in the way she lives her life. As a woman with little formal education, she has a fighting spirit and I got my hustlin directly from her. Mom, you are a living example of God's grace. Farid, on the other hand, has the *mind* of an activist and he is constantly researching the understory and untold facts. Farid's critical consciousness and brilliance have been a source of pride for me as far back as I can remember. Dad, I still vividly recall the way you schooled me about the realities of Christopher Columbus when I was in first grade. In honoring what these two very different people have raised within me, I hope that both the heart *and* mind come together in this work.

I found out I was pregnant on my first day of graduate school—the very first day. And I was convinced that the child inside me would help me reach my goals. But Tsadiku Solomon Obolu is a child who exceeds expectation. As we like to call you, Stax: I want you to know that all that I am able to do is because you are standing next to me as a true warrior and testament of all that is right in the world. Your righteousness, strength, and intellect are glorious.

As I began to collect the data for this book, I gave birth to Adiyah Ma'at Obolu. When I was pregnant, I felt a jewel growing inside me that was in me, but not of me. I never dreamed that something so beautiful or bright could exist on earth, and then I met you. As we like to call you, SisterBear Didi: you saved my life because you taught me how to laugh and smile to the core of my being. Your love is soulful, joyful, and transformative.

Together, my children inspire my fight; they are ever-present with every word I write and every act I take to improve schools. But I could not raise them without you, my dearest Solomon. This book feels like a small accomplishment compared with our blessings. Although we have two doctorates and have beaten the odds, the greatest achievement of our lives is the seeds we planted together, not just in having kids, but also in raising them in one family and with one love. The tireless pressure of the research process was lightened by your patience, your kindness, and especially your heartbeat—for it is this sound that soothes my soul in this weary world.

Within my extended family of friends, colleagues, and comrades, I need to give a special shout out to Amaya Kesi Noguera-Mujica. When I was drowning in the politics and stress of our day job, you would hold up a critical mirror and encourage me to look back and push forward (*Sankofa*). Your steadfast sensibility and relentless strength as a *sistar* and road dawg are challenging and inspiring. Thank you for your ingenuity, continuously finding ways to bring marginalized youth into the center of school reform.

My passion for knowledge and my quest for truth were ignited in high school by a conscious-radical-healer-educator-extraordinaire: Mr. Hodari B. Davis. When I was 14 years old, I was in his African-American History course at Berkeley High School; from that point onward, he mentored me into teaching. To this day, I have never seen a classroom teacher able to revolutionize learning and transcend classroom walls the way he did . . . I am hard-pressed to describe it as anything but magical.

The greatest teachers lead by example. And one man, in particular, lifts as he climbs. I first met him in eighth grade and over the past two decades he has been a genuine guide and a source of encouragement. Pedro Noguera: you showed me that scholarship and community organizing can go hand in hand; better yet, they always should. You have influenced my work and life in more ways than I have space to acknowledge—but please accept my heartfelt thank you.

Mark Warren was my doctoral advisor and demonstrated unwavering support from conception to finish line. Mark, you not only helped me feel at home in the academy, but befriended me as a colleague. You even prodded me to publish when I felt blinded by intimidation. I am eternally grateful on so many levels, but especially for your compassion and commitment to activist scholarship.

Sara Lawrence-Lightfoot, as a woman, a professor, and a dignified diva, you helped me fall in love with writing. Thank you for training me in a research methodology that included—rather than denied—the fullness of my senses and the depth of my experiences. I hold tight to the tools you have provided me: research with integrity, depth, and respect. It is an honor to stand in your shadow for you are a trailblazer for generations to come. You have my sincerest gratitude, admiration, and applause.

Helen Snively believed in my abilities as a scholar even when I stopped believing in myself. She was both a cheerleader and careful reader throughout this entire process. Rest assured, Helen: I could not have done it without you.

When I was living in Massachusetts for graduate school, Mama Patricia Vattuone opened the doors to her family and heart. She soon became my mentor. I watched intently as she used music and dance to create community right there in her living room. And around the dinner table, Patricia would gather together various talking heads and then prod them to act: "Help build a Nelson Mandela University for Social Justice in South Africa!" Beautiful Mama Patricia: even when you were ill with cancer, your body, mind, and sense of purpose never stopped. Now, every rainbow I see is your smile.

There are still others to honor and appreciate. Specifically I want to thank L. J. Dance and Michael Apple as well as Georgette Enriquez and Catherine Bernard at Routledge and Andrew R. Davidson at Prepress Projects Ltd. It is an honor, privilege, and pleasure to work with each of you, even if just by email. I thank you all for being champions of the liberatory praxis found inside this book.

Further, a big thanks to my little brother Barak, step-dad Jamie, Grandpa Richard, and Aunt RickaMae. A few words of praise are also due to Horace Kendell Harris: your heart is my sunshine and I am so proud that you are back in school. I know you will make an excellent x-ray technician (make that money, but don't let the money make you). I love you and Emmett James Harris IV unconditionally—we all we got (*Self Made*).

Yet even these acknowledgments cannot do justice to the army of allies, haters, and the like who pushed me onward in this fight to the finish line. I appreciate all of you. I thank my colleagues at the UC Davis CRESS Center as well as those folks I work with on a daily basis in various schools, organizations, and neighborhoods, among them Nicole Martinez, Estella Sanchez, Kindra Montgomery-Block, bel Reyes, Zenae Scott, Jazz Kaur, Ed Aguilar, Matt Cervantes, Ramona Bishop, Stephanie Au, Leslie Lipman, John Jones, Sandy Holman, Kahlil and Eli Jacobs-Fantauzzi, Michelle Seijas, Anna Trunnell, Jeanette Providence, Wesley Marshall, Yolanda Jimenez, Mary Sandy, Marlene Bell, Renee Newton, Terry Westover, Michele Hamilton, Karen Smith, Irvis Orozco, Amy Page, Jonathan Young, Chanda Chhin, Sammy Nunez, Motecuzoma Sanchez, Oscar Cardenas, Julie Lee, Assemblymember Victor Manuel Perez, and many others.

I am grateful to work alongside my SAYS family. In particular, I am indebted to the poet-mentor educators who are changing the face and purpose of education: Stephen Dimal (Bolo), Laura Cook (Mystic Mama), Denisha Bland (Coco Blossom), Patrice Hill (Mama Afrika), Ayla Dozier (Rainbow), Guillermo Torres (Intense/Esq), Richard Jackson (Black Star), Amaru Yawo-El, Alexay Wright, Victor Carreon (DJ Amp 1), Travion Cotton (T.R.E.), Ijeoma Ononuju (Professor), Andre Tillman (Dre-T), Trouble and Coon (E-Legal Tag Team), Emmanuel Padilla (EJ), Ebony Grant, Sasa Afredi, Dahlak Brathwaite, Nosa Ikponmwonba, Mannie Rizvi, Jeremi Roberts (Preach), and Shane Salter. I am also deeply thankful to my former University of San Francisco credential students—you know who you are—and I simply love the way y'all continue to love teaching. A shout out to the middle and high school students who are ignited with passion, perseverance, and power: Charday, Jelintha (Brownie), Adrian, Caitlyn, Canela, Jarron, Alexander, Truth, Ronee, Tatiyanna (Tatti), Jenny, Gabriel, Alexis, Nate, Zany, Mikey, Don-Jesus, Jagger, Shabrielle, Antheus, Miya, Sammy, Joe, Keiona, Maleek, Rashaad, Amori, to name just a few.

My extended circle of sisterhood cannot be overestimated. Here's to the aunties: Amina Meyer, Donna Justice, Stephanie Wolf Bravo (LikiLikiBoomBoom), Dr. Jann Murray-Garcia, and Carolyn Caldwell. On the academic side, Jabari Mahiri at UC Berkeley was extremely helpful in the first stages of this project along with my graduate study group (Susie, Anu, Jen, and Dana). Here's to the scholars who keep me grounded: Daren Graves, Kofi Charu Nat Turner, Louie Rodriguez, Jean Wing, Victor Rios, Pablo Gonzalez, Matt Horton, Dorinda Carter, Heather Harding, Michal Kurlaender, Richard Reddick, Frank Tuitt, Erin Murphy-Graham, Zeus Leonardo, Antwi Akom, Angela Booker, Tara Brown, Julie Reuben, Wendy Luttrell, Gloria Rodriguez, Antonio Cediel, Shawn Ginwright, Julie Figueroa, Kerry Enright, Jeff Duncan-Andrade, Rebecca Ambrose, Chris Faltis, Maisha Winn, and Lila Jacobs. Finally, I stand on the shoulders of my grandmother Alvina, an amazing teacher; Mama Doris, a real angel; and King Haile Selassie I, a true savior. Altogether and in unison, this network of people made it possible for me to complete my first book. From the core of my being, I thank you and the Most High for this privilege. May it never be in vain, but always for the power of the people.

I believe we live in an era of emergency. The perils of our time are defined by draconian neoliberal economic policies and politricks that insure the rich get richer and the poor get poorer. Our generation is marked by the ever-present threat of nuclear weapons and the ever-expanding (in)justice of the prison industrial state. Yet hegemony is not omnipresent; there are always cracks in the concrete where roses, weeds, and life itself survive and thrive. At the dusk before dawn, I rest assured that David will still beat Goliath. And if we only get one shot, may we aim for the jugular. So I give thanks for our deep personal and collective awakening that is rooted in love and resistance. And I pray for I-n-I; in other words, I pray for those at the top, those at the bottom, and everyone in between.

My prayers are for humanity, but I write for Diezal Boss (RIP), J. Redd (RIP), Shadondee Williams-Harris (RIP), Yusef Campbell (RIP), Ronnie Easily (RIP), Zillion Cash (RIP), Baby Doug, Ronnell Phillips (Ski Da Lo), the larger M.O.B./Cuzos, and all the youth around the world from Libya to Egypt to Brazil to the corner of Ward and Sacramento Street in B-Town and back, who need a Dereca-Rudy-Victor-Jack in their life so that they can be all that they were born to be. To the teachers and youth-serving practitioners on the front lines, thank you. You are in one of the most vital positions to make a difference. Therefore, I hope that this book makes a small contribution to help transform minds, guide hearts, and inspire our feet to improve the systems that impact our lives.

1

INTRODUCTION

Gangstas, Gunshots, and Grades

Youth Voice
What are the youth to accomplish when they don't have a voice?
And what do they acquire when they don't have a choice?
Who asks the children, the youth what they need?
Who gives them the chance, to say what they mean?
Who takes the time out to answer their questions?
Who looks deep inside their anger and aggression?
Who gives them their love, support, and their trust?
Who gives them the courage, to keep going when stuck?
Who gives them the voice when the voice is too weak to be heard?
Who picks up the voice and not kick it to the curb?
What, you don't see violence and you don't see rage?
That's all the voices yellin, cuz they've yet to see change
And when the yellin gets loud, y'all cover your ears
Instead of hearing the words in the eyes behind tears
They beggin for quality, not quantity hear
But instead of getting books, they get cases and years.

By Yusef Campbell

This poem about youth voice contains provocative insights for anyone work-ing with young people, and thus is a powerful entry point into this larger examination of community-based educators. Like Yusef, I wanted to know *who* is making an impact and successfully moving our most disadvantaged students toward positive goals. Over the years, Yusef's questions have echoed in my mind at odd moments as I was collecting data for this book; his bright contagious smile would appear, as if etched into my heart, in the most unlikely of places.

Yusef is as much a part of this story as anyone else. Like Kenny, whom I introduced in the preface, Yusef was one of my students. Not that long ago I helped him fill out his financial aid application for San Francisco State University. Yusef returned a few months later to say he had received a full scholarship. His face beamed with accomplishment. Seeing young Yusef beat the odds and graduate from high school, and then go on to college, was the greatest thank you any teacher could ask for.

Then, one midnight, the phone rang and Yusef's distraught girlfriend told me that he had been murdered. On January 15, 2007, the *San Francisco Chronicle* reported that he had been shot, and died, on the concrete of the 400 block of Haight Street the previous Saturday night. The article painted a bleak picture, mentioning 14 homicides in the past 17 days in San Francisco. It said very little about Yusef as a person, about the eager student I knew. He seemed to be just another number—the 11th homicide—whose life and death were so dehumanized that I had to wonder: when and how will this epidemic ever end? I ask this question because, like Yusef's untimely death, it haunts me. We are losing a generation.[1]

In 2007, 5,764 young people across this country were murdered—an average of 16 each day (CDC, n.d.a). And for "every person who gets shot and dies," reports the physician John Rich (2009), "another four get shot and survive" (p. x). In 2009, homicide was the second leading cause of death among people aged 15 to 24. In this age group, homicide remains the number one cause of death among African-Americans, the number two cause among Xicano/Latinos, and the number three cause among Native Americans. The homicide rate is 19 times higher for young Black men than for young white men (CDC, n.d.b).

As we all know, death rarely occurs in isolation. When any of us loses someone we care about, we experience great sadness and feel tremendous loss. We mourn. And to the extent that our grief becomes perpetual—because so many people in our lives are dying—it can affect our overall social, emotional, and academic wellbeing. Many students are living amidst the sounds of these gunshots, the pain of constant bereavement, and present (not post) traumatic stress disorder (Breslau, Davis, & Peterson, 1991; Cooley-Strickland et al., 2009; Tucker, 2007).

Yet even in some of the most violent neighborhoods, schools remain safe havens. Fewer than 1% of all homicides among school-age youth occur on school grounds (Anderson et al., 2001). The absence of physical violence, however, does not imply the presence of learning. Many schools contain a different type of violence: an *intellectual violence* in the form of low expectations, an irrelevant curriculum, and zero-sum discipline policies that can actually push young people out of school, often into the streets (Anderson, 1994; Anyon, 2005; Apple, 1995; Fine, 1991; Orfield, Losen, Wald, & Swanson, 2004; Watson, 2004). "Students who frequently get into trouble may have so many negative experiences in school that they conclude school is not for them and that the rewards associated with education are beyond their reach" (Noguera, 2008, p. 134). During 2006–2007, California's public schools produced one dropout for every three graduates (California Dropout Research Project, 2009). Each time a student disassociates from school, society experiences larger casualties. Researchers have found that, over their lifetimes, dropouts depend more on public assistance and have lower earnings, poorer health, and higher rates of unemployment, mortality, criminal behavior, and incarceration than their peers who complete high school (Breslau, 2010; Orfield, 2004). Thus, finishing high school can mean the difference between life and death, between a dorm room and a prison cell. Education is a gateway to survival.

From Reproduction to Resistance

Educational attainment is critical to the lifelong health and success of students, but there is little consensus about the type of education young people need. Interventions abound based upon the latest technological craze or the newest learning theory, but the failure rate of students, disproportionately low-income students of color, continues to rise (Anyon, 2005; Kozol, 1994, 2005; Lipman, 2011; Noguera, 2003; Orfield & Kornhaber, 2001). Perhaps particular students fail because they were never supposed to succeed. This conundrum is as American as apple pie.

Across decades, even centuries, the same question arises: what is the purpose of school? The answers have differed, from Horace Mann's (1848) promise of school as the "great equalizer" to the analysis by Bowles and Gintis (1976) of the ways schools structure inequality. Throughout its history, public education has been subject to constant criticism and debate as the ideals of meritocracy face off against the realities of inequity. Since a capitalist economy relies on income stratification to function, its educational system must sort and categorize students in order to perpetuate the social order (Oakes, 1985). This is simple and straightforward. However, because this country's democratic principles fuel rhetoric about equal opportunity, social institutions have always served a complex purpose. School is no exception; it is a contentious arena where these ideologies often collide.

From a historical perspective, compulsory education has been used to socialize students using market-based ideologies (Angus & Mirel, 1999; Apple, 1995, 2006; Aronowitz & Giroux, 1993). A prime example is demonstrated by Adams (1995) in *Education for Extinction: American Indians and the Boarding School Experience 1875–1928*; he thoroughly documents the rationale that superintendents, policymakers, and reformers used to dismantle an indigenous worldview. He writes, "A major objective of Indian schools" was to insure that students "say 'I' instead of 'We' and 'This is mine' instead of 'This is ours.'" In fact, the barometer of a student's success was based upon the school's ability to "awaken in him wants . . . The desire for property of his own may become an intense educating force. Discontent with the tepee and the starving rations of the Indian camp in winter is needed to get the Indian out of the blanket and into trousers,—and trousers with a pocket in them, and with a pocket that aches to be filled with dollars!" (p. 23). As debates lingered about *how* to exterminate indigenous nations in this country, schooling became viewed as a powerful and effective weapon to oppress.

In the current push–pull dynamic between capitalism and democracy, many leaders of school improvement continue to err on the side of the market; that is, they educate to create an economically divided and complacent citizenry (Apple, 2006, 2010; Lipman, 2011). This was made quite visible in the 2010 movie *Waiting for Superman*. Demonstrating the film's neoliberal framework, Geoffrey Canada states in the movie that we need school reform because "we are not preparing our children to be the leaders of the free world." Although freedom sounds good, it can be misleading. Lipman (2011) would argue that Canada is referring to freedom as a concept within the market (p. 10). In other words, freedom is simply associated with the ability to purchase things; which parallels the approach used at the Indian boarding schools described above.

In further critique of the movie, Swalwell and Apple (2011) contend that as a "(supposed) documentary" (p. 369) it completely "neglects the impact of No Child Left Behind and other educational policies that have cut off funding to schools labeled as *failing* . . . and further marginalized children who are predicted to drag down test scores" (p. 373, italics in original). Thus, Canada, alongside the other voices highlighted in *Waiting for Superman*, such as Davis Guggenheim and Michelle Rhee, reinforced a common yet dangerous philosophy toward schooling: some lucky impoverished children can win the lottery and escape their poor neighborhoods and become highly academic in a charter school setting (Swalwell & Apple, 2011). However, not all children can leave their environments or avoid their neighborhood schools. So how, then, do we empower poor Black and Brown children with tools to advocate for, rather than escape, their communities? This is not simply a question of access, but rather a demand for equitable and authentic community-based democracy.

Education in this country continues to perpetuate the cycle of social reproduction: in large part *because* of school the disenfranchised will grow up to be disenfranchised (Angus & Mirel, 1999; Apple, 2004; Bordieu & Passeron, 1977; Kozol, 1991; MacLeod, 1995; Oakes, 1985; Willis, 1977). But this is not our only option. Education has also been used as a liberatory tool—especially within the African-American community (Anderson, 1988; Fisher, 2008; Payne & Strickland, 2008; Perry, 2003; Woodson, 1933).

Decades of research reveal that, to effectively democratize learning, student-centered instruction is essential (Dewey, 1916; Freire, 1970). Often called critical pedagogy, this approach argues that education must be multicultural, emancipatory, and relevant to the needs of students (Adams, 1975;

Apple, 2011; Darder, Baltodano, & Torres, 2003; Duncan-Andrade & Morrell, 2008; Giroux, 1997; Ladson-Billings, 1994, 1995). Furthermore, to close the achievement gap, many critical scholars argue that urban youth need strategies that help them decode the power structure—including school—and their place in it (Conchas, 2001; Delpit, 1995; Ginwright, Noguera, & Cammarota, 2006). Yet even these types of lessons can sometimes embrace middle-class values in ways that fail to address the particularly disturbing inner-city problems of poverty, crime, drugs, gangs, and other ills. This was the case in my example in the introduction, of teaching Ethnic Studies; for Kenny, the topic did not do justice to his reality. For many urban youth, an effective student-centered pedagogy must embrace—rather than deny or demonize—street life (Dance, 2002; Dimitriadis, 2001; Duncan-Andrade, 2004; Ginwright, 2004, 2009; Mahiri & Conner, 2003; Whyte, 1943).

Unfortunately, many teachers enter the urban environment without any real understanding of their students' lives outside school. And even those who know about certain challenges might not have the tools to help. In order to significantly impact young people's life trajectories—from the classroom to the block—we need to broaden our conceptualization of education and refine our academic partnerships. It is here that the work of community-based organizations comes into clear view (Anyon, 2005; Blum & Rinehart, 1999; Fisher, 2007; McLaughlin, Irby, & Langman, 2001).

In *Identity and Inner-City Youth*, Shirley Brice Heath and Milbrey McLaughlin (Heath & McLaughlin, 1993) analyze the role of community-based organizations in the lives of urban youth. They explain: "most of the youth who come to these organizations . . . regard school as a place that has rejected and labeled them by *what they are not* rather than by *what they are*" (p. 4, italics in original). Youth link up with these programs for the "security that comes from accomplishment as a member of an active, supportive group" (pp. 8–9) and because they "embrace the whole person, not just a single issue" such as "school success" (p. 217). Furthermore, the authors make the important distinction that these organizations are not "mere adjuncts to school" or "youth-serving agencies," but "establish young people at their center—as resources" (p. 4).

Although schools and community-based organizations share an obvious connection in serving young people, an unfortunate divide and philosophical tension can exist. In a later study McLaughlin (2000) wrote: "Adults working with youth organizations frequently believe that school people do not respect or value their young people. Educators, for their part, generally see youth organizations as mere 'fun' and as having little to contribute to the business of schools. Moreover, educators often establish professional boundaries around learning and teaching, considering them the sole purview of teachers. Yet adults working in community organizations know that youth have many teachers and that learning does continue in non-school hours" (pp. 34–35). To date, few researchers have examined the pedagogical contributions from community-based educators, who often act as important alternative teachers and mentors in the lives of youth.

Building upon this gap in the literature, I understand that relying solely on traditional classroom practices has limited our understanding of how youth today are learning and what is possible. As Freire and Macedo (1987) contend, we must realize that "it is impossible to think of education strictly reduced to the school environment . . . we have to recognize that historically there are times when the school environment provides more or fewer opportunities" (p. 61). In a city landscape that is both violent and nihilistic, schools and society throw some troubled teenagers away. But even amidst gunshots and abandonment, the four community-based educators in this study demonstrate that despair is not deterministic, because agency is always present. Accordingly, these educators not only break the cycle of social reproduction in the lives of poor urban youth; they replace it with *social resistance*.

By intently examining these nontraditional educators I hope, on the one hand, to dispel and demystify the notion of a "miracle worker" and, on the other hand, to reveal practical tactics these educators use daily, in their flourishing programs. Yet there is another critical layer to consider: the bridge between the community-based educator and the classroom teacher. To excavate the sheer possibility of transformative teaching and learning, I left the schoolhouse and went into the community in search of answers. Without stringent standards and the obscenely overloaded schedules that most teachers face, the four educators in this book have the freedom to create authentic social justice praxis. Focusing on their efforts helps us imagine alternatives and, equally critically, it underscores the types of training that urban teachers need to be effective.

Finding the Best of the Best

Years ago, I began my earnest quest to uncover best teaching practices, but the answer was not where I expected it. One day, as part of a research job in San Francisco, I visited a community-based organization, one of many groups that provide direct services to youth either within or beyond the walls of school (Connell & Gambone, 1998; Gambone & Arbreton, 1997). To my surprise, many of the young participants demonstrated an array of leadership abilities and skills, and a genuine excitement about the work they were doing within these groups. But when I spoke to them about school, they expressed discontent, disengagement, and a boredom that all too often correlated with very low grades and dropping out. Why weren't these same students feeling connected and excited about school? What were their leaders, the community-based educators, doing that their classroom teachers were not? Can the lessons derived from their work inform the practices and pedagogy of high school teachers in low-income urban communities?

To answer these questions, I sought out practitioners doing exceptional work throughout the San Francisco Bay Area.[2] Specifically, I used specialized listservs and personal contacts with teachers and researchers to elicit names of people and programs. I also examined the results of a youth development survey to identify various model programs (Catalano, Berglund, Ryan, Lonczak, & Hawkins, 1999), and then combined these lists to yield a group of community educators. Essentially, I wanted people who, in my estimation and that of knowledgeable researchers and colleagues, had proven their capacity to move youth toward positive goals. A dozen individuals fit these criteria. To shorten my list, I visited the sites, met with the staff, and spoke informally with the teenagers. Finally, I chose these four people because they work with high-risk students and, perhaps most importantly, the youth constantly told me that *their* community-based educator is the best of the best.

The findings I report throughout this book result from 3 years (July 2003 to July 2006) of ethnographic research on community-based educators and their successful programs for disenfranchised youth. Throughout this process, I used Sara Lawrence-Lightfoot's (1983, 2000; Lawrence-Lightfoot & Davis, 1997) methods of portraiture to document and analyze each educator's teaching techniques, to understand their philosophies and strategies for working with students, and to see how their personal experiences and the institutional context shape the way they engage troubled teenagers. The tools of portraiture—observation, thematic in-depth interviews, and document analysis—allowed me to scrutinize the emerging themes in several ways and bring the central story of each educator to light (further information on my research methods is available in appendices B, C, and D).

Portraiture is a unique methodology rooted in vivid storytelling; it invites you, the reader, into each moment, where a lively, authentic, and multi-faceted reality unfolds. My intentional perch of human-as-instrument lets you discover the universal within the particular and thus absorb the lessons in these exceptional teachers' lives. Since portraiture anticipates a co-construction of the narrative, the story is deliberately participatory. Given this dynamic, I ask that you become a part of the process by asking yourself three guiding questions:

1. How do I do *my* work?
2. What do I *believe* about today's students, teachers, and schools?
3. Do the community-based educators use any strategies that might affect *my* perception of and relationship with disenfranchised youth?

I asked myself these same questions and the answers were not always pretty. But I knew I had to look in the mirror critically, courageously, and honestly because this is what I was asking of my participants and this is precisely what the educators ask of their students. This process was simultaneously informative and introspective, analytical and heart wrenching. To gain insights into their world, I had to join them—physically, emotionally, and spiritually.

As a result, the educators not only opened the doors of their organizations to me, but they let me deep inside their lives. I was fortunate to have the opportunity to delve into their personal idiosyncrasies and family stories, which enabled me to uncover the ways their upbringing shapes their strategies, their political beliefs inform their practices, and their expectations guide their outcomes. Allowing me to mine them for answers, in what Lawrence-Lightfoot and Davis (1997, p. 139) call human archaeology, took enormous trust, but they did trust me with their voices and experiences so that I could authentically share their remedies to the ills of our time. On every level, this is serious, intense, and provocative work. I made every attempt to depict their effectiveness in a way that is nuanced, accurate, and authentic. If I fail to accomplish this, I take full responsibility; these educators became vulnerable to me so that they might become real to you.

Overview of the Journey

This book describes my journey into the lives, lessons, and curricula of highly successful community-based educators. In chapters 2 through 5, I devote an entire chapter to each person, but I would like to introduce them officially, though briefly, now.[3]

Dereca Blackmon is the executive director of Leadership Excellence (LE). LE provides year-round grassroots community-organizing and leadership skills to African-American children and youth from urban neighborhoods throughout the Bay Area. The organization has been recognized nationally as leading the way in the field of youth development because of its innovative programs that bring together education, community engagement, and social justice.

Dereca's colleagues and the youth she serves describe her as "somethin amazin." As I watched her teach at Camp Akili, I witnessed her unconditional love for these young people, coupled with her high expectations. She is an artful speaker and her lessons resemble a good conversation because of the inquisitive conversation she inspires. This is Dereca's external persona, but we go much deeper. Through interviews and observation, Dereca allows me into her life history: the family story that drives her tireless effort to change students' lives.

Rudy Corpuz Jr. is the founder and executive director of United Playaz (UP), a violence prevention and youth leadership development program for youth aged 14 to 18 in San Francisco. In collaboration with schools, detention centers, and communities, UP promotes the development of youth leadership and critical life skills, and provides alternative recreational activities to improve the health and wellbeing of youth who are most at risk. A key strategy of UP is to place the program in the hands of the youth. From its inception UP has been driven and led by students. Its participants take responsibility for planning and organizing activities, conducting outreach and recruitment, and providing education and violence prevention advocacy to their peers.

Rudy's life history makes him uniquely qualified to work with troubled teenagers. He grew up in the South of Market District in San Francisco and dropped out of Mission High School in the tenth grade. A former gang member, drug dealer, and drug addict, he spent over 9 years in prison. Using what he has learned on the streets of San Francisco, he connects with youth and encourages them to serve their communities.

Victor Damian is the designated "coach" of the Youth Task Force (YTF) within San Francisco's Department of Public Health. The YTF is a group of teenagers who work as advocates for youth-driven care in the city systems that provide services in child welfare, juvenile justice, mental health, special education, and substance abuse. All the task force members are themselves receiving two or more of these services. The YTF works successfully with public agencies and organizations to make the system more youth friendly. They have produced a youth rights guide to help children navigate the foster care system, organized several conferences for service providers, and won a national award for their spoken word poetry CD entitled *I Am That Youth.*

Victor strives to facilitate a partnership of empowerment with the youth. Although he did not grow up in one of the systems of care and in many ways feels different from the students he works with, he uses empathy alongside his own story to open his students' hearts. Because of his compassion, he inspires youth to share their stories and perhaps heal from the strife in their lives. Significantly, Victor is a former slam poetry champion; he uses his gift with the written word and performance poetry to engage the young people in rereading their lives and resurrecting their personal power.

In 1987, *Jack Jacqua*, a middle school counselor and coach, co-founded the famous Omega Boys Club in San Francisco, with Joe Marshall, a middle school teacher and administrator. Both were concerned about the number of African-American youth who were dropping out of school and/or becoming involved in the drug trade. The club's mission remains the same, and simple: to keep young people alive, unharmed by violence, and out of jail. To accomplish this goal, Omega hosts weekly family meetings, offers intensive academic classes and tutoring to teenagers, provides youth with scholarships to college, facilitates a radio show (*Street Soldiers*), and teaches inside incarceration centers.

Now in his seventies, Jack is the oldest participant in the study—and the only white person. He is legendary on the streets of San Francisco and in the prisons. Since he has been doing this work for decades, his success stories are now intergenerational. Jack sees himself primarily as a community activist and revolutionary. He spends his time at juvenile hall, at several youth and adult prisons (850 Bryant Street, Log Cabin Ranch, San Bruno, San Quentin

State Penitentiary), and on San Francisco street corners. His tough-love, no-nonsense approach is rooted in Afrocentric principles and an extended family model that supports young people in succeeding academically from the jail-house to the schoolhouse.

Following the individual portraits, in Chapter 6, entitled "What Does (Not) Work," I examine some of the inconsistencies between what the educators espouse and what inevitably happens in their learning spaces. I also spend this time analyzing the types of students these educators have helped and those they have lost along the way in order to complicate and challenge any one-size-fits-all conclusions. Nevertheless, I found some provocative answers and common tactics that all four educators utilize to school and empower disenfranchised youth. I present these in the form of a toolbox for anyone interested in being part of the solution in the lives of urban students. Chapter 7, "Community-Based Urban Education," delineates layers of community engagement, from the classroom to the ivory tower, that are necessary components to truly changing the school system. I move from practical tactics to policy recommendations in the last chapter, "Grindin for All We Got from the Bottom to the Top." This final integrated analysis demonstrates my sense of pragmatic optimism in the power and plight of today's students and their inner-city schools.

Risking Change

Dereca, Rudy, Victor, and Jack have remarkable conviction in their resolve to work with troubled teens. For these educators, the fight is to save lives, but it is nearly impossible to save someone if they do not want to save themselves. Since all human beings have choice—even in the most dire of circumstances—the goal becomes awakening students to their own self-determination, personal power, and collective agency. Guiding young people to transform their lives is connected to helping them decode systems of oppression while simultaneously empowering them to climb out of poverty and beat the odds. For many, the odds are stacked against them. But these children are not inmate numbers or case files or statistics; they are living breathing human beings with potential and brilliance.

Given the unique personalities and diverse needs of students, it is unrealistic to think that any one teacher or community-based educator can effectively meet the needs of every child. Now, more than ever, partnerships are pivotal to the academic and long-term wellbeing of students, especially those who are apt to drop out of school. And since no single person or magic formula can completely remedy the academic and social ailments of this generation, we need to work together in new ways to increase learning and change lives. So I invite you into the stories of four community-based solutions to the crisis in education so that together we may shift the status quo and courageously reach, teach, and transform rough, tough, misled youth.

This work is not easy, but it is imperative. When I think about the untimely passing of so many of our young brothers and sisters, I try to remind myself that our future will be defined not by these wretched experiences of children dying, but rather by what we choose to do about it. Ideally, we use the devastation we see around us to spur creativity and innovation; we become even more motivated to take risks because our children are at risk. I am not advocating that we layer multiple piecemeal reforms onto one another in ways that actually fuel our burnout. No, I am referring to a deeper paradigm shift rooted in the very purpose of school.

The four community-based educators you will meet in subsequent chapters demonstrate an approach to education that is engaging and empowering. In their work, leaving no child behind is not a political catchphrase; it is a call to action and a way of life. As I watched, listened, thought about, and felt the ways these particular community educators work with young people, I was challenged by the soul-wrenching love they showed. Despite the differences in their approaches and styles, their love was palpable when I stepped into their classrooms. From juvenile hall to the basement at Balboa High School to the conference room at the San Francisco Department of Public Health to a lecture hall at Sonoma State University, their spaces, no matter how dark and grungy or pristine, became filled with the light of love. It was powerful. I have come to believe that to *really* see each young person, educators must fall in love. For these teachers, education *is* an act of love. Through this love, and because of it, they succeed with the so-called unreachable and unteachable. Love is central to the improvement of our schools, but it is only part of the answer.

More often than not, as teachers, we develop skills as lecturers, but often what we need is to learn how to hear. And hear from the voices Yusef so painfully described as being silenced. The best educators are able to teach this generation *because* of their ability to reach them, listen to them, and learn with them. If traditional schoolteachers are to hold ourselves to the highest principles of pedagogy—the art and science of teaching—we must recognize that lessons can come from the most unlikely of places (those gems in the gutter). Although teachers are often trained in content expertise (the science of our profession), we are rarely equipped with tools in *communication, community building, compassion,* and *commitment,* yet these are some of the characteristics that define the art of our craft. And these are not merely tools for the classroom teacher, but are cornerstones of change for us all. Nourished by personal awareness and collective consciousness, we can each participate in the solution. Let's start by learning from Dereca's pedagogy of *communication.*

2

DERECA BLACKMON

Pedagogy of Communication

A True Fighter
Ima fight until I win
Yaa Asantewaa fought
She was a fighter
She wanted victory for her kingdom
Dedication poured through her skin
Survival memories flowed through her mind
And she chose to keep her eyes set on the prize
A choice that would forever make the Ashanti tribe
A legend in most West African Ghanaian lives.
Who would have thought
That this righteous woman would have fought
Well I did
Seeing blood gushing from your children's neck
I would have said "Hold up, I'm not finished yet!"
Ima Fight
Ima Fight until I win
Yaa Asantewaa fought, she was a fighter
So when are we going to fight?

Excerpt from a poem by Simone, a youth participant at
Leadership Excellence

Simone's poem, *A True Fighter*, makes me think of Dereca Blackmon and her reputation as a fierce activist and advocate for African-American youth. Her status in the community and the reputation of Leadership Excellence excites and intimidates me as I prepare for our first interview. I recall the many stories I have heard over the years about Leadership Excellence. When I was in high school, many of my friends participated in LE's famous summer camp and returned to school with a profound consciousness I admired. Now, nearly a decade later, it's 2005 and I am about to meet the executive director.

Leadership Excellence is located in downtown Oakland, California. Although Dereca's office at 1629 Telegraph Avenue is relatively easy to find, I circle the block a couple of times competing with all the other drivers to find parking in this busy area. I worry about being late and worry how Dereca will perceive me. So my palms are a bit sweaty as I turn the steering wheel sharply to pull into a parking space.

This afternoon the city streets are full of people. Some rush into offices while others wait at the bus stop. Hurrying down the street I pass a shoe store, hot dog eatery, and café, and make my way to the small metal door. As I enter the corridor, I see it is dark and dirty, and paint is falling from the ceiling onto the concrete floor. I push the button and wait for the old elevator to come down slowly to street level and take me to the fourth floor. When I step out, I am struck by the contrast between the gloomy corridor and this large, light-filled space with hardwood floors and bright colors. LE shares the floor with Diversity Works and Global Education Partnership and each organization has intricately detailed political posters and collages on display.

When I first come face to face with "Sista Dereca" I am taken aback. I do not know exactly what I was expecting but, as I shake her hand, I am struck by how disarming she is. What is it about her? Though she is relatively short, at 5'2", and somewhat petite, it is her compassionate brown eyes and wide bright smile that are comforting. Dreadlocks frame her face and fall freely past her shoulders. She could even pass as a teenager in the right clothes and definitely seems younger than her thirty-something years. Though she works around the clock, her face is not worn, wrinkled, or tired in any way. Quite the opposite, her expression is energetic and enthusiastic. I feel immediate warmth as she welcomes me into her professional space to appreciate, study, and learn about her life's work.

We take a seat in her cubicle, our knees almost touching because the space is so small. As she clips the microphone to her sweatshirt, I take out my notebook. I begin by asking Dereca how she got her name, and she answers by describing, in rapid succession, details from her family history. I quickly realize that tradition and history are essential to Dereca. She comes from a long line of strong Black women and boasts that the birth of her daughter, Nia, makes five generations of women currently alive. Since the 1920s, this matriarchy has held together her large family in Detroit. Before that, it was the women who kept the Blackmons close during the trials and tribulations of living and surviving in the Deep South. This ancestral memory is ever present in Dereca's story about her own life and the lessons she brings to African-American youth.

Dereca has hundreds of relatives, and countless inspirational men and women in her large blended family. As she puts it, "lot of divorces in my family, lot of blended family as we like to call them." Of all her relatives, Dereca's paternal grandmother, Delores Blackmon, now in her nineties, is the one who most nourishes Dereca's sense of community and passion for social justice. She is a "huge equal rights advocate" and "a legend" in the community thanks to her commitment to Black people. When Dereca was young, Delores took her on many adventures, ranging from the Dance Theatre of Harlem to rallies to the voting booth. When Dereca became a young adult, Delores took her to Africa: Ghana, Côte d'Ivoire, and Senegal.

Now Dereca tries to share as many as she can of these same kinds of experiences, which were so influential in her own development, with the youth at Leadership Excellence. When meeting with Oakland Supervisor Keith Carson or Congresswoman Barbara Lee, Dereca makes it a point to bring young people with her so they can be involved with politics at first hand. Moreover, following her grandmother's example, once a year she takes a group of young African-Americans to Africa. Delores Blackmon's acts of courage and resistance instill in Dereca a relentless dedication to fight for what she believes in.

Dereca has an aggressive, passionate belief in the capabilities of *all* young people. As she looks back over her life she realizes that she has always felt drawn to them. "If you're called to this work, you know you're called . . . I don't know how to explain it. It's like any other thing you're called to do." This intense commitment has always been a part of her. Even at 15, she was a peer educator for Planned Parenthood. Her ambition to reach and teach also carried her into jobs for which she was technically not prepared. For instance, just after she received her bachelor's degree from Stanford University, she returned to Detroit and was hired as the art director for a large community development corporation. Using photography, she started a cross-cultural exchange program involving urban and suburban youth. "I did a multi-cultural photography program where we had kids from the inner city take pictures of kids from the suburbs of their lives" and vice versa. The program became nationally recognized and Dereca received the very prestigious Telly Award for her efforts. She was shocked by this accomplishment because "I knew zero about photography." But she smiles, "I knew about people."

Dereca's zeal to work with young people, particularly those commonly deemed high-risk, drew her to LE. In 2002 LE's founders, Dr. Shawn Ginwright and Mama Nedra, hired Dereca to develop the organization that was already known for its "extraordinary transformational summer programs" into a more "comprehensive organization." Today, Leadership Excellence provides year-round grassroots community organizing and leadership skills to children and youth from urban neighborhoods throughout the Bay Area. Dereca mainly oversees four programs that direct youth away from high-risk behaviors and toward constructive activities for themselves and their communities. The first is *Oakland Freedom School*, a 6-week summer literacy and leadership program for children aged 5 to 13. The second is *Camp Akili*, LE's renowned summer camp. This 6-day consciousness-raising overnight retreat is designed for teens between ages 14 and 18. The third is a new group of programs (*Rise, Drop Squad*, and *Decision Time*) that developed to support the youth once camp was over. This aspect of LE provides year-round academic and social support. The fourth and culminating activity is *Camp Alkebulan*, a 2-week summer-abroad program in which African-American youth travel to West Africa to volunteer on community improvement projects.

In the 5 years that Dereca has been its leader, the organization's annual budget and capacity have nearly doubled. For the upcoming year, LE has secured over $800,000 to provide direct services to approximately 500 children and youth. Dereca has a team of six staff members (three of them former LE participants) and a cadre of volunteers to help fulfill these responsibilities. As she runs through these figures I comment, "That's a relatively small budget for the number of young people you're serving." Nodding her head she replies, "Yes, yes, yes, it is," especially when so many organizations have exorbitant budgets and no young people. She says, "I call an organization that I know that had like two million and ask em to send a youth to something we had, and they were like 'we don't have any youth.' I was like what?" I concur; the primary obstacle for most community-based organizations—especially those working with so-called at-risk and high-risk youth—is recruitment and retention, but this is not an issue for LE. Dereca continues, "If you look at [the] asset assessment of our kids, they are the most high-risk of all the kids being served by Oakland Fund for Children and Youth. And it's funny cause I didn't even write that on my last grant proposal. I meant to. Because it's like hello, we get the best outcomes and we work with the, quote unquote, hardest kids to serve. You know, you hear all these hard to serve, blah blah blah. And I'm like I can't use 'hard to serve' cause they're *not* hard for us to serve." Based on the hard-to-serve indices, LE should be doing some of the most challenging work in Oakland. Dereca knows that this is not the case.

Dereca's natural ability to relate to people is a central theme throughout her work, particularly when building relationships with youth. I immediately realize she is a gifted storyteller and am intrigued by the many details and anecdotes she brings to our conversation. It seems she rarely even takes a breath before continuing her enthusiastic recounting of times and places. Happily I manage a few notes when she finally does take a break in her narration.

When I ask Dereca to describe the youth she works with, she grows quiet for the first time since we sat down. She takes a moment, looks off to the distance, and then a joyful smile fills her face. "They're raw, hella real. They're really, really, *really* beautiful, just like incredible lovin spirits who just haven't had an opportunity to shine." She quickly moves from her personal belief to the work of LE. "It's really part of our organizational mission to outreach to youth who have otherwise not been engaged with youth programs. So we try to do outreach to probation, to foster care, to street corners." I learn that her organization will also partner with churches and other groups such as the Center for Young Women's Development[1] so there's "always a mix" of Black youth. Dereca recognizes that some families send their children to LE's programs "because they want them to know about their culture and their history." But many of the "kids don't have, necessarily, like a family situation, and they stay with us because they get that here." She surmises that perhaps, most importantly, youth stay because they are "loved unconditionally."

Although the atmosphere of love and family is central, I also want to learn about LE's curriculum. The teachers at LE, including Dereca, intentionally try to awaken African-American students "to the fact that they're not personally to blame for their condition in this society . . . That there are things in the society that are designed to exploit certain aspects of their personality and their history and their culture." As youth learn about these injustices, "they just become hungry. So our youth that are here are hungry for knowledge. They're excited about the opportunity to have a positive social environment where people care about them."

Dereca's words are powerful and inspiring. Driving home, I consider her perspective. With fervor she told me that high-risk African-American youth are not hard to serve but rather have not had opportunities to shine. Accordingly, at LE, students are loved and taught about oppression and racial pride, and this motivates their desire to learn. This method allows young people to realize their agency—to recognize that they *are* capable of greatness. But what does this look like? Only when I visit Freedom School a few months later can I fully appreciate the ethos she describes.

Relationship Building

I arrive at the single-story dilapidated West Oakland Elementary School at 8:15 on a chilly morning in July. Today is visitor's day at Freedom School, and I am eager to see for myself what Leadership Excellence looks like in action. But I see no signs and only hope I have the right location. Venturing toward the main building, I see Brother Saleem, whom I recognize from the LE office. Along with some other guests, he welcomes me and directs us to the auditorium. The room is filled: over 70 children, aged 5 to 13, are standing in small groups on the periphery having quiet conversations. A few adults rush about to prepare a table of fruit and bagels. Simultaneously, the coordinator, Brooklyn Williams, walks slowly around the space, holding a stick of burning incense.

After I engage in a few minutes of small talk with various people, Dereca enters the auditorium. She is wearing a long, flowing white skirt and a yellow Freedom School shirt. Her long locks are now gone; in their place is a beautiful, short, two-inch Afro. Holding her daughter's hand, she immediately begins checking in with her staff and greeting people. She seems to notice me from the corner of her eye and within seconds makes her way across the gym floor. Before I know it, she is giving me a big, welcoming hug. Dereca then checks her watch and yells abruptly, "You have one minute to clear your plates cause we're about to need our hands!" I take a few last bites of cantaloupe and just as I am throwing out my plate Dereca roars, "Harambe," KiSwahili for *come together as one.*

The children promptly form a large, wide circle and everyone present follows their lead and holds hands. As I watch the circle expand, I take in the number of people present (well over 100) and bask in the sea of faces. In the room I see every shade of Brown, every hue of Black. I notice that no one is outside this circle; all the visitors, parents, children, and teachers are gathered together. The group is intergenerational and, besides me, there is only one other white person; everyone else is African-American. Dereca provides us with a brief orientation to LE and what to expect this morning at Freedom School. She then welcomes us to "the greatest program for Black youth in the world."

Sister Brooklyn proceeds to walk into the center of the circle and starts to chant: "OFS [Oakland Freedom School], we'll manifest, we choose the path that's the best from East to West, we put ourselves to the test and refuse to settle for less, Jah guide." The greatest part of this chant is the crazy excitement it creates in the children. In this call-and-response exercise the energy in the gymnasium seems explosive. I notice one student who is wearing a backpack that seems as big as he is. The bag appears to weigh him down, but it does not stop him from jumping up and down, shouting the words. Another chant starts. I immediately recognize the beat as a remix of one of Tupac's raps. In unison the children sing, "I can't deny it, I can't deny it, this is how the tide is comin, comin from the Freedom School. And you know I won't act a fool, cause I'm livin by the golden rule."

I am mesmerized by the joy. One child looks like his jugular vein is literally going to pop out of his neck because he is chanting so loudly and passionately. These kids have so much energy at 8:30 in the morning and are so thrilled to be here, at school. I stand chanting along with everyone, but my mind wanders. Although I feel I should be happy about what I see, I find myself feeling a bit sad. I try to remember a time when I visited any school and saw this much collective positive energy. I have done many site visits for the teachers I work with and I have taught at both elementary and high schools. In most of those schools I have been overwhelmed by the students' feelings of despair and boredom. Freedom School provides a stark contrast.

Freedom School appears to be an oasis of joy and in many ways, is a unique and alternative kind of learning environment. On a personal level, for Dereca, it is also drastically different from the "predominantly white schools" her four daughters attend where "they're not having conversations in the classroom at all from the perspective of cultural consciousness . . . the whole concept of I'm an African, that's just not introduced to them." I am surprised that this does not bother her, but she explains that her priorities are clear: "at the point at which my daughter feels uncomfortable at Freedom School, like I have to change her regular school." But, according to Dereca, she does not need to choose. "My daughter is like very, very smart by the school standards. But she's also very, very conscious. And if I had to choose between her being very, very smart or her being very, very conscious, I would choose very, very conscious. I don't have to choose, though."

Dereca believes her daughters are enriched and empowered, though in different ways, by both contexts of learning. She goes on to tell me that, when it is time for Freedom School, her children are ready and willing to attend. "We have conversations about . . . whether they can have a choice to go to Freedom School, even when there are other strong options for them. I'm blessed to be able to have other options for my kids. They're like, damn, but I don't want to miss Freedom School." To be an executive director on the one hand and a mother on the other, "that's just a great feelin." Dereca wants her children to feel at home in the Blackness and cultural consciousness of LE's programs. Inevitably, Dereca wants for all children what she wants for her own: a place, like Freedom School, where they feel "love, connection, and challenge" in a way that supports their cultural heritage while maintaining high expectations.

How is this implemented? At Freedom School, Dereca and the staff insure small class sizes (a 1 to 10 ratio); they provide literature that is historically and culturally relevant (e.g., *Run for your Life*, about a girl growing up in the West Oakland Acorn Projects), and they design daily activities that are both fun for the children and at the same time educational. Students at Freedom School make significant gains in reading. But, Dereca explains, that does not occur "because we're such great literacy specialists. That's not why." She has discovered that "they love reading *because* we love them." Although love is central to the learning process, it is sustained through the ways "we create an environment of community," as illustrated in the daily Harambe circle. I am eager to learn more about how this community is created and sustained.

When I question Dereca about this, she explains that the quintessential success of Freedom School, true for all LE's programs, is the relationships fostered between teachers and students. Dereca recognizes that her daughters "bond with their teachers, like they love them" and that many LE participants have a similar experience. "LE's biggest asset, I think, is our relationship building." This is a recurring theme for all of the community-based educators.

As executive director, Dereca understands that if she wants positive outcomes—that is, deterring high-risk behavior by motivating students to combat social injustice—she must create a climate in which her staff is able to foster strong, healthy relationships with the young people. Throughout her impressive career, Dereca has overseen a myriad of programs, from *Upward Bound* to *Girls Inc*. In each endeavor, she has incorporated time and salary for "what I call youth development hours" to compensate her staff for the practical need to "stay after class or before class or take a kid out to lunch." Dereca believes these activities are imperative. She acknowledges that most people who do this work—from community-based educators to mainstream teachers—already have their plates full and "it feels like you don't have time," but, she stresses, "you have to, you have to." Often as simple as 15 minutes of conversation after class, this one-on-one time is crucial to get to know every child more intimately, especially those who might be struggling or who do not have many positive adult role models. Therefore creating an authentic connection is the top priority: "if you want to cover a lot with these kids, you better get that relationship straight cause if you don't, you can forget it." This is especially crucial for students who are disengaged: without connection, "all you're ever going to get are the people who had the aptitude in the first place." At LE, Dereca wants to ignite in every person an interest in learning and, for this to occur, she understands relationships are the catalyst.

Strong relationships are not static but are instead a continuing by-product of "the way you interact with them, what your power dynamics are with them, what your respect level is for them." Dereca tries to personify this behavior, being honest about her own experiences and inquisitive about their lives. I witness an example of this respectful reciprocity when our interview comes to a close.

While I am packing my bag, a few teenagers come into the office. Dereca jumps up to greet the three young African-American women and one young man. The ladies give Dereca a hug as the guy stands back and says nothing. He almost fades into the background except that his two sparkling bling-bling earrings are just too large not to notice. After speaking with the girls, Dereca goes over to the young man and asks, "Have we met before?" He replies with a solemn "No." She beams, "Well, welcome," smiles wide, says "I knew I would have remembered you," and gives him a hug. I watch a smile creep slowly onto his serious face. Small acts of warmth such as this seem to make all the difference for the African-American children of the LE family.

Clearly, relationship building is a central theme for Dereca. As I left the building, I watched her greet a so-called hardcore young African-American man. I was struck by the look of sheer jubilation on her face when she welcomed him into LE. However, this interaction was not about relationship building because she did not know him—it was about love. Just as she told me earlier, the kids at Freedom School love reading because their teachers love them. For her, love is an essential component of reaching young people, but I am not convinced that this is all that teachers need to be effective.

Real People

In January of 2006, I arrive at the LE office for our next interview. I ask the first person I see where I might find Dereca. I am told she is on the phone but that I can take a seat in "The Spot." The Spot is a multi-purpose room that has the usual necessities of a community-based organization such as chairs, TV and VCR, old couches (draped with red sheets), and a whiteboard. This space, however, is exceptional with its all-encompassing multi-colored mural. On every wall there are symbols, words, and visions for and by youth. As I wait for Dereca, I take this opportunity to walk around the room.

The top perimeter of the wall reads "Respect Each Other and The Space, Value All Thoughts, Give 100%." There are life-size silhouettes of youth with poetry written within each frame. I am drawn to one of the images of a person with dreadlocks and a fist in the air. Red, black, and green stripes give shape to the arm and within the body of the portrait I read, "If I dream natural dreams of being a natural woman doing what a woman does when she's natural, I would have a revolution." There are other powerful images. On yellow pad- locks are written words such as *oppression, violence,* and *poverty.* Near them are drawings of keys overlaid with words such as *culture, education, unity, health,* and *spirituality.* I see another silhouette that moves me because the person's arms are outstretched. I walk closer to read the text inside the body:

> With my eye that's at the top of the sky shining rays down on
> my people . . .
> And making my people realize that they are no longer a token,
> cause every word, every speech and every verb can change
> lives because of the words that will be spoken and have
> been spoken.
> With my eye I can see what most others can't and will not
> want to see.
> For me this is a world of wonderful and talented young
> people.

Other pieces of poetry captivate me. Bold purple words state:

> No rubber glove to go through our pockets for something we
> didn't do.
> No more brutality . . . No more thug gang banging mentality.
> We want peace for our streets and schools.
> No more cops acting like fools thinking it's cool to beat and
> cheat.
> No more killing. No more blood spilling.

On the back wall is a life-size image of a tree with thick, deep roots and a heart in the center.

As I make my way around this room, I am inspired because the space feels so young, exuberant, and energetic. When I worked at a nonprofit organization that encouraged youth leadership, I fought to no avail to have a similar "youth space" in our fancy downtown San Francisco office. I dreamed of having a mural like the one before me. Although the organization I worked for is ostensibly engaged in youth development, it did not attempt to make the office celebrate youth or even look youth friendly because, I was told, that might make funders feel uncomfortable. LE, under Dereca's leadership, seems less obsessed with what funders might think and more concerned with its work on the ground with African-American youth.

When Dereca finally arrives for our interview there is a rush about her. She has overbooked herself and is in juggling mode trying to multi-task through her day. Feeling her distraction, I ask if she would like to reschedule. Without hesitation she says no and focuses her attention as we take a seat on the soft, worn couch. I am excited to find out more about the vibrant mural that surrounds us. Whereas I see bright colors and am enthralled with every symbol and word, Dereca has a very different impression and interpretation. She does not talk to me about the beauty but, turning to face the wall of silhouettes, states matter-of-factly, "I could tell you who these different people are cause they're *real* people." She describes the struggle and debate that went into every image. "They had lots of debates about stuff . . . there was a problem for folks that the [all-seeing] eye was blue . . . and it was just interesting. We had a lot of interesting debates about just the women in like different positions and the men. It was really interesting."

Where I see the displayed art, Dereca is more intrigued by the issues of gender, race, and political symbolism that the youth debated about while creating the mural. Although the final product is aesthetically pleasing, it is the *process* that excites her. As I re-examine the mural through her eyes I think of the behind-the-scenes mess of this work. It is easy to romanticize LE's accomplishments. Through our discussion of the mural, Dereca reminds me to look underneath the accolades and get into the trenches with her. I do this at Camp Akili.

How Do You See Yourself

Thick gray clouds define this early August morning as I make my way up Highway 101 in bumper-to-bumper traffic from Richmond to Sonoma State University. In a little over an hour I am in Sonoma, where the sun has broken through and vast expanses of fragrant eucalyptus trees line the road. The university is surrounded by farmland and rolling hills, so different from the cold weather and urban sprawl of the Bay Area. I make my way toward Stevenson Hall to experience Camp Akili and soon hear Dereca's voice coming from the auditorium.

It is 9:00 a.m. and class has already been in session for an hour. Dereca is just starting her lesson on the use of the word "nigga." I take a seat in the corner and glance around the room at the sea of stern faces. Eighty-eight high-school-age African-American youth sit on plush, light-blue, movie-style chairs. Counselors, who range in age from their early twenties to mid-fifties, are dispersed throughout the room. All eyes are on Dereca. She is wearing a tan *I Shot the Sheriff* Bob Marley t-shirt and a tan cap that fades naturally into her pale yellow-Black skin. In a calm tone she is explaining the history of the n-word and saying that it became popular "through acts of genocide, through acts of people being killed." She surveys the room and her voice gets deeper: "and now young people want to defend the word, wanna flip it. In some parts of the world it now has a positive connotation."

She relates a couple of anecdotes. Dereca and several LE youth were getting off a plane in Ghana when they immediately heard the popular rap song "Tell Me When to Go." When their car broke down in the desert in Mali, someone rode past on a camel with a boom-box blasting another rap song, "21 Questions." She comments, "We have to be careful what we export to the rest of the world." She continues, "In Senegal, where there is a war raging, the townspeople dress up like Bloods and Crips before going out to battle." After taking a few questions and comments from the students, Dereca plays a Chris Rock video that lightens the mood and brings spurts of laughter from the group. Though the nature of the video is comedic, it is not off topic; Chris Rock talks about the difference between "Black people and niggaz." With piercing prose he examines "the civil war going on between the Black middle-class and grimy niggaz." He quips, "I just love Black people but hate them niggaz. I wish they'd let me join the Ku Klux Klan so I could go kill me some niggaz . . . Books like kryptonite to a nigga, cause niggaz love to be ignorant . . . People wanna blame the media. I'm not lookin around my shoulder when I go to the ATM talkin bout the media gonna get me." As Chris Rock jokes, Dereca overlays a statement in bold white print on the screen: "It's the media! Are you a nigga?" The video stops, the screen rises, and the lights come back on.

"How do you see yourself? Are you niggaz or not?" Dereca uses provocative questions to challenge her students to analyze the n-word and Chris Rock's portrayal. A young woman says, "I still feel like changin the connotation of the word is justified," and tells us about the origin of Capoeira; slave-owners and overseers believed the people were dancing when in fact they were practicing martial arts, but had disguised it. Young people begin talking all at once and Dereca shouts, "Ago" (KiSwahili for *listen*) and everyone yells back, "Ame" (*we're listening*). As she refocuses the class, she assigns a number to each person with their hand in the air so they understand they will have a chance to speak. One guy remarks, "One of my Mexican patnas be like what's up, my nigga? . . . How can *they* use it?" Dereca repeats the comment and asks a follow-up question. "Well, did you like it when he said it?" He explains that he did not like it and ended up calling his patna a wetback. Dereca asks the campers to think critically about his racialized comeback and to consider whether or not it achieved anything constructive.

This issue of who can use the n-word hits a nerve with the students and stories pour out about all the non-Black people they know who use the term. Dereca challenges: "Where's the miseducation coming from?" A young man replies, "The miseducation comes from us," which leads another very young-looking boy to ask, "If we don't know we're miseducated, then how can we teach another race?" He continues in a slow whisper, "It's just like we stabbin ourself with a knife but don't feel it and don't realize it's killing us." The room explodes with clapping. "It's how we feel it," explains Dereca. "It's how we feel the word. Is this the word you want to feel good about? Today I just want you to think critically about this." As if in rebuttal, one of the young women challenges, "Well, shoot, we all brainwash cause no one on the street, no one on the corner tellin us about the word."

Dereca assures her that Camp Akili is designed to teach about the past precisely so each person has the power, at least the choice, to act consciously. Dereca then asks, "How many y'all know about the Holocaust?" A camper responds, "Which Holocaust?" Dereca grins, "Yes, exactly. Which one? If you know your history, you know yourself. We about to get into it for real, bout to give you all a history lesson." She walks over to the computer, pulls down the video screen and begins showing us images and artifacts from the on-line Jim Crow Museum. "Did you ever know that Agatha Christie, who's a famous author of mystery stories, is also the author of the book *Ten Little Niggers*?"

With every derogatory image we see on the movie-size screen, the mood in the room grows more serious and somber. One slide has a picture of a dark-skinned baby eating out of a bottle of ink. The caption reads, "What does nigger plus milk equal? Ink, black baby ink." Dereca comments, "This isn't that far back. This is our grandparents' age. This is in the last sixty years. This is Beatles, John Lennon. John Lennon wrote a book called *Woman is the Nigger of the World*." I try my best to write down what I see, but the pictures are too grotesque, too full of white supremacist hatred. My stomach is in knots. This is the unspoken history of *my* people.

In a timid, innocent voice a young woman in the front row asks, "Are these things [for] white people houses or Black people houses?" Dereca says, "All these things that I'm showing you were made for white people's homes and purchased for white people's homes . . . Now, some Black people collect these things so that we will never forget the history that we come out of, the strug-gle that we come out of." Students spend the next couple of minutes in deep discussion. Dereca then asks for the lights to come back on. She encourages everyone to take a short break and stretch: "Reach for the sky. The sky's the limit."

Within a minute, everyone is seated, quiet and stern. The room is con-centrated on Dereca. "How many people believe that Black people could be

racist?" A few hands go up and then a student asks, "Well, how are you defining racism?" Dereca loves this question "because the essence of all of this is to
challenge, to criticize, to think." She encourages the kids to speak and engage
in dialogue because that is what brings the conversation "to a higher level."
On the blackboard she writes, "institutional, interpersonal, and internalized"
and defines each: "Institutional is about systems. Interpersonal is that you're
only able to affect your sphere of influence. It's much more one-on-one. And
internalized is what's going on within you." She then asks for examples of each
of the terms. At the institutional level the group talks about "systems of power
[such as] economics, education, the military, media, the law." Then she asks,
"What does internalized oppression mean?" A young man in the center calls
out, "It's about oppressing yourself," and a female chimes in, "If you use the
n-word you internalizing oppression." Dereca facilitates a conversation about
systems of oppression and then, once again, pulls down the video screen.

The 2-hour lesson plan comes full circle when the words "Abolish the
n-word" fill the screen. A slideshow of Black men being lynched begins alongside the sounds of Nina Simone's version of "Strange Fruit Blowing in the
Summer Breeze." At one point, in small type, it reads "But many Black men
that were lynched were castrated and their balls were stuffed in their mouth,
and they would actually die choking on the blood from their own testicles."
Nina Simone's voice echoes through the room with such clarity I feel like she
is sitting in the corner singing about bodies hanging from trees. The music
fades out but the pictures continue. We travel farther back into history to auction blocks where African men, women, and children were sold to the highest
white bidder. These images are jarring, the scars on naked backs enraging.
Bold red letters on the screen ask, "Why would you use the n-word today?
These are acts of hate. This word was made popular on a daily basis. So why
would you use the n-word today?"

At this point the auditorium has a peculiar, stunned silence. The only sound
I can hear is my pen on paper. I wonder if I'm being too loud just by writing
these words down. Next we see an image of a white man stabbing a Black
man with an American flagpole. Underneath this image is the caption, "Hate
is the author of the n-word." A Black man stands naked on an auction block.
Bold letters again: "Abolish the n-word." In a melancholic tone Dereca closes,
"This is not about hate, it's about love. Loving yourself to heal what people
been through, survived, and where we are going. It's a personal decision." The
young people begin to clap. I set my notebook down and begin to clap along
with them.

Sister J. Braggs, this year's camp director, walks to the center of the room.
Her auburn locks are pulled back in a ponytail and her voice sounds hoarse.
"Everyone stand up and stretch. We're about to go do our nation debriefs.
Ashanti counselors to the front. If you are in the Ashanti nation, go outside."
She continues with the Hausa, the Ibo, the Zulu, and so on, naming the

nations that the young people belong to while at Camp Akili. The youth and counselors go outside, sit in circles, and talk through the morning's lesson.

I make my way out of the building. After years of hearing about the famous Camp Akili, I just experienced a piece of it for myself. In her lesson Dereca used imagery (the Chris Rock video, Jim Crow slides, and brutal images of slavery) alongside thought-provoking questions ("Are you niggaz or not?") to facilitate a critical conversation. For 2 hours, over 80 teenagers participated enthusiastically in Dereca's lesson.

The students' behavior today was drastically different from the stereotype. In fact, a common perception of "urban teaching" is that discipline problems will overshadow learning. Dereca shows that youth can and will engage. But is this possible in schools? What makes Dereca's approach so effective? When I sit down with Dereca's student, Scid, I get some answers.

Start Fightin

Scid's circumstance, unfortunately, is not atypical of many disenfranchised urban youth. After being kicked out of Fremont High School for poor attendance and bad behavior, he only cared about "bein a dope boy, sellin dope on the street, makin money so I can buy me some car rims." Scid (pronounced "Sid") first attended Camp Akili when he was 17, at a time when he was "goin thru my misguided problems." At first he was "shocked. I wanted to go home bad, cause I wasn't used to this. Where I'm from Black people don't love each other." Throughout the days and nights at Camp Akili he pushed away and questioned, but eventually, "towards the end of the camp, I was beggin Dereca, like can we *please* have an extra day." During the 6 days in between, Scid describes having an awakening. This was in part because of the knowledge he was receiving. "I remember arguing with Dereca about the word nigga. I told Dereca I'm a nigga. Nigga means Never Ignorant Getting Goals Accomplished. I changed it. She was like no. Then we watched a clip of Sankofa.[2] Then we started talkin about the ancestors. And she took us to a room showin a lot of men bein hung by their necks off trees—that's called strange fruit. She wrote on the bottom, 'Are you a nigger now?' and I was like wow. Maybe I'm not a nigga."

For Scid, this was a thorough history lesson that made him question his language and lifestyle. However, though the information was highly conscious and relevant, it was only a part of what made him change. The constant attention and care he received made him feel part of a family and gave him a sense of community. He describes what happened: "Towards the middle of camp I guess [Dereca] noticed me kinda tryin to avoid em. So what she did, she stuck to me like glue . . . She just opened up her arms and accepted me and that kinda made me feel special because she accepted me for who I were . . . Instead of judgin me, criticizing me, and pushing me away, she took me in." This acceptance reinforces the notion that genuine relationships can have a profound impact.

After camp, Scid began sticking to Dereca like glue and would come to the LE office, his oasis, nearly every day. From my experience, I think many nonprofit organizations would be thrilled to have a young person eager to be active in their organization. Dereca was no exception, but she was also very direct and practical: he needed to finish school and get his driver's license. I think about Dereca's staunch position on this as I sit with Scid. She does not want Scid to end up like some LE students who can tell her about the origins of civilization but do not have basic skills to get a job. Dereca explains this to me: "Sometimes youth development organizations, especially youth organizin groups, they get these kids out here and they got them all focused on makin changes in the community, and it does give them self-esteem and it does make them feel good but when they walk away from those kids or the kids walk away from them, they don't have the ability to take care of themselves. I've had way too many homeless kids graduate from LE." She looks directly into my eyes and proclaims, "That's a failure." This sense of somehow failing students haunts Dereca because she wants them to succeed in all areas of their lives.

Dereca has good reason for this fear. One day some months earlier, Scid completely disappeared. This happened after he had been coming to the LE office regularly for over a year. Dereca was in a panic, fearful that somehow the "LE family" did not provide him proper support, or worse. She remembers, "He just disappeared and I was so scared that somethin had happened to him cause he had had gang problems and other things that had gone on in his life. I was just terrified." She explains, "I went out driving in the neighborhood lookin for him . . . And then one day he walked in the door, and I just started cryin." Scid told Dereca: "I just thought about what you said and I got somethin for you." Dereca was thankful that Scid was alive and well, and overwhelmed when he handed her a photograph of his graduation ceremony, along with a copy of his GED and his driver's permit. Scid had disappeared because he wanted to surprise Dereca; he wanted to demonstrate to her that he could, on his own, complete his goals. This is an example of empowerment.

It is hard to imagine that not too long ago Scid believed his whole life revolved around his boys and the notorious corner of Fairfax and High Street in East Oakland. Before he came to Camp Akili, it never occurred to Scid to do well in school. However, Leadership Excellence, coupled with Dereca's tough love, was transformative. When he focused on his goal, he went to "Berkeley Adult and got my high school diploma like the snap of my fingers . . . I'm in college to this day . . . I have one more year before I get my AA[3] degree." When I ask Scid to describe his new lifestyle, he declares his clothes a metaphor for the new man he is becoming: "I wear my grill because this is ancient, like African kings and queens used to wear gold teeth . . . My locks is my king's crown. I wear glasses to help me to read . . . I wear button-up shirts and slacks and dress shoes . . . Basically to show that I'm going to keep my gold teeth and locks and Black skin, just to show the police that don't everybody dress [in] white T, blue jeans, and Nikes." Scid, now a conscious, determined young man, is an active participant in LE as a camp counselor and is pursuing his education.

Scid credits Dereca for his awakening because she is "very powerful" and "somethin amazin," a warrior consistently giving him strength to conquer circumstances. "She was like . . . livin in this society you gonna fight or you're gonna be a victim . . . Dereca, she pushes you real, real hard . . . as a victim you may want to feel babied," he says, but "Dereca gives the impression like stop crying, start fightin. Stop cryin n start fightin!" Scid knows he has a lot to fight for, especially since the vast majority of the youth he grew up with are either dead or in jail. In fact, "two of em got killed the other day." He leans forward and speaks with intensity: "Dereca been through the struggle . . . I want to run something too, cause I been through the struggling." He champions, "I can haul in kids . . . you never know what we might spark out there. We might spark another leader or another anything . . . Malcolm X was a pimp and a hustler before he was who he were . . . like they did with me . . . you never know what you're gonna spark just by opening eyes." Scid's spark is strong, courageous, and contagious. I am inspired.

From Scid's perspective, Dereca is effective for several reasons. Unlike his teachers at school, Dereca fully accepted him with love, taught him about African history, and convinced him to be a warrior. Scid sees himself as a warrior for social change; this means not falling victim to his circumstance but instead excelling in school and in life. It is almost hard to picture him as a hardcore grimy 17-year-old. But then again, the room is full of students who are more like Scid than one might think, and I see them the next time I drive to Camp Akili.

Critical Thinking

On my second visit to Sonoma State to experience Camp Akili, I think about the intensity of the previous lesson on the n-word. It reminds me of the eye-opening curriculum I received as a student in the Black Studies Department at Berkeley High School. In ninth grade I crossed the racial divide at school when I enrolled in African American Studies. Instead of Economics, I took Black Economics; instead of (Western) Psychology, I studied Black Psychology. For the next 4 years I supplemented my schedule with a range of such classes: African-American Literature, Black-Gold Black-Soul Black-Dynamite, African-Haitian Dance, African-American History, and Black Leadership. I did not enter these courses in search of some Black experience, but was cognizant that I would be pushed (and I was) to learn about being white.

Because of my high school experiences, I feel at home at Camp Akili and comforted by the content and pedagogy. However, as I make this drive toward camp, I remind myself that one of the things that makes Camp Akili so healing and empowering is its *for Black people, with Black people, by Black people* approach. To the extent that this component is what makes it so successful, I do not want my (white) presence to distract from the task at hand. I am humbled by this thought. Even if I want to stay the entire day, I know that, after Dereca gives her lesson, I must leave so that the youth and elders have *their* space to reflect, heal, and grow. The drive goes more quickly than I expect and before I know it I am walking toward Stevenson Hall.

As I make my way to the entrance, I notice an Akili student lying down on a concrete bench. I walk toward him because I want to ask if everyone is in the auditorium. As I get closer, I realize he is sound asleep, snoring. I remember Dereca telling me that last night was *The Middle Passage*. During this exercise the campers are awakened at 2:00 in the morning, blindfolded, and then taken into the foothills of Sonoma. In this setting, African music is playing, incense is blowing, and the youth are standing together in their assigned nations. Suddenly they are forced from one another, disrespected, and dragged away. They remain blindfolded and are taken to new locations, isolated and alone. When the sun begins to climb over the hills, the blindfolds come off and they reconvene to reflect on the horrific experience of slavery, the strength of their ancestors, and the power of their possibilities. Numerous LE graduates have told me that it is a terrifying, painful, and life-changing experience that every young Black person needs to go through in order to wake up. I can almost hear the conviction of their words as I make my way into the building.

An African-American professor, Brother Mutu, stands at the blackboard talking about power, oppression, and change. He is dressed casually and is attentive to the youth; he seems not to even notice me taking a seat in the back row. "Let's talk about your environment." He asks the tired kids, "What's your environment like?" Although the youth have been up the entire night, they start pouring out descriptions: "crackheads, smoking, poverty, ho's, scrapers, bad ass kids, ignorance, weed, school, liquor stores, drug dealers, police, guns." Writing quickly, he can barely keep up with the barrage of images describing their crime-infested neighborhoods.

"Okay," he concludes, "here is the lie. We act like that's how people are," and points back to the words on the board. "Seeing is believing. The human mind believes what it sees. There's a difference between reality and the truth." He conjures Morpheus from the popular *Matrix* movie: "One pill will give Neo reality, one pill will give him truth. Truth is being offered to you at this moment at Camp Akili." And he continues, "See, the opposite of the truth would be a lie. And the lie is that people think that crackheads, smoking, poverty, ho's, that that's who we are. But it's not true. What if that reality is based on falsehoods? The way you self-identify is the way someone made you to self-identify. Shoot, [in] *our* neighborhoods, we think we control the liquor licenses. Who controls who can open a liquor store? Cause white people make sure there ain't a liquor store on all their corners. Shoot, where's the grocery store in West Oakland, people? Albertsons don't know where West Oakland's at? When the color of the people in the community change, they clean it up, the stores move in. Why is that?" Brother Mutu continues, sprinkling facts with dialogue. He seems mindful, like Dereca, to carry on the lesson like a thoughtful conversation. It is not yet 9:00 in the morning, and already the campers are engaged in a critical analysis of West Oakland.

I feel a tap on my shoulder. Brother Jason, an LE teacher, asks me to come to the back of the room. "Vajra, I don't know if you should be writing everything down because the youth don't really know you like that and we're trying to build trust." Although Dereca has invited me to Camp Akili, many of the other adults are concerned about how the students will perceive me and if my note taking will disrupt their process. I understand their unapologetic commitment to build trust with the youth and agree to take notes only when Dereca teaches.

Brother Mutu concludes his lesson and during the short break I watch the counselors interact with the young people, noticing the friendly gestures, intense conversations, and warm exchanges that fill the classroom. Many of them were once campers, and now they return each year to volunteer at Camp Akili. A few staff members are paid, but all of the camp counselors are volunteers. "The 'thank you' you get from those kids," one says, "is priceless . . . I'm passin down the toll . . . that's worth more than anything, that's global change."

When it is time to turn the class discussion over to Dereca, she is nowhere to be found. While we wait, Sister J-Braggs plays a few popular E-40 songs. The music finishes, but still Dereca is missing.

Finally she explodes from the back door looking furious. "What could have gotten her so upset?" I write, picturing some drastic event. Did a kid get hurt? Dereca rushes to the front and steps into the aisle. Her eyes are blazing. She begins to recite vulgar, misogynistic, hard-hitting rap lyrics. The youth are aghast. My mouth hangs open, I am so startled by her demeanor. Dereca does not look like herself. She is no longer Mama Dereca, sista, and conscious. Instead she is grabbing her crotch and walking side-to-side with an "I don't give a fuck" attitude. In offensive, nasty language she rants on for 5 minutes and then, instantaneously, she steps out of the persona and appears to be herself again. She moves slowly and sits down on top of the front desk. Her back is straight, her body is still, and her eyes are scanning the silent room. Dereca uses everything she has to her advantage in her work with young people. Her small frame belies her capacity to speak so loudly. She once told me how she loves using the shock-and-awe factor when teaching.

A few moments later, as the dramatic impression settles over the quiet audience, she resumes a strong tone, "It must be your butt." The youth immediately recognize the phrase and in an impromptu chorus finish the Nelly song by responding "cause it ain't your face." In call-and-response mode, Dereca starts sentences from popular rap lyrics and the young people, with no preparation, complete each one. These lyrics are so integral to their daily reality and vocabulary that they do not miss a beat. Just when I think a discussion will ensue, she roars, "I tol you all about the ten little nigger book yesterday. Well, we're about to watch the ten little nigga video right now!" She pulls down the screen.

Dereca proceeds to play the uncut version of the Nelly video, "It Must be Your Butt Cause it Ain't Your Face," in which a dozen women in little or no clothing dance obscenely. Immediately after the video, Dereca asks, "What's somethin that was put on or in a woman's butt?" Hands go up around the room, as the youth name items: a credit card, a hand, a video camera, a chain, drink, and money. She listens carefully to their answers and then, in what feels like a tangent, begins to discuss the crack cocaine epidemic. She tells us, "I know about it. Ask me about it." Dereca describes the ways crack dismantled "our" community and says that "we" are the crackhead generation. "The result," she teaches, "is a Nelly video." Dereca's voice reverberates through the room as she reminds the youth of their history lessons: "Thousands and thousands of years of civilization. Look at us now. Why us?"

A young woman in the third row replies, "Cause of broken homes." Dereca nods and then challenges the girl's comment: "Mexicans have broken homes. A Jordanian might have a broken home. But why us on the video like this?" A young man responds, "The video is so degrading it hurt to watch that. The men and the women are both oppressed in that video cause the men been tricked and it's like they don't know who their role model is . . . who's watchin uncut? My little brother." Dereca comments on his observation and then goes on to explain that if she went to an elementary school and began the same type of rap call-and-response the children would be able to complete it. Why?

Over 15 hands go up across the room. The overall commentary from the students is either in support or ridicule of the Nelly video. This dichotomy splits along two themes—those who admire Nelly because he is rich, and those who consider him an exploiter of Black women. Dereca pushes the class to examine the socio-economic and historical context that gives birth to the Nelly videos of the world. She points out: "He already made the video so the analysis can't be so trivial and simplistic as dissing Nelly. That is not critical thinking. That is reactionary."

In a forceful tone, the young man sitting in front of me challenges Dereca. "This shit's really not our problem, ya feel me? Whateva's happenin, you know, all you puttin all this shit down our throat. We can't control nothin!" His comment causes nearly every hand in the room to go up. The young people begin to discuss, debate, and critique their lives and whether or not they *really* have power to make a difference. Dereca says, "I want you to think about the influences in your life. And I got Houdini (I'm a ho you know I'm a ho) in my iPod right now. It's about all of us."

She continues with a personal example from her years in college. At her sorority's party she stepped to the tune "Hey, We Want Some Pussy." A few weeks later an article in *Vibe* discussed Dereca's step show. The author challenged her and her peers (college-educated Black women) to have higher standards for themselves and their people. She admits, "That article checked me." Following Dereca's lead, a counselor with long locks and ebony skin talks about his family: "I'm learning not to judge my family. I used to get frustrated because I got family that smoke and drink and, you know, family members that got a baseball team of ho's. I used to really judge them. But now I work at McClymonds[4] and I live in my community to stand strong *with* them. It's not about separating myself from my family, it's about loving them for who they are and loving myself for who I have decided to be." The mutual sharing between counselors and students that ensues truly creates group conversation.

Dereca recognizes the honest communication and encourages the youth: "Best part is not just what me and the counselors talkin about but what y'all talkin about." She heats up the discussion. "What's my favorite word?" mimics Dereca from Too Short's new song and everybody yells out "bitch." Someone admits, "I didn't know bitch was a bad word till I was nine." Dereca walks around the auditorium, encouraging students to speak about their lives and experiences.

"Okay now," she hollers as she moves to the blackboard, "I need some quick definitions of pimps and hos." The youth come up with attributes of a pimp: "no conscience, dependent, illusion, manipulative, vulnerable, one-track mind, money, low self-esteem, lazy, self-centered, hustle-minded, trick they mind." For whore they offer: "dependent, conform, use drugs, vulnerable, insecure, gullible, hustle-minded, insecure, low self-esteem." In the pimp column Dereca places a star next to no conscience, illusion, and manipulative. On the ho side she puts a star next to gullible, hustle-minded, insecure, and low self-esteem. She then shouts, "How many in here hoin for a shoe company?" She takes a short pause, looks around the room and then explains, "The pimp–ho relationship is about money and control, whether that's between a man and a woman on the block or between you and the corporations. The pimp is hella insecure and hella lazy. A pimp is lazy and cannot survive in the world of men so he goes into the world of women as a predator. Corporations do the same thing! Nike costs about 43 cents to make, but you pay over $100. That's some pimp shit."

Dereca pops her collar with fierce attitude. "What y'all makin ain't shit! The real pimp game, not many people know what a bottom bitch is. Who know what a bottom bitch is? That's the main chick who recruits other females. How many bottom bitches for the companies we got up in here? Recognize yourself as the bottom bitch that you are!" She is on fire. "How many of us know who we are beyond what we're wearin? If you do not know who you are, you're vulnerable to being pimped. It's all about money. America is based on capitalism. We vote with our dollars, but we're not poor. We got our clothes, we got our hair done, our nails . . . Go to jail, risk your life for that car, just to buy those shoes. You're a good ho! . . . You got to be the first one on the block with the shoe . . . then you clown other people cause they don't got em. You don't like it when your girl got some dude's name tattooed on her arm. But then again, you basically are a walkin tattoo with all the name brands you got on." A wave of "Damn, she clownin" and a lot of "ahs" come from the students. "I'm not askin you to live outside your community. I'm asking you to wake the fuck up. Wake the fuck up!" Dereca's voice cracks with intense emotion. Her passion is palpable. This commitment to raising the consciousness of African-American youth is demonstrated repeatedly in many touching moments. Using everything she has, everything she knows, she gives all of herself in these lessons.

As I watch her, I wonder if she ever gives too much of herself. Later on, I ponder how she is able to sustain her round-the-clock fight for young people alongside her many responsibilities as a wife and mother. Through my research I have had the opportunity to meet some remarkable and unique community-based educators. But when I interview Dereca, there is a distinct tone to our conversations compared with the conversations I have with my male participants. Though Dereca and I are different, we share a common bond as mothers. Sometimes, before our interview can even begin, she says she just needs to speak to me "mother to mother" and we sit, talking back and forth, about raising our children and co-parenting. Even though Rudy has three children, I cannot imagine our conversations going in a similar direction. As I watch her and the other community-based educators do their work there is something different about Dereca—yet very familiar to me—in the ways she must balance, and more often than not juggle, home and work. Should she get out of bed in the middle of the night when the phone rings to bail a kid out of jail? Rudy, Victor, and Jack receive similar phone calls but do not seem as torn between the push and pull between their personal lives and serving youth.

Give Something of Yourself

The rewards and challenges of being "Mama Dereca" is one of the topics we explore during our third interview. Dereca is "head of the LE family" and feels a motherly connection to the youth and families she works with. But it does take a toll on her personal life. As she tries to be mother to all, it is sometimes difficult for her to find time to be at home nurturing her own children and her relationship with her husband.

When I ask her colleagues about any areas Dereca could improve upon, they assure me that her work ethic and effectiveness are stellar. They do, however, tell me that it is difficult for Dereca to "take time for herself." A colleague says, "She works so hard I don't really see her takin that time to just be the mom or just to be the wife and I think that's where her struggles come in." Another person in the office explains to me that Dereca will receive a call and have to drop everything to go to the emergency room to "hold someone while they bleeding" and that that constant care "sometimes gets her in trouble because she has a life, she's married, she has kids." Dereca recently got married, though she has been with her partner for over 7 years, and is aware that she has to get better at "that personal piece." A number of community activists are encouraging Dereca to go into politics, but she will not, precisely because "I spread myself too thin" and "my family needs me"; this is a serious challenge for her. Nonetheless, African-American children are in crisis and this motivates her exhausting commitment to Leadership Excellence.

Identity-based programs are, in general, a hard sell, and Dereca works incessantly to convince people that they are necessary. "I don't think Camp Akili could happen," she says, "if it was integrated. It's like trying to talk about what's goin on with your family on Jerry Springer [and] that's not something that's easy to talk about in a mixed setting. It's hard enough to talk about it just with Black men and Black women." As she speaks about the exclusivity of LE, I gain a deeper appreciation for her willingness to let me in. However, this does not change her perspective that African-American youth need spaces where they can develop *their* specific consciousness. And this concentration is not without controversy. Dereca has had to fight and defend her perspective, even with other Black organizations.

Dereca told me about going to a Children's Defense Fund meeting at Alex Haley's Farm in Tennessee, where she joined with African-American organizations from across the country to discuss putting together a Black Community Crusade for Children. During one of the workshops someone mentioned that it was "a Black community crusade for *all* children." Dereca was quite confused by this comment and raised her hand: "I understood you to say that it's a Black community crusade for *all* children and when we signed up to be a part of this program it was because it really focused on Black children, providing literacy opportunities that really reflected *their* culture and *their* experience . . . I just want to make sure that I understood you correctly and if there's going to be a shift moving away from that to focus more universally on all children?" Dereca did not want their efforts to be integrated and did not want to spend time strategizing about how to help children from all racial backgrounds.

Dereca thinks back to this moment and says, "I thought I was very polite . . . it wasn't attacking. I just asked the question." But she shakes her head and says, "Then it went down." When one of the event coordinators stated that no one else was confused, Dereca faced the hundred-or-so people in the auditorium and suggested, "Let's ask because if I'm the only person who's confused, then I'm happy to have a side conversation." The facilitator begrudgingly asked the question and "hands went up all over the room," indicating the need to clarify whether the campaign was exclusively for African-Americans or for *all* children.

Now in storyteller mode, Dereca imitates each person's voice and mannerisms. "It went down so bad" that an "older, Black woman minister" stood up in the middle of the ensuing debate to proclaim "We just goin to pray now because we don't hate white children." Dereca took to the floor, determined to address the minister's point. She faced the crowd of African-Americans: "What is the issue with us when we try to love ourselves, always being accused of hating? We have nursed white babies at our breast. We don't have anything to prove about our love for humanity but we do have to prove whether we can effectively love ourselves." Dereca breathes heavily as she recounts the discussion. "I don't hate white children. My record is clear on my love for children. That's not the issue. The issue is that I'm trying to put together something specifically for my children who are in a special crisis situation." Her statement did not go over well. Another elder stood up: "You were not alive in the '60s, you don't know." Dereca ("I was like fire. I was right back") retorted passionately, "But I'm alive now and if you don't let go of the baton and pass it on, your whole movement will die."

Dereca is unabashedly committed to Black people and she is ready to take the baton. Perhaps she already has. When I ask her if she had to choose a particular cause to work on, she is quick to tell me about the prison system. Angry, intense, and sad all at once, she teaches me about the prison industrial complex and the criminalization of youth: "The criminal justice system is the worst enemy of youth, of urban and poor youth in this country." Through her efforts to reach young people she has found that it is "a very huge enemy of their consciousness. They are living in a police state and it's really bad . . . They really feel like they can't break free and they can't in many cases . . . I just really believe that right now that is the stronghold, the chokehold of the enemy on our community, on our people. Like we're losin a whole generation of Black . . ." Dereca stops mid-sentence and it looks as if she is trying to blink away a few tears. She swallows, takes a breath, and continues, "We're losing a whole generation of Black men. It's straight genocide. That shit right there hurts like no pain. That's my family."

This struggle is about *her* family. From the outside, Dereca is an accomplished African-American woman. But underneath her smile and quick-paced demeanor a deeper story emerges. Dereca's life is a pendulum of experiences. The communities that developed her into the strong person she is today were often in stark contrast to one another. On the one hand, Dereca was raised with a "very strong Black consciousness." This sense of pride came in part from her immediate family but also from her larger community. On the other hand, she was educated in predominantly white schools while her parents struggled with their addiction to the streets.

In Detroit, the city council, police chief, and mayor were African-American and the experiences she had within her city were relatively isolated from white people. She does, however, remember quite vividly when the Ku Klux Klan wanted to march in her neighborhood. "Have you heard the Ku Klux Klan is coming? . . . It was a big old thing. Everybody was talking about it in all the barbershops and all the corners. Even little kids were talking about it." There was a great debate; should we let the Ku Klux Klan march? Dereca's eyes sparkle with enthusiasm as she recounts what the mayor, Coleman Young, declared: "Let em march down Mack Avenue on the lower east side . . . I'm not goin to deny you your permit, but if you want to march, you goin to march in this neighborhood—let them deal wid you." Everyone felt the weight of his statement because "Mack Avenue was not someplace [you] wanted to mess with . . . and they didn't want to march. They did not march! That's the climate that I grew up in." Although the KKK incident captures the ethos of Black solidarity in which Dereca was raised, it stands in stark contrast to the predominantly white schools she attended throughout her life.

Dereca attended affluent, elite institutions from private schools in Detroit to a boarding school in Massachusetts because her mother wanted her to have a prestigious education. In these environments she was one of a small handful of African-Americans in a sea of white people, white culture, and white ignorance. In these spaces she was asked all kinds of questions including "How come you don't wash your hair everyday?" and "What do Black guys smell like?" In fact, at the boarding school a classmate called her the n-word. Although the isolation and racism were harsh, Dereca was raised to accept any opportunity and achieve. She remembers, "I was raised to be shooting for the teacher," and in these environments she excelled academically. However, Dereca does not see her educational prestige as a special accomplishment because her teachers had such low expectations for her. She tells me about "the pity factor." Teachers were amazed that "I could write and I could talk and I could add . . . and that was such a miracle . . . that I never had to do work."

Although Dereca did not find school especially challenging, at times she did find it hard to navigate her distinct worlds: Black Detroit and white schools. Her mother was keen on making sure Dereca knew her place as a strong African-American woman: "I would call home and if I said something" like a white girl "she was like . . . let's just be clear, like don't get out there and have them think, have you think you can just talk any kinda way or act any kinda way cause that's not for you. That might be what *they* do, but that's not for you." Dereca developed code switching into an art and I am always struck by her ability to navigate vastly different environments with ease—from a cut-throat one-on-one situation with a kid on a street corner to guest speaking at UC Berkeley about hip-hop to a debate with Jane Fonda about women's rights.

Although the environments that raised Dereca were drastically different from one another, it is the behind-the-scenes, behind-closed-doors juggling that deeply impacts her outlook on life. For example, while Dereca was going to lily-white schools, her parents were selling drugs and she was "totally exposed to street life . . . cocaine . . . my father was incarcerated . . . it's a crazy kind of combination." While her stepfather slowly transitioned out of the life, her mom "had a harder time," and even when she was at Stanford, "my mama was cracked out."

Dereca is not ashamed of her family's turmoil but believes it is an important component of how she is able to reach LE youth. Part of her teaching philosophy is to be upfront and personal about her struggles. Accordingly, she will tell them "my daddy was a pimp . . . because I don't carry necessarily shame with it [and] I think it helps them feel validated too. Like I'm not ashamed that my mother was on drugs . . . I think sharin that wisdom that I've gained over the years is really helpful for them because . . . there's nobody in their lives usually tellin them how do you navigate havin a mom who's on crack." While she speaks intimately and frankly about these perils, she simultaneously encourages the youth to succeed in spite of—possibly because of—what they are able to survive. She affirms to certain teenagers, "Just because she's on crack doesn't mean your life is over." Although Dereca was touted as "the exception" and "the gifted child" her entire life, she makes it clear to youth that success is not contingent upon a certain type of family or background. She confides in the kids that "nobody wants to be the exception, that's not a good feeling and I have been that for most of my life . . . I know so much more about my community than the people who labeled me that way. I know I'm not that exceptional . . . but for the grace of God, everybody in my community would be doin the same thing I'm doin but the system doesn't allow them to do that." As Dereca says this, a picture of Scid flashes through my mind. It is Dereca's deep-seated belief in personal agency and the inadequacies of the system that prompts her to consistently raise the bar for youth. She knows that when they succeed it is not because they are exceptional. Rather, it is precisely because they are innately excellent.

Dereca offers me an illustration in an LE student named Lafia. Many of the adults in Lafia's life can hardly believe she can maintain a GPA above 3.0 because of her circumstances. But for Dereca a 3.0 is not even adequate because "Lafia is capable of a 4.0. She should be valedictorian of her school cause she's that smart." Dereca is disappointed and frustrated with adults who only "want her to go to *a* college. I want her to be able to go to Stanford or Harvard" if she wants. Dereca can see Lafia's potential partly because of her own life experiences. She also tries to treat every child at LE with the same high academic expectations she has for her own children. In order to see the greatness and possibility of youth, Dereca believes you have to see "them like they're your own kids." This is key to her philosophy: if adults working with young people are unable to genuinely identify with youth, they will never be able to recognize their intelligence and potential.

I ask Dereca to speak further about her tactics as a teacher. She explains that she loves, listens, and shares stories from her own life as a way of reaching students. At the outset, she fundamentally cares for and believes in the young people: "I love, I love, I love the youth that I work with and I think that always shows through." Moreover, "I *really* believe in their ability to take control of their destinies." Her basic strategy as a teacher is to "listen to them." This is true for all the community-based educators. In Dereca's case, listening to young people helps her design relevant, thought-provoking lessons. For example, based on conversations she had with LE students throughout the school year, she knew that showing the Nelly video at Camp Akili would spark an intense discussion. Dereca sees this responsiveness as one of the most important tools she uses because it allows her to "get the barometer," learn about them, and then create curriculum "based upon what they're thinkin about." She clarifies that this does not mean she is trying to seem "cool" to them, but it is instead about having lessons that "resonate with their own experience."

Dereca realizes that she cannot ask young people to open up about their own lives if she is unwilling to talk about herself. She recognizes the need to be "really honest and vulnerable about my own experiences . . . I been raped . . . or even just mundane little things, like procrastinatin hella bad." Dereca's colleague states that Dereca is constantly able to model her belief that "if you want the youth to give something of themselves you have to give them something of yourself." This creates honest dialogue because Dereca is exposed along with the young people. Dereca has a vociferous style and is able to instigate conversations that are both political and interpersonal. The result, as I witnessed at Camp Akili, is dialogic. Dereca champions a *pedagogy of communication*; she intentionally creates a classroom where conversation and debate are paramount.

Even when Dereca is able to carve out spaces for honest communication and critical thinking to occur, she is not content. She is constantly asking herself and those around her what can be improved. Dereca is not afraid or unwilling to admit when she is wrong or out of step with her own teaching philosophy. Recently her younger brother checked her: he said she did not facilitate enough of a conversation with the youth during the sexism workshop at Camp Akili. "My brother, who is my ultimate critic, was like it was wack . . . you came too hard so that you didn't create the space like you normally do where they could acknowledge where they're at." She recognizes that was "great feedback." Though Dereca shuns being a didactic teacher, she has a natural, forceful tone that sometimes makes her too direct. This is an instance where the ideals of her pedagogy and the reality of her classroom sometimes clash. However, she is very open about this dilemma in her teaching style. This self-reflective quality is an important part of her character, and carries into her leadership style.

Dereca is constantly refining LE's programs so that they can best serve the needs of African-American youth. Camp Akili, for example, will now only accept teenagers from West Oakland. This was a hard decision for her to make because she wants to provide services to any kid in need, but she realizes, "if it's the seventy in West Oakland versus seventy in Richmond or the seventy all over the city, it doesn't matter to me. The difference is that if I take seventy in West Oakland, I have the capacity to be there for them" after camp. This sensitive flexibility seems to make Dereca a reflective teacher and farsighted leader.

Show Them an Option

It is time for our final interview and I am eager to sit down with Dereca once again. Over the past 2 years Dereca and I have become fairly close and, because of the sheer busyness of both our lives, we can rarely carve out space and time to come together and reflect upon the work she does so well. Once again I am circling the block trying to find parking when my cell phone rings. It's Dereca. "Did I tell you we moved?" She gives me directions and I turn my car around. Miraculously, I find parking in front of their new building and, before I know it, I am jogging up the two flights of stairs. The new office space is larger, very bright and airy. Although there are boxes everywhere, a few pieces of fabric and African batiks adorn the walls, giving it a homey feeling.

While Dereca is preoccupied with a staff member, I walk down the sunlit hallway and turn right into an office meticulously decorated with African and African-American regalia. I take a seat on the plush chair, lean back, and think about how the many images reflect Dereca's passions. Then, to my surprise, the office intern walks by, leans in and tells me, "This is *not* Dereca's office. You need to go next door." Feeling a bit thrown off, I gather up my tape recorder and backpack and make my way to the adjacent room.

This office next door could not be more different. It is sparse with no decorations of any kind. Two large desks are pushed together in an L-shape and each desk has a computer on it. A corkboard of pictures leans against the back wall but has not been hung. When Dereca comes in, she proceeds to check email on one computer, look up information on a grant on the other computer, make a phone call about an upcoming speaking engagement, and simultaneously look over at me from time to time to check in. I laugh to myself as I watch her and wonder how I was able (even after learning so much about her) to confuse the offices. Of course Dereca's office is barren; she is not overly concerned with the aesthetics of her job or the appearance of her office. She is too busy with the crisis, the state of emergency at hand. Dereca feels this urgency as deeply as her soul can reach. When the war is over, and all youth have genuine opportunities to excel, then perhaps she will take time to decorate. For now, she is seeing how Leadership Excellence can help improve McClymonds High School in West Oakland.

Leadership Excellence has always been on the periphery of schools, as a staunch critic of the inadequacies and as an advocate of the possibilities. Only very recently is LE partnering with a school and trying to have its transformational success occur within the confines of an institution. Dereca resisted this union: "It's just failed and diseased and it's just sick . . . it really bothers me to have to tie our work to that system . . . I wouldn't let my kids go to McClymonds so why am I tryin to get kids to go there more . . . [but] if I don't get the attendance up, these kids won't have a good school but I see why they don't want to come cause the school is so bad . . . it's a very bad chicken-and-egg situation over there." Alas, this is the dilemma and crisis of urban schools. Applying Dereca's strategies to the confines of public education adds another critical and difficult dimension to her work.

With my research questions in mind, I am interested to probe further into her advice for teachers. To that end, I ask her what she views as the similarities and differences between the mission of LE and what they encounter at McClymonds. She says with frustration, "The expectations for the youth are so low . . . the mistreatment of them, the disrespect that they receive in terms of the way people curse at them and talk about them and belittle them. For that to be going on in classrooms is sick."

I prompt her to pinpoint ways she thinks teachers in the traditional school setting can improve. She begins to vent about the inadequacies and power dynamics that make teachers ineffective. "If your whole thing is about your power in the classroom, like you really don't have no power. One of these kids will get up and whoop yo ass . . . if you tryin to control kids, you shouldn't be a teacher . . . Like if you're tryin to influence them, that's a different thing. Like you should be tryin to influence them, but don't try to control them cause it's not real. You have no control. You got a little hour and a couple of flimsy passes that you can use to send them to the office . . . like these kids are facin bullets, they're not trippin off you." Dereca seems hard-pressed to draw any comparison between McClymonds and LE because school is such a "different environment." She talks further about the noticeable differences, then abruptly pauses mid-thought to change the tone and direction of her answer. She realizes that she *does* have practical advice for teachers: some essential elements of LE are transferable.

Dereca wants educators to understand that the didactic "teacher in the front of the classroom" way of teaching "is dead. I think that the more teachers can find a way to flip that [didactic] paradigm on its head, whether it's project-based learning or whether it's the way that they take the kids out of the classroom." She actually begins to get excited about the possibilities. "Take a field trip as your first day. Go to the park for free and sit down outside the classroom as your first day and actually talk with the kids." Or, if that is too awkward or infeasible, at least "be willin to put the desks in a circle." Making these changes, she suggests, will help "break the barriers and the walls of the classroom" that inhibit the learning process. She is confident, perhaps too idealistic, that such small shifts would "just change everything."

Teachers are hard-pressed in today's environment because of stringent curriculum standards and policies ("these stupid tests now") that they must adhere to. Despite these constraints, Dereca insists that teachers can still accomplish a lot, particularly in the area of relationship building. "People are so afraid of losing the time on task, and school districts are so afraid of not gettin the outcomes, that they don't realize that you get the better outcomes when you have the relationships built." Creating an environment that nurtures strong relationships alongside the traditional school curriculum is challenging, but it is possible. Dereca draws on her experience: "A lot of the kids I have these breakthrough conversations with, I talk to for an hour or two, but that hour or two investment builds a relationship, builds a connection between us that I can come back to." Dereca re-emphasizes that a connection makes anything possible and opens up more achievable results. I nod my head, realizing the importance of her statement. "Ah," I comment, "You can't have a classroom without community. People tend to think you need content and then a community. But what you're saying is that you have to have a community and then you can have any type of classroom content you want." Her eyes glisten: "Exactly!" Finally, tying together the institutional component with her sense of community building, she asserts, "The relationship building aspect of what we do in youth work is critical for classrooms."

"What about your personal vision of teaching and learning?" I ask. She thinks back to her own education. "The learning that was most important to me was the learning that raised my consciousness . . . it wasn't because I could correctly identify—as I can—all of the capitals of all of the states in the country. That's what people think is teaching, but that's not what teaching is. Teaching is giving you the tools and the thirst for learning . . . that right there is a lifetime journey and when you can really, really give a kid that, that thirst for knowledge, that's what learning is." It is to inspire interest. *Real* teaching, Dereca continues, is about "exploring things with the classroom, exploring their lives, exploring their ideas, allowing them to bring their unique experiences into the class."

As Dereca talks about her idea of a classroom of exploration, I ask how these notions relate to the ways LE works with young people. As Dereca mentioned before, the relationship component is key to their success. She builds on this idea, going on to say, "We have the experience, we have the boldness—the balls truthfully—to go in and deal with the young people where they are. And not just assume that where we are is the place they need to be. Because of that, we learn together. I learn every single time I'm with kids and if you can't say that, you're not a good teacher." Dereca speaks about reciprocal learning. Every community-based educator will reinforce this theme.

Dereca, in her typical fast-paced tone, lays out several important points. According to her, effective teaching and learning does not flow in one direction; it is not, as she says, didactic. Fluid and exploratory, it involves everyone in the classroom, including the teacher. But what if teachers are not ready, or willing, to learn from the students in their classes? What if teachers are afraid of their students the way Scid believed his teachers were absolutely scared of him? Then what? At LE, Dereca's staff is a very diverse group of African-Americans with the "boldness" necessary to meet the young people where they are—and for many of them it is a world that is racist, classist, and sexist. So how, for instance, does a white woman teaching at McClymonds High School reach and teach her students effectively? Is it possible?

Dereca says yes, believing adamantly that anyone ("I don't care who you are") can do this work if they are mindful that "race, gender, and class always matter." Dereca recognizes that public school teachers are overwhelmingly white and she reinforces that they have an important job. She does not undermine their valuable and important work, but at the same time she recognizes that teachers have to be cognizant of their identity. Identity is an explicit topic at Camp Akili, but that type of introspection about one's race, gender, and class is rarely a mandated topic of discussion among teachers. The result is classrooms of cultural mismatch; schools often perpetuate the "silenced dialogue" (Delpit, 1995, *passim*).

Dereca has discovered that many people who wish to work with youth of color are driven by the desire to save kids by helping them with their issues. To her, this is a problem. She elucidates, "Most of those people who come [into our communities] haven't taken the time or don't even understand the importance of workin out their *own* issues. What are my issues around race? What are my issues around class? What are my issues around gender?" Once that is addressed with sincerity, "you can come from a place of being able to be honest and make relationships and connections with kids" and avoid merely projecting outside beliefs and (mis)perceptions onto the youth.

This type of personal and professional introspection is a critical component of preparing teachers to succeed in schools. Dereca provides an example from her life. A particular class at Stanford, Group Communications with Professor Helen Shrader, was vital to Dereca's development as an educator-activist. In this course students broke into groups based on their race, gender, birth order, and class. Each sub-group wrote down questions for all the other groups, after which they took turns answering. One of her pivotal moments in this class came when she made a white woman cry during the interracial dating conversation "because I could be very angry in my militantism back when I was 19. I was fire."

Although Dereca cannot remember precisely what she said, what she does remember is that "every other class, she and I were in a group together." While they were in the lower-class group this same white woman told Dereca "stories of being from Appalachia [and] I wanted to leave the poor group because I ain't never ate no mayonnaise sandwich." This conversation made Dereca realize she cannot make assumptions about people and the privileges they might have. It inevitably made her more open to working with a broad, diverse group of allies. Although Dereca's focus is African-American students, her comrades come in all colors and from all economic backgrounds.

Another critical moment in Dereca's education in this same course came when an affluent white male student asked her point blank, "Why should I care what happens to Black people or poor people?" Her rebuttal was automatic: "You can't build enough fences and gates to keep your grandma safe when she walks in the street . . . Cause you're goin to want to go outside at some point and we are goin to be der . . . You're going to be the one livin in the prison . . . Keep cuttin us off and see what happens cause that's not natural. People are goin to fight to rebalance and nature is goin to fight to rebalance . . . and you might want to make sure that we've had some education, some opportunity, because otherwise we're going to rob you. Like real talk, that's what's goin to happen." Dereca's gut reaction to his question reinforced her commitment to "speak truth to power" whenever she has the opportunity because "people need to understand . . . they don't just get it intuitively, the connection between them and the poor people around them." Dereca began to recognize that her strikingly different experiences growing up are actually an asset, qualifying her to be a powerful ally of the marginalized and misled.

Dereca believes that the information she learned in elite schools allows her to question authority in unique ways. As a prime example, she tells me about the time she confronted Congressman Dan Lundgren. Lundgren is an advocate of incarceration and stood at the podium bragging about crime reduction in California. Dereca asked him, "Have you ever stopped to calculate the opportunity cost of the crime reduction?" Mr. Lundgren looked baffled and commented, "What do you mean opportunity cost?" Dereca described a sort of X–Y graph: "Well obviously if you lock up all of the people, the crime rate will go down significantly. If you lock up everybody you won't have any crime. How many people will be too many people to lock up to justify the crime rate going down?" He could not answer.

Since Dereca was "educated with all these people," she sees it as part of her duty to challenge them because "I speak their language . . . I'm bilingual in that way and that bridge aspect is a responsibility I feel I have." Another layer of Dereca's pedagogy of communication is her eloquent code switching, which enables her to talk with all kinds of people. Without even pausing from the Lundgren story, Dereca reveals that working with those at the bottom grounds her. She says, "My whole career I wanted to work with kids that was locked up. They kill somebody, they've raped somebody, they child molesters.

Give me the kids that nobody wants to work with, that's who I want to work with because I think it's a responsibility." She looks directly at me and declares, "If you can see the good in anyone, then you have a responsibility to work with the ones nobody else will work with." Dereca does not take this job lightly nor does she view it as a burden. In reality, the challenge "makes me hungry."

This theme is recurrent. The hunger Dereca describes comes out of her earnest passion to work with young people. It is "what keeps you goin once somebody straight trips out on you, when somebody throws something at you or even somebody is like fuck you and what you talkin about. The passion is what makes you sit and work it out and not resort to your control and your defenses." Although this passion is key, she understands it is just a part of working effectively with teenagers. Dereca believes that many adults have the innate zeal to work with young people but lack adequate training; that training might include analyzing one's issues around race, class, and gender. "When you have passion and natural ability," proper training allows you to "develop it [and] sustain it in a way that makes you excellent. Without one of those sides, you might just be good." These two stages Dereca outlines—passion and training—are quintessential components of her effectiveness. She sees a third element as equally critical, and it has taken her years to fully comprehend.

The third element was harder for Dereca to actualize because, in truth, Dereca wants to "save everyone" and it is always a harsh wake-up call to her when she cannot. After over two decades of doing community work with young people, she has learned that "I'm not a savior." Although she has a bold, vociferous personality, she is quiet and humble when she speaks of the natural abilities of youth. Many hard lessons have taught her that she is not responsible for a young person's failures and/or achievements. She admits, "It's taken me a long time to really just get to that level of maturity and to recognize that if they don't want it, they don't want it. I'm maturing to the point where I no longer feel like it's my responsibility to save them. My responsibility is to show them an option," to emphasize that they have a choice. She wants youth to become more "conscious and aware" of what their lives can be. Summarily, to the extent she can "expand the expectations they have for themselves and their community" and awaken in them a "sense of positive possibility," she feels successful.

I appreciate Dereca's aspirations for young people, but I still do not completely understand how she defines success. I try to bring it closer to home, asking exactly what she hopes to accomplish at McClymonds High School. "I want kids in West Oakland to have the choice to go to a good high school in their neighborhood," she starts. "But that's a choice thing," not an external imprint forced upon them. Of course "I have visions for communities, I have a vision for the country, but I don't have visions for individual kids cause that's what I want for them: to have their own vision for themselves." It's about empowerment. "To do what?" I ask her. She urges me to trust the young people. At Leadership Excellence the participants "get to choose what it is, whether it's crack pipes bein sold in liquor stores or on the corner, whether it's police, whether it's their school, whatever it is, they get to choose what issues LE is going to work on. They are LE." Once youth at Leadership Excellence have the tools to critically analyze society, the issues they choose to work on are up to them. Essentially, Dereca and her colleagues trust the students' leadership and direction toward social justice.

Nodding, I continue, "Now tell me about what it means to be effective . . . what does it look like?" I am pressing her to describe her personal approach. She moves her chair a little closer and for a moment I feel like she is my older sister or a long-term mentor. Her tone is advising and loving. "Vajra, all I ever really do when I'm at like my very, very best is hold up a mirror to their life and say what do you think about that . . . And that's it. That's really all that it is at its core. And [the youth] get it cause they're so damn smart . . . and then if, like if I'm really ballin, if I really hella succeed, then I give em a mirror and I'm gone. And they got a mirror that they can always check it out . . . You know, you can use a thousand metaphors. It could be a telescope, it could be a magnifying glass, it could be whatever . . . it's just activating what's in them . . . I have to remember, I'm frostin, I'm not cake." She sighs, "They cake. They're life . . . they're real people." I grin and remember her description of the mural in "The Spot." Dereca wants me to see what she sees—the raw amazing *realness* of young people. At first I only saw the bright colors of this work and the glamour of the mural. Today I see the comprehensive services LE offers, the complexities of accomplishment, and the philosophy of empowerment Dereca espouses.

Dereca is on a lifelong quest for equity. She tells me, "I'm a revolutionary and I really believe that systems have to be overthrown." She does not talk about conventional notions of revolution that involve violence and bloodshed; she speaks in terms of a different war. Dereca's acts of resistance come in the form of her daily interactions with young people and the innovative ways she fights for their rights. Her sense of revolution is both introspective and interpersonal. "I believe to check yourself is a revolutionary act," she declares, "cause that's the hardest and most important . . . If you could check yourself and get yourself in shape, you become a role model, you become an advocate."

Dereca Blackmon is a woman warrior. As head of the LE family, she is on the frontlines battling on behalf of, and as a comrade with, African-American youth. She will never forget when Professor Shawn Ginwright, LE's cofounder, taught her and all the Akili campers about Queen Yaa Asantewaa. As Simone's poem expressed at the beginning of this chapter, Asantewaa was a fierce leader, head of a strong matriarchal community. When the Ashanti were prepared to surrender, Asantewaa led her people to war to protect the very soul of their nation. In this shero, Dereca finds profound familiarity and inspiration. To this day, she will invoke the name Asantewaa to gather courage and strength to keep fighting.

I imagine Asantewaa's fiery brown eyes as I look at Dereca. I sense in her a heart that beats with revolutionary love. In her battle to empower youth, the methods are clear. As I leave her office, I take these approaches with me: to reflect on who I am and my experiences so that I can present myself in real, honest ways to youth; to constantly talk with the youth I work with about their lives, experiences, challenges, and goals so that I am attuned to teach them better; and when I teach to be sure that it raises their knowledge, understanding, and curiosity about this world in critical, conscious ways. Throughout, I must promote the innate potential of all students in order to encourage their aim for achievement, challenging them with higher expectations. Teaching entails a commitment to youth that, as Dereca shows, requires that actions speak louder than words. I need to be reflective of this entire cycle so that I can refine my pedagogy. Finally, I need to trust the choices the young people make, because they are *real* people—ultimately, they have power over their own aspirations. So, even when I am the teacher, I am also the student. By examining Dereca's best practices, I am starting to discover a transformational praxis where all involved learn, grow, and change.

Balboa High School in San Francisco has learned first-hand about the benefits of supporting a community-based program *within* the school. During a wave of "turf wars" at Balboa in the mid-1990s, Rudy Corpuz set up a meeting with the leaders of the warring sets; from this peace talk, United Playaz (UP) was born. Over a decade later, UP has grown into a comprehensive, grassroots violence prevention and leadership development program. Acting as a bridge between the streets and school, Rudy is a "freedom fighter" for the "street cat" of any color. I turn to him now.

3

RUDY CORPUZ, JR.

Pedagogy of Community

When I set out to find community-based educators who were successfully reaching and teaching high-risk youth, I kept hearing that I had to meet Rudy Corpuz, Jr., founder of the United Playaz (UP) program in San Francisco. Both youth and adults lit up when they spoke about his unique strategies, hardcore manner ("little bit rough around the edges"), and compelling persona. I was intrigued. I began trying to contact him but all I had was his pager number. This old-school method of contacting him did not work and for months we played phone tag. I became accustomed to hearing his deep voice on my answering machine: "Waz up Vajra. This is Rudy. Get back at me. One love, one thug."

I was struck by the strength of his tone on the phone, but I could not picture him. I had no idea of his looks, ethnicity, or style. All I could uncover was that UP offered a comprehensive grassroots violence prevention and youth leadership development program in various schools and detention centers in San Francisco. I was told that Rudy works with youth and families "from really challenging situations" and has helped them make "amazing" changes in their lives. UP's reputation was reinforced in an article in the *San Francisco Chronicle* (March 1, 2003). It described a dance, *The Playaz Ball*,[1] where over 300 teenagers from warring turfs came together for a night of peace. It read, "This is a group of kids who you probably wouldn't allow at the prom" who are, through United Playaz, "really excited" to have this event, and included a full-page photo from the evening. I scanned the picture hoping to get a glimpse of Rudy, but no one stood out as the leader. Everyone was holding hands in a large circle, heads lowered, and they appeared to be praying. The caption finally let me pinpoint Rudy. His long jet-black hair was pulled tight into two long braids hanging half way down his chest. Wearing a colorful silk shirt and sharply creased pants, he seemed a bit stocky, not much taller than the young people he stood with. I held this image in my mind as I set out for my first United Playaz meeting.

The UP family meets every Wednesday at lunch at Bal (Balboa High School). During our phone conversations Rudy urges me to just show up *any* Wednesday and "we'll be there." On a brisk sunny day in the spring of 2004, I pull up to 1000 Cayuga Avenue and am struck by how enormous the school feels, perhaps because it takes up an entire city block in the middle of a residential area of small houses. The 20-foot iron fence around the rusty-orange building adds to its dramatic feel.

It has been a while since I set foot on a high school campus and I am excited. As I approach the perimeter, a security guard immediately motions me to the entrance. I make my way through the only opening in the gate (about 15 inches wide) and head toward the office to get a visitor's pass. When I enter the office, all the adults are busy at work. I ask for a pass and the secretary barely looks up from her pile of papers. She simply points to the sign-in book and hands me a bright orange-and-black Balboa sticker. I stick it on my bag, ask for directions to the UP room, and then make my way down a flight of stairs to the ground floor.

I have not yet seen a single student. The school grounds and dim hallways are bare and silent, making this large building feel even emptier. I can hardly believe that over 1,000 students are in attendance. But then the bell rings and, before I can blink, the hallways are packed with laughing and shouting teenagers. A few students rush over to the UP door and I follow them in. They immediately take seats at the large wooden oval table at the front of the room and begin spinning around in the black swivel office chairs.

Bob Marley's "One Love" is playing in the background as more students start flooding into the room. "Where's Ru at?" a young woman asks. "Takin care of business," another responds. Within minutes an amazing mix of people are checking in with each other. The demographics of Balboa—approximately 55% Asian, 21% African-American, 20% Xicano/Latino/Native, and 4% white—seem proportionately represented in this small space. There are also a number of adult visitors who seem to know the kids, judging by the way they are getting along. The forty-or-so people are busy with each other, giving me an opportunity to jot down some initial impressions.

As I walk around this unique high school classroom, I notice a handwritten sheet on the wall:

Q: What is United Playaz main purpose?
A: To stop violence and enforce education.
Q: Name 3 ways UP attains its goals . . .
A: Find answers throughout the room (i.e., articles, letters, etc.)

I am eager to find answers. Posters and messages throughout the room espouse UP's philosophy. A 10-foot black-and-white mural hangs above the computers announcing "UNITED PLAYAZ: Power to the People" to anyone who enters. Hip-hop posters featuring artists such as Tupac and a group of local Samoan rappers are as much a part of the wallpaper as the political posters with messages like "California is 1 in prisons and 41st in education" and "the youth ain't the criminal, the institution is." The provocative and blatant revolutionary messages urging young people to "upset the setup" seem to reflect the program's desire to awaken students toward personal agency and community transformation. I wonder how this happens and what it really looks like. I continue to explore.

Amidst inspirational letters from prison inmates taped and thumbtacked to the wall, I find a poem that intrigues me. It reads:

> Our country's wealth is not given to all.
> Because lacking knowledge, many communities will fall.
> Today a sense of confusion has really risen.
> Therefore, many teenagers are getting locked up in prison . . .
> It's time to rise up and restore our land.
> Let's all become educated to meet this demand.

This message explains the importance of using education as a catalyst for social change. But, regardless of the provocative and inspiring statements, a larger question occurs to me: Is United Playaz actualizing these ambitions? Furthermore, if some elements in this particular program are effective, what are they? And how, if at all, can these strategies improve the ways educators communicate with, teach, and support students? I am determined to unearth some answers. But, for now, I sit down on one of the old, well-used black couches and introduce myself to a few of the students.

Although the youth are ethnically diverse, they share a general street style. The attire of baggy pants, tattoos, and grills is the norm for both the students and adults. The room's aesthetics also add to this urban hip-hop feel. Rudy strategically uses items from the streets "to make the room look pimperish." Red velour car seats (which Rudy found in an abandoned van and carried into his classroom) are among the most popular chairs in the room. There is a weight-lifting station in the corner, four old computers along the back wall, and a three-foot-tall stereo system that sets the mood with R&B, rap, or reggae music. Music is critical, Rudy explains in a later meeting: "Regardless of what color or ethnicity you are, whether a man is somebody, a man who's from the gutter, everybody can relate." Rudy uses music to connect people, to create unity. This is significant because his main concern is the incessant killings ravaging local communities.

The twenty-plus pictures that cover an entire wall reinforce this message. The photographs are of people who have been murdered in San Francisco: overwhelmingly African-American young men. Each 8″ × 12″ headshot has the young person's name and lifespan written below it. I am struck. These are familiar faces; the names are real to these students. In fact, many are former UP participants. Others are family members of current UP members. The presence of these faces in the classroom reinforces the need for UP: the "gang to end all gangs . . . a movement hoping to end violence among the youth" (Espinosa, 2006, p. 5).

While I consider Rudy's reputation and the work of UP, I continue to gaze at the captivating pictures. I cannot help but think about the people in my life who have died because of the extreme violence on these streets. I feel angry, sad, and often overwhelmed. In 2007 alone, over 140 people, the majority of them youth, were murdered in Oakland. What can be done to curtail the violence consuming young people's lives?

Suddenly the door flies open and Rudy, his partner Misha, and their 2-year-old daughter Sadé (whom everyone calls Mookie) rush into this packed classroom space. Mookie runs over to give a few students a hug and then bounces into her special Winnie the Pooh chair. Misha lights up the space with her smile as she puts down a stack of pizzas. Rudy nods his head as a greeting, paces over to the stereo, and cuts off the music. He then strides to the front, adjusts the podium so that it is front-and-center, and glances over at one of the students. Without further ado Evangela, an outspoken senior, steps to the front. She does a quick welcome and then says, commandingly, "Who wanna go over the rules for me?" Responses come from every corner of the room. Youth call out the guidelines: "One mic," "No freeloadin," "Be on time," "Turn off the cell phone," "Step up to the plate," "Be respectful." Evangela checks the agenda on the blackboard: "Okay then, do we got any new guests? Introduce yourself." There are four newcomers and we each say our name and explain how we came to hear about United Playaz.

I say my name, explain that I am excited about UP's work, mention that UP reminds me of the Vice Lords,[2] and sit back down. I do not discuss my research agenda but try to fit in and observe what's going on. I can feel Rudy's eyes on me. It seems he is also checking me out—observing me back—because at this point he has not even agreed to participate in my study.

After our introductions, Rudy remarks, "Show them some UP love y'all," and loud applause ensues. "For the people who just came in today," he continues, "can you tell them in a nutshell what the United Playaz program is? Step up to the podium." He looks over to a young man sitting alone in the corner. The teenager stands and walks to the front. "The United Playaz is," he pauses and then proclaims, "We are a tribe that is organizing to save our community." The students clap. Rudy tells the young man he did a very good job and proceeds, "Is the sign-in sheet goin around? Did everyone sign in? Courtney boo, we need you to take the notes." With quick directives he ensures everyone is on task and then nods to Evangela, "All right, go ahead."

Evangela gives an update on the upcoming basketball tournament between students and teachers, which UP is organizing. After deciding what still needs to be done, various youth volunteer to take charge of particular tasks such as reserving the gym. Evangela then welcomes to the podium a guest speaker, Xavier. Xavier graduated in 1997 but is "UP4Life." Although his voice is soft at first, he quickly gains momentum and begins telling us in a persuasive tone that "Rudy the reason I graduated. I was wild in ninth grade."

We learn that Xavier was known as one of the Dice Kings because he ran the craps games at Bal. Rudy was "always in my ear. I didn't even know what a credit was because I was so caught up in the streets and the life . . . I never went to class but then I got turned onto UP." He looks around the room. "UP can give you tools for what you will need in life. This is a lovely thing. What you doing right here gonna get y'all away from the street." I watch the students as Xavier talks. All eyes are on him but they do not seem overly excited about his statements. Their expressions are a bit subdued. Rudy steps in and says, "See me and Xavier we go back like a hot bowl a grits," and he adds that UP is "official like a pistol." His quick metaphors bring smiles and a few laughs from the teenagers; he livens up the feeling in the room while reinforcing Xavier's points.

Evangela looks up at the clock, gives Rudy a nod, and then quickly rolls through the rest of the agenda. She closes, "Who wanna facilitate, run the meeting, next week?" Everyone looks around the room and the group collectively picks two people "who haven't ran it in a minute." Courtney, the note-taker, reports on what happened during our short 30 minutes and closes by letting the group know that at next Wednesday's gathering "we have to follow up on the basketball game." Rudy then tells the youth to stay focused in school and invites everyone to "break bread together" and share pizza. The pizzas are still being distributed when the bell rings. The vast majority of young people rush out. Within minutes the space is calm.

As I get up to formally introduce myself to Rudy, I realize he is still busy. Although the meeting is officially over, he remains preoccupied with a particular student. He is sitting at the table completely engrossed in a conversation with an African-American teenager wearing an oversized Akademics outfit. Rudy's piercing dark brown eyes stare into the young man, and as long as I look over at Rudy, I do not see him blink. His face looks serious, his concentration penetrating: I recall Xavier's comments during the UP meeting. What was it about Rudy's tactics that made such an impact on Xavier's outlook on life? Although I am eager to understand this, for now, I sit waiting for my turn to speak with Rudy.

When Rudy has a free moment, he turns to me, and with a stern expression says, "So you're Vajra." I get up to introduce myself and he asks me point blank, "What did you think about the meeting?" I explain that I've never seen anything like it on a high school campus and that I am really excited to learn more about what he does. Rudy looks directly into me, smiles, and then turns completely around to face his daughter. In a teasing tone, he chases Mookie around the room and tells her she is the most beautiful girl in the world and then looks over at Misha with a twinkle in his eye and says, "but you the most beautiful in the Universe," which causes her to blush and giggle. Even though Rudy is entrenched in the sad, heart-wrenching violence on these streets, his spirit is jovial.

My first impressions of Rudy fascinate me. In the meeting, I saw first-hand how students respond to his "gift of gab." I also witnessed the way young people *are* UP—they run the meetings and seem to organize the activities, such as the basketball game. Also, the street style of *everyone* and *everything* (like the style of the room) is prominent. Although street life does not seem glorified, it is not necessarily vilified; I am reminded of the popular phrase, "don't hate the player, hate the game." Rudy seems determined to change the game, but loves the player. As he will later tell me, "We're not the kind of players who do gangster stuff and have all the nice cars and gorgeous women. We are the kind of players who are positive and productive for their people in the hood."

I want to learn more. I am eager to set up our first interview, but it feels inappropriate. Whereas Dereca welcomed me with open arms, Rudy is a bit hands-off. I sense I will have to earn his trust in order to be let into his world. Before long I realize that I have to *do* the work if I want to begin to understand it. For a year (October 2004 to September 2005) I attend nearly every Wednesday meeting at Balboa and also participate in their community outreach efforts.

Really Down

"How many y'all down for freedom?" Rudy roars during a subsequent UP meeting. Hands go up around the room. He insists that everyone with a raised hand should attend the annual march in honor of the Rev. Martin Luther King, Jr. My hand is in the air, so I feel compelled to participate in the 3-mile walk through San Francisco.

Early on a Saturday morning in January, my husband, my 3-year-old son, and I take BART (Bay Area Rapid Transit) to downtown San Francisco to meet with United Playaz to march in the MLK parade. When we arrive I immediately spot the group because they are wearing their black UP t-shirts with bold white letters that proclaim, "Straight Playaz Not No Haters."

We gather in a circle and Rudy talks about our presence being important. He promises us that nothing happens by sitting down; we have to "keep it movin" and fight for what we know is right. "Because y'all came out today I'm gonna pass out t-shirts. Who doesn't already got a UP shirt?" A few hands wave in the air. The youngsters are thrilled when they receive a shirt because only people who are "really down" and have invested time and commitment get to wear these shirts. This particular attire, or "uniform," as one student tells me, carries significance within the community because it acts like a type of armor. Essentially, the United Playaz logo provides a protective pass because of UP's stellar reputation for creating peace on the streets. A person wearing the shirt can walk safely through any neighborhood or territory in the city. Even though many people will try to purchase these shirts, Rudy is firm that they can only be earned.

My family and I stand on the periphery watching the proceedings. I am surprised when Rudy calls me to the center of the circle and presents me with a shirt. I can now relate to the kids' beaming expressions because I find myself overwhelmed with enthusiasm. I quickly put the shirt on over my sweatshirt and get ready to march, not as an outsider, but in my UP attire.

The parade is already under way so Rudy weaves the 50 of us through various side streets in order to catch up. I doubt that we will find a place in the thicket of marchers but, as if it were planned, we slide right in. As we walk I feel the intergenerational and interracial unity of United Playaz. Rudy's older brother blasts old-school R&B from his boom box and shouts out the lyrics. An Ethiopian woman in her twenties and her Latino partner push their son in a stroller. An older African-American man walks with his nephew. Kids pop in and out of the line in *their* UP shirts that have Nas' popular rap lyrics, "I know I can be what I wanna be," printed on the back. A white teenager wearing a red doo-rag marches alongside the Asian, Black, and Latino youth. The atmosphere is celebratory. I look up at my son sitting on top of my husband's shoulders and appreciate that we are all able to participate in this event. Glancing over at Rudy, I notice the way he lovingly holds Misha's hand and simultaneously talks to everyone.

Every UP event I participate in during the course of this study, from the annual Magic Backpack give-away in Hunters Point to the cookout for mothers whose children have died, is fun and strategically celebrates life. Misha explains that it is important for young people to understand that "community service doesn't have to be like this huge sacrifice," but that it can be a "good time for everybody." Evangela reinforces this point: "I learned I can help out my community and also just have fun while I'm doing it." It is clear that people like to participate in UP events. United Playaz has over 100 members locally with chapters at Balboa and Thurgood Marshall High Schools, as well as at recreation centers in the South of Market neighborhood. United Playaz also extends to the Bronx in New York. In addition to the number of youth still in school, others, such as Xavier, become "UP4Life" members to increase the total. A unique aspect of the program, explains Misha, is "how much people who have been involved in the past stay involved." This accounts for the intergenerational presence I witness on nearly every occasion.

Creating an atmosphere that welcomes and encourages participation from the entire family reflects Rudy's concept of community. Even when Rudy has a critical meeting with Mayor Gavin Newsom, he brings his toddler. When I visited Leadership Excellence or other programs in my study, I had to arrange childcare, but at UP, I would have been out of place if my family did not participate in the events. For Rudy, unity genuinely means there is a place at the table for everyone—young and old, new school, old school, and no school. His drive to include everyone is related to the way he was raised and the intense struggles he has faced along the way.

Be Loyal

The day of our first interview has finally arrived. I have been up the entire night with excited anticipation. I drive across the Bay Bridge, park quickly in front of Balboa, and rush toward the UP room to have my first formal sit-down with Rudy. I step into the classroom and expect to see Rudy sitting at the table waiting for me, but of course not. As always, he is surrounded by people and is running a bit behind schedule. This must be his day for interviews because a film crew is here and Rudy is preoccupied with the newscaster. I find a comfortable seat at the oval table and wait my turn. I watch Rudy look directly into the camera and forcefully recite UP's mission and function. He seems to thrive in front of the camera, but, even more than that, he appears to shine just by being around people. I try to remember a moment over the past year when I saw Rudy alone, quiet, and not on the move—but cannot recall a single such moment. I wonder, what drives Rudy to do this work? It is obvious to everyone in his presence, including the youth and colleagues, that something drives him. But I remain unclear about what exactly makes him want to do this work 24 hours a day.

I hear Rudy from across the room: "What's up Vaj-ra, what's *really* going on with you?" A smile spreads across my face because I know we're about to get started. We sit down across from one another at the table. He devours a fish sandwich I brought him from the Black Muslim Bakery and seems uninterested in the details I explain to him about the interview process, for example that we can turn the recorder off at any point. He is ready to get down to business.

We begin. "Is there anything I shouldn't say?" are the first words out of his mouth. "Hell nah," I respond. Rudy leans forward, "I trust you." I thank him for allowing me to document his valuable work. He turns his face as if to brush off any compliment I am trying to give him. "It's for the struggle," he says, "I know that's the intention . . . everything you do is for the power of the people and the movement and it's an honor for me to know that and to be a part of this." We enter into this quest for best practices and I recognize the justice that we both seek for the youth on these streets. Yet Rudy's tactics are original and I have a lot to learn.

Rudy Corpuz Jr. is "110%" Filipino "with no cut." The youngest of nine children (seven boys and two girls), he was raised on the streets of San Francisco, in the South of Market district at Ninth and Howard. In this tough neighborhood he grew up with African-Americans, Latinos, and Samoans. Because of this, he "was kinda embarrassed about who I was cause I didn't know my identity" and never learned, for instance, to speak Tagalog. Although Rudy did not necessarily have ethnic pride, he knew about his family. In the 1950s, his father was the first Filipino sergeant in the United States Army. Rudy smiles as he explains that "It was really rare to have a person of color in charge of white folks back then." He looks off to the distance and says, "My father had to be super strong."

Rudy Corpuz Senior managed his family like a small army and raised all of his children "like soldiers" with "tough love." As the youngest, Rudy received discipline and advice from everyone and he believes each of them shaped him. Rudy's sense of family is central. "I can't go wrong if I got all them in me." Even as a grown man in his mid-thirties, he continues to see himself as a direct reflection of his mother, father, brothers, and sisters.

Since Rudy comes from a large close-knit family, I can see how United Playaz is a natural extension of his upbringing. I think about the ways youth explain UP. On a questionnaire that over 50 teenagers filled out, I asked for "3 words that describe UP," and the most common answers were *family* and *love*.

Whereas Rudy's sense of discipline and leadership came from his father, it was his mother's giving "open heart" that turned their home into a recreation house for the neighborhood kids. "After the recreation center would close, everybody would come over all the time." Looking back on this, he reckons that other children appreciated that his mother and father were in the house because many of them did not have that. When these young people would come around, his mother would be sweet and feed them while his father would "drill they ass." To this day Rudy's father is remembered with admiration. "It trips me out that some of the dudes I knew back then who are currently straight up riders, who's locked up in the pen, who are never coming home, I see them and they say, 'How your dad doing? Man, he sho was a tough dude.'"

Rudy begins to ramble a bit, lost in his own thoughts, immersed in his memories. "When my father talked, you would know. When he'd walk into a room, the animals would walk out. He had that presence." He continues in a monotone, "My father passed away." There is an abrupt silence between us. Rudy appears in deep reflection. "My dad was the type of person that would never tell you he loves you." He looks away and then down at the table before telling me, "To this day, when I seen him dead at the hospital, I'm like, damn, he never told me he loved me . . . I never got to tell him that. Was I supposed to tell him that?" This question seems to haunt Rudy for a moment, but he reconciles with it: "I knew it because of what he did." It was through actions, not mere words, that Rudy's father taught him how to be a diligent, loyal soldier in this life. Rudy straightens his back and declares, "If you gonna stick through something you gotta stick through it all the way. From the beginning to the end. From the womb to the tomb. From the cradle to the grave. You have to be loyal to what you do because that makes you part of a man."

In Rudy's search to be a man, he understood that, whatever he chose to do with his life, he had to do it absolutely. When Rudy was 12, his oldest brother explained it to him clearly: "If you gonna be a straight doctor, you be the best doctor. If you gonna be a gang banger, be the downest gang banger. If you gonna be a bank robber, then you be the best bank robber." At this relatively young age, Rudy had already made his choice: he was the leader of his gang. His oldest brother, who was already established in the "dope game" and "thoroughly respected out here in the city and throughout the nation," began teaching Rudy about the streets and how to make money. Taking his father's philosophy about being "loyal to what you do" to a negative extreme, along with his oldest brother's street connections, Rudy became rich and renowned. "I used to be on Turk and Leavenworth, 200 block. My whole MO back in the days when I was out there hustlin was straight money, mack, and murder."

As a freshman at Mission High School, Rudy could barely grasp what his teachers were talking about. He concluded that because the education he received at Potrero Hill Middle School "wasn't even up to par" there was no point in continuing with school. Simultaneously, the lures of the street were too strong. Rudy spent his school days across the street at Dolores Park getting high, selling drugs, and gang banging. He rationalized that there was no need to be "really trippin off school because I made more money than the teacher." In many ways he felt he was living the good life. "I was drivin at 15. I had enough money at 17, Vajra, to travel the world." But Rudy was not in a state of mind to travel. Instead he stacked his hundreds in a fireproof metal safe and would "take my whole gang shopping" to purchase troop suits, tennis shoes, or whatever they wanted.

Although his hustles were very lucrative, they were also life threatening. One night an undercover cop put a pistol down Rudy's throat and yelled "I'm gonna let this loose on yo ass!" For some reason unknown to Rudy, "maybe just the grace of God," the police officer did not pull the trigger. Rudy can recall many instances when his life flashed before his eyes. But none of these struggles on the street prepared him for the death of his father. Around this same time his closest friends were getting locked up or killed. Unable to cope with these immense tragedies, he "slowly started getting high off my supply. I became my best customer." Rudy's severe addiction to drugs caused his life to spin out of control. "I was climbin in people's houses, sticking dudes' guns down they throat and sayin 'break yourself, give me yo shit,' for drugs." During this time, he was going in and out of the penitentiary. He ended up spending over 9 years of his life behind bars. "I done been in every type of lock-up you can think of, mentally and physically. I done laid in my death bed three times. I been on both sides of the world and I done hustle."

Then, in a search for sobriety, Rudy participated in nearly every recovery program San Francisco had to offer, from Cracks on Cracks at Glide Memorial Church to Horizons Unlimited. Rudy acknowledges that the programs were strong and temporarily helpful. His continuous problem was that "it helped me out until I got home and I got back into that environment . . . The first day I got back from the camp they sent me to, I broke into somebody house and took they dope." Becoming clean was a slow process of "one day at a time" and two important, cataclysmic events made it possible. First, he became close to someone who was a Jehovah's Witness and began feeling a connection to God that made him want to get sober, want to change, and want to live. Second, his probation officer got him a job at City College. However, while he was holding this steady job by day, he was still selling drugs and getting high at night. "Dr. Jekyll in the morning and Mr. Rob Yo Ass at night." I recall how Rudy was raised to be loyal. He knew he could not live a life of contradiction but he continued to straddle the fence. That is, until he began working directly with young people.

"I never thought I'd be working with youngstas that was going through the same stuff I experienced in life." In 1994, Rudy saw a sign that Bernal Heights Neighborhood Center was looking to hire a Filipino gang counselor. He thought, "I'm Filipino. I used to gang bang. Why not apply?" When Rudy showed up for the interview, the first question he was asked was, "Have you ever been locked up?" He hesitated, but finally said "yes" and was hired on the spot to deal with Filipino students at Balboa High School. In a forceful tone he asserts, "I knew what I needed to do . . . When I took on that job I made an oath to myself that I was gonna have to stay clean as Clorox. I had to because I'm not going to be advocating to these youngstas don't sell these drugs, and then you see me in the Tenderloin at night sellin dope."

The Leaders that They Are

On Friday October 7, 1994, soon after Rudy began his job at Balboa, a race riot broke out between Black and Filipino students at a school dance. In the following weeks, the violence grew to the point that everyone in the school was endangered. "Every day somebody at Balboa would get stabbed or would be knocked out or would get shot at. The school was outta control. And the administration there, the principals, the teachers, counselors, they didn't know how to deal with it. And the only way they would deal with it, they would put band-aids on it. And then the next day, boom, the riots would occur." Balboa "was considered the battle zone," remembers the school's police officer; it was the "toughest school in the city."

School staff and teachers were distraught, afraid, and not equipped to squelch the violence. In contrast, Rudy was uniquely qualified. "Me coming into the battlefield, I'm thinking, damn, how could I slow the violence down just in the school?" He decided to use the skills of survival he learned on the street and in prison to work with the main antagonists. "So like we would do in the penitentiary, when there's a war between different ethnic groups, we would sit one group down and we'd get the other group. So I got in good with the Filipinos. Got their shot caller, they leader. Sat him at the table. And I got this brotha, this dude who was a football coach, Black dude, who knew the brothas, got them at the table. We sat down and we broke bread. We talked about, what can we do?"

Rudy did what no one else dared: he asked the youth for the solution. At this monumental meeting, he let the teenagers do the talking. "I was just ear hustlin," trying to gauge what it would take to stop the madness. The youth were clear that they did not want to speak with adults they did not trust. "They said, 'We don't want the police in here.' We got the police out. 'We don't want the principal to sit in on this.' Got the principal out." Rudy believed it was essential to listen carefully and respond attentively to their concerns. In the next few hours, through intense dialogue, the youth—who were, moments before, entrenched in a war against each other—worked together and came up with a list of demands that they believed would lead to peace among the students.

What did they suggest? Activities. The students wanted to know, "why don't you guys provide us, man, with something at lunchtime?" Rudy felt their demands were simple and necessary. "At lunchtime everybody just hanging out like wet laundry. There's no activities going on. The teachin that was going on there wasn't up to par. The teachers that they had up there was not teaching the kids. They was scared of the kids. So the everyday activity was the violence, was the gang fight." Rudy wanted to insure that violence would no longer be the everyday activity at Balboa High School.

Rudy took it upon himself to secure sports equipment and began organizing tournaments. Youth from different turfs started playing together and the fights "started slowing down and slowing—and it worked." Barriers were overcome between students. Additionally, Rudy got teachers involved in the games. This drastically improved the school environment because students began having stronger, more cordial relationships with their teachers. This reminds me of Dereca's insistence that teachers need to have authentic relationships with their students. Rudy actualized this at Balboa High School. He explains, "Instead of them just seein them just teach and talk about English, or math, or writing, they were seein them in the battlefield playing basketball with em or football or at the car wash."

Rudy understands that students need opportunities "to see teachers other than just teachers" but as "human beings." Consequently, these relatively simple sports activities at lunch changed the culture of the school. In Rudy's words, it "started crackin" because students started having a genuine investment in learning. According to the principal, Ms. Gray, "before Rudy teamed up with us" many of Balboa's students "were dropping out," but because of Rudy's interventions "they stayed and finished high school." She affirms, "that's success" for the students, school, and Rudy.

Once the lunchtime sports were under way, Rudy began hosting weekly meetings so students could organize the activities. Quite naturally, planning these events created a bond between students from different backgrounds. Rudy remembers, "It was not only Blacks and Filipinos; we brought the Samoans, Latinos in. We all had different cultures and everybody talked about it and everybody started sharing. We grew into our own program: the United Playaz." From that point on—"to this day, 11 years and 20 days"—UP has "been in full effect."

From its inception in 1994, UP's presence at Balboa High School has been enormous. Once the turmoil subsided and the school became relatively calm, Rudy began working with the administration to bring in additional "community-based organizations that were from the Hunters Point community, that was from Sunnydale, and from the Mission and from the South of Market." Having people from "they hood" was critical because students "could see their own peoples"; as a result students began "feeling mo comfortable." Balboa really began to turn around. However, this shift did not happen overnight and it was not easy. Despite positive changes, a number of obstacles persisted—for the school and Rudy.

In 1995, the State of California reconstituted Balboa High School. The entire school went through an overhaul. Only 4% of teachers[3] were allowed to return and nearly all extra-curricular activities were canceled. United Playaz was the only program that survived this change. Rudy was retained because "I knew his contribution and valued it as much as I valued the teaching of the students," remembers Ms. Gray. "That might sound like I'm not being true to my calling to education," she says, "but you can't teach the students if they're unsafe." Rudy kept the school safe by forming strong, genuine relationships with the young people.

Rudy has an exceptional rapport with the students. He "connects with them, understands them, knows how to get their attention" and, continues Ms. Gray, knows "how to connect with the people in their communities." Rudy's links to the neighborhood cannot be overestimated. Balboa's school resource officer, Bardoni, reasons that since Rudy "knows so many former gang members" he is able to "get word out to the outside sets not to bring the gunfire around" the school premises. This became poignantly clear to the teachers and administrators when students from the Sunnydale Housing Projects and Lakeview area started fighting. Even though Rudy is not from these areas, recalls Ms. Gray, "he knew where to go so that they could help us make the difference" and "that's how Rudy got the credibility around town." On countless occasions Rudy has proven that making peace among warring groups is possible—in the school and on the streets.

Rudy instigates peace through listening, which he calls "ear hustlin," and by working with the main antagonists. At Balboa, he values students' insights and trusts their decisions. He also understands that peers relate better with peers. Consequently, every aspect of United Playaz is youth-driven: they decide who runs the meetings each week, what activities the group will do, and who will be in charge of organizing the events. This strategy "teaches them leadership skills and responsibility." Furthermore, these activities are designed to show them, through experience, "the leaders that they are. It gives them power." As one student tells me, Rudy is "empowering." Although youth empowerment is not a new idea, Rudy's approach is noteworthy because he is able to involve at-risk and high-risk students. For him, leadership development is gang prevention.

Rudy taught teachers and administrators at Balboa that some of the school's toughest students were also the school's greatest leaders and, when given an outlet, they became vital partners in Balboa's change. Ms. Gray acknowledges Rudy's important contributions and suggests that "without his interventions" the school's transformation would have been "highly unlikely." Because of the insightful suggestions from these rough teenagers, such as having sports activities during lunch, Balboa became a more harmonious learning environment. While Rudy recognizes that Balboa now has a good academic reputation, he also knows that, more importantly, "lives have been saved. Lotta lives been saved."

Inspired by the notable changes at Balboa, UP participants started working within and beyond the walls of the school to spread their message of unity. Sports are still a component of United Playaz, but many of today's activities revolve around community service and take place throughout the year. During the summer, UP's weekly meetings are held at various community centers. At one particular meeting, Rudy asked the students if they should meet twice a month during the summer instead of once a week. Appalled by his suggestion, a young man turned to his peers and shouted, "There's too much that needs to be done!" When the vote was taken, every teenager raised their hand and voted to meet weekly. I was shocked. I had wondered if maybe students come to UP meetings just for pizza. During the summer, there is no pizza, but youth still attend; the numbers are impressive, with 30 to 50 youth attending each week.

Watching the young people's ambition to improve their school and community revives my hope. I know so many youth who might have graduated from high school if UP had been on their campus. Rudy engages students on a different level from the traditional schoolteacher; he involves them in activities—from feeding the homeless to going bowling—that directly impact their lives. The lessons are eye-opening, hands-on, and life-changing. Students consistently tell me that these activities "saved my life."

Rudy's life has also been saved. Once he began working with youth, he was able to get sober and become a new man. However, just as Balboa High School has gone through some monumental changes in the last decade, so has Rudy. He explains to me that when he was a gangsta he made a lot of enemies and transitioning out of the life has been hard. "I've been stabbed while I've been doin this work. Right here in my chest." When his past came back to haunt him, he considered striking back because "I know how to retaliate and how to get people back if I wanted to but I knew that I had a higher calling and I would stick to my loyalty that I'm not going to do that." When the streets would test him, his allegiance to peace was clear. The confines of this job also tested Rudy's loyalty, but in other ways.

The financial burden of doing youth work stresses Rudy and for the last 11 years he has made under $30,000 per year. During this time his workload has increased substantially, but he has never received a salary increase from the organization that originally hired him. Providing for his family—four children and Misha—is very difficult. I ask how he is able to make it. "The best way I can . . . selling CDs, selling Misha's jewelry." Though Rudy lives below the poverty line and knows how to make money by selling drugs on the street, "I did not resort back to sellin dope. I knew it would be hypocritical. I'm a man befo anything."

As I listen to Rudy's declaration, I insert my perspective. I explain the potential benefits of turning United Playaz into a non-profit organization. Rudy is interested in the possibility and has been considering going independent. Following this conversation, I arrange for him to meet with a grant writer. As a result, UP is now an official non-profit and Rudy's salary is over $60,000 per year.

Although earning a living wage is important, it is not Rudy's primary motivation. As executive director, Rudy has the freedom to dream about new possibilities for UP. In the future he wants to have a central UP office and recreation center in the city. He also envisions UP chapters in elementary, middle, and high schools throughout the country so that, at each tier of school, children and youth will have "somebody to connect with."

Creating programs for high-risk youth definitely benefits the participants, but Rudy also wins. United Playaz is his redemption. No longer does he live and die for the block. Rudy is now committed to helping uplift the streets: "to create more love, create more harmony, and more peace." With passion he exclaims, "I go all out just trying to make it better for my community." This is not a 9 to 5 job for Rudy; it is his life.

Rudy's life revolves around helping those in need. On many occasions I saw groups of kids come to his apartment to purchase food. For example, Rudy and Misha charge 25 cents for a container of Top Ramen. Though this barely covers the cost of the purchase, they tell me that the real payback is lending a helping hand. I recall the way Rudy described his home growing up as the neighborhood recreation house. When Rudy and I sit down outside his apartment in the SOMA (South of Market District) for our second interview, I begin to hear, see, and feel the context of his work.

Unconditional Love

There is no mistaking which apartment is Rudy's. A large handwritten poster in the window to the left of the front door reads "United Playaz." When I enter, Rudy is busy in the kitchen preparing spaghetti for the kids (his three who are here today, plus a few cousins). While he gets them settled at the table and leads them in a short prayer, I look at the various wall decorations. A large red flag of Che Guevara is covered with taped-on postcards of Malcolm X and the Dalai Lama, and photos of family and friends. A framed image of the Black Panthers, a Bruce Lee photo, and a Bloods and Crips truce poster adorn the walls. The ambiance of the house is welcoming and I feel comfortable plopping down on the couch.

Kids from the building are constantly coming in and out of the living room. A few of them play with toys in the corner and it seems everyone considers it *their* house. Because of the number of people in the apartment, Rudy suggests we sit outside. For the first time, I see him turn off his cell phone and I know I have his full attention. Under the hot sun and constant noise of sirens, I inquire about his work.

Rudy has a demanding schedule that never seems to stop. "I be up to fo or five in the morning, somebody else's neighborhood dealing with somebody else's kids or dealing with another adult cause they just want to kill somebody." I ask how often this happens and Rudy is clear: "It happens every time. Happen last night. Day befo that."

The sacrifices Rudy makes for people are enormous and extensive. One student's family was so involved in warlike gunplay that Rudy confiscated the young man's pistols and arranged for him to go to school out of state. "I made the phone calls to the kids, to the UP bank, to the president, I say, we got a 9-1-1." The response from the UP members was unanimous; they needed to "charge it to the game" in order to save one of their peers. The youth used their emergency funds to purchase the young man's plane ticket.

Two months later, in the middle of the night, Rudy received a very distressed phone call from this same student. The young man had tied up a few people and was standing with a gun in one hand and the phone (with Rudy on the line) in the other. "I'm goin to kill somebody," he kept repeating. "Tell these mothafuckers who I am!" Rudy remained on the phone and tried his best to defuse the situation. The young man began confiding in Rudy that "UP is all I got" and that, without the love and stability of the program, he could not maintain his wellbeing. After a long conversation, Rudy convinced the young man to put the gun down. In subsequent weeks, the teenager moved back to the Bay Area and re-enrolled in school. He is now 27 and works as a case manager at a local non-profit, guiding high-risk youth toward positive pursuits. He acknowledges that he would be "in jail or somewhere dead" without Rudy's guidance. This is not atypical. More often than not, these are the types of situations that make up Rudy's days and nights.

One way Rudy stays abreast of the needs of his students is through home visits. One young man's father was HIV positive. "I used to go to they house to kick it with the kid." On one particular Saturday the father called Rudy and asked him to come over to spend some time with his son. When Rudy arrived the father was cleaning his guns and sent his wife to the store to buy more gun cleaner. Rudy stayed in the living room with the youngster. The father got up, took his FBI Rugger to the bathroom, and blew his head off. Rudy was the person who opened the bathroom door and saw pieces of brain sprayed on the wall, and he was the one who had to console the traumatized child. In retrospect, he realizes that the father called on him out of desperation. To this day, Rudy has a tight relationship with the son.

On another occasion, Rudy was called to the hospital because a 17-year-old high school student had tried to commit suicide. He had an intense heart-to-heart with her for over 3 hours and—he smiles widely—"she's alive to this day."

As Rudy remembers and tells these stories, there is not a hint of arrogance in his tone. He passionately and humbly believes that every struggle in his life has led him to this moment. "I ain't used to be [able to] walk in San Francisco by myself in certain neighborhoods cause I knew it would be on, on site. But now I feel that the Man up there is guiding me to do this work and he's giving me the tools that I have . . . I believe everybody has a purpose in life . . . And to me it's not a job, it's my life." I begin to understand Rudy's relentless dedication. Each time Rudy is put in a position to help someone it reinforces his mission. His jarring struggles on the street, surviving drug addiction, and his time in prison actually prepared him to make an impact on some of the "hardest cats" around.

Rudy's colleagues believe, like Ms. Gray, that this constant drive comes from the "very deep love" he has for people "from really challenging situations" because "he was just like them and was given a second chance." She continues, "He does not want to see them do what he did. He emerged victorious and he's giving back to his community." In order to constantly be of service, Rudy maintains a very adaptable schedule. He tries not to get bogged down in meetings because with one phone call he might have to jump into his car and go in the opposite direction. When that happens, he smiles, "I was supposed to go that way." This flexibility is unrealistic for teachers but critical to Rudy's effectiveness.

Whichever direction Rudy's day takes him, he enters every encounter with the same underlying philosophy: "love." Whether on the street or in a UP meeting, "the atmosphere I like to bring is that unconditional love." He elaborates: "whether they wrong or they right, we there to listen to em and accept em for who they are." As I probe this part of his character, Rudy reveals that his outlook is deeply spiritual. "I believe God doesn't judge you for how you dress but I know He loves you and He wants you to do the best that you can do to bring out love in you and other people. I think that's what God is: Love." This loving philosophy is embedded in all the work he does to reach students.

The students explain to me that United Playaz is not an organization but "we family" and "it's unconditional love." When I ask Courtney and Evangela about Alex, a young woman who no longer comes to the UP meetings, they declare that "no matter what there's always unconditional love . . . we goin to always be here regardless. If your boyfriend leave or your car break down, we still got your back." Alex left UP for nearly a year and everyone believed she got caught up with her boyfriend. Evangela explains that no one got mad at Alex but always accepted her. Regardless of whether or not she was participating in UP, they did not pass judgment. Consequently, Alex got re-involved and brought with her a new UP participant: her boo. Recently, United Playaz had two commitments on the same day so Alex, along with the rest of the UP females, went to a grant-writing workshop while her boyfriend went with the guys to feed the elderly. For Evangela, this confirmed UP's power, positive influence, and inevitable growth.

Love is a real strategy for Rudy. It allows a family bond to exist between UP participants. But how does he create this bond when he first meets a group of students? Rudy was recently called into a local middle school to mediate between a group of Latino and African-American boys. The first question he asked the group was, "Is any of you guys ready to die?" One of the African-American students raised his hand. Rudy recalls, "I don't know if he was clownin or he wanted some attention so I went over and I said, 'first of all I want to say you're brave enough, I give you props, cause you brave enough to say that. Most people won't even go there. Why you want to die?'" Rudy was very direct and "started getting on his line, 'is there something going on?'" The student smacked his upper lip and began to get a strong attitude with Rudy. The student said, "You better get up off me man. You better get back now!" Rudy looked him straight in the eye: "If you wanna die, I'm concerned. I wanna know why you wanna die man cause I wanna live." The student got angrier, "Back up." Rudy stood his ground, "I'm not gonna back up!" The youth asked, "Why you ain't gonna back up?" With conviction Rudy responded, "because I love you and I care for you too much to want you to die." These caring words "shut him down." The student did not know how to answer and instead gave Rudy a deep, solemn look. Rudy put his hand on the boy's shoulder: "You know what brother, we need to talk more about this." The student looked up toward Rudy: "Why you pickin on me?" "Because," said Rudy, "I'm tryin to give you some love. There's a difference, homie."

Intrigued, I ask Rudy why his approach stopped this student in his tracks. "I think that stopped him because he ain't heard it like that . . . It's that tough love." Most classroom teachers, he explains, have a different approach like "get away til you cool down." Rudy sees an "emergency. You ready to die? I ain't gonna let you die, homie. I am not going to let you die! Hell nah!"

After the mediation, the student came up to Rudy and said, "Can you call me?" Through subsequent phone calls Rudy learned about the enormous difficulties at home: when the youth spoke to his family members about dying their response was, "Die then muthafucka. You already dead to me anyway." So "basically when he told me—I wanna die—he was tellin me he wanted to live. I threw him a muthafuckin life preserver." Rudy showed this young person he cared by not backing away; he saw the misbehavior as a cry for help.

When the teachers in the room saw the young man's misbehavior a few of them shrugged, "ah . . . there he goes again." They watched in amazement at Rudy's approach. When Rudy mentioned love and said he was "not gonna back up off" the student, the teachers were startled. Rudy suspects "some of the teachers prolly get scared cause he's a little kid but has dark glasses on, all his hood shit, and to me that's all a mask." When the meeting was over, the teachers told him "that was some great stuff." Reflecting on this encounter Rudy observes that "many teachers are not able to love and care for their students because they are afraid of them."

Teachers are fearful because they do not know or understand their students. All they see is the mask. Since Rudy used to wear a mask, he can see, as Dance (2002) writes, beyond the "tough fronts." He elaborates, "Most of the kids out there are just lookin for somebody to help them out or to give them some love. There's a lot of these kids out there that front like they violent or they act like they will get on you, but a lot of them just want to be heard." This sounds simple enough; Dereca also encourages adults to listen. But many teachers never see beyond the mask and, consequently, never listen.

Most teachers, insists Officer Bardoni, are "intimidated" because "they don't understand how the kids are talking" and "assume it's bad behavior." But the situation is usually more complex than teachers grasp. "Cause all these kids are angry, just about, and they don't understand why they're angry. And it's because of the piled-up trauma [in] their short 14 years on this earth. They've had no life experience to understand why they're mad or what's influencing it. Cause when their family members get blown away, killed, none of that trauma is ever released." Since Rudy is "one of them," reckons Bardoni, he accepts them for who they are and creates a space where "they can be themselves."

I ask Bardoni to compare Rudy's tactics with those of the teachers at Balboa. I continue to try and uncover how teachers can successfully reach and teach high-risk youth. Bardoni's answer is distressing. "You've had to live somewhat of their life to understand. It's not a color issue, it's where people are from . . . I don't know if it's possible sometimes to change a leopard's spots, because they've been brought up with a certain moral understanding of the world. Cause what they've been taught," he says of most teachers, "is the polite world where they've never had to worry about . . . puttin' their babies to sleep in bathtubs" to protect them from stray bullets. He shrugs, "you could explain it to em but most of the time I find they just draw a blank stare."

Rudy agrees with Bardoni's analysis in some ways, but his perspective is less daunting. He believes that teachers have a unique and essential responsibility. Rudy deeply respects the role of the traditional schoolteacher. In his role at UP he does not try to substitute for the imperative work of classroom educators. He does not see himself in front of a class teaching, for instance, English literature. He salutes educators who teach students how to read, appreciate, and analyze books. Nevertheless, a teacher with a profound ability to discuss literature might have little opportunity to actually teach, if (s)he cannot communicate with the class. Again, Rudy and Dereca agree. "It's about communication skills as an educator," Rudy says, "learnin how to communicate with somebody and if you not getting it to them in the right language, it's gonna be a rap." As Ms. Gray mentioned, Rudy speaks the same language as the students and knows how to relate to them. This is how he reaches them. On the contrary, many educators know the content—that is, teaching—but are unable to reach. Here is where a natural bridge between these two types of educator is necessary, especially for students who are disenfranchised.

Teachers can benefit from Rudy's tactics. At the bare minimum it is important for educators to recognize that some of their "bad" students can excel in other places, such as UP. Further, many young people are failing in school not because they are unteachable, but because they are not engaged. Through UP, Rudy offers youth a place on campus where they can connect. What other insights can he give classroom educators? With this question in mind, I invite Rudy to speak to my students at the University of San Francisco (USF).

Being Misled

On a fall evening in 2005, Rudy spoke to my credential classes at USF. The majority of the students are first-year teachers in San Francisco with a limited knowledge of their students' neighborhoods and community resources. I brought Rudy to class to try to fill this void, to act as a bridge between the school and street. I was surprised to see that the discussion made some students reconsider teaching as their profession. However, for most, his unmitigated advice reaffirmed their commitment to the communities and students with whom they will be working.

At 7:15 p.m. the students begin filtering into the classroom, which is located in a renovated church. The 50-foot cathedral ceiling is punctuated with elaborate stained glass windows depicting saints and other Biblical figures. A small wooden crucifix hangs to the right of the front door. Without the blackboards, television, tables, and podium, a visitor might not believe this space is a classroom.

By 7:35 p.m. the room is packed with first-year teachers. Three of my classes are coming to listen to tonight's talk. Every seat is taken and many people are forced to sit on desks in the back of the room. Although I know that Rudy is true to his word and is coming, I begin to worry that he is lost because his presentation is supposed to begin promptly at 7:30 p.m. And knowing him, I specifically told him it would start exactly at 7:00 because I did not want him to be late. Finally, my phone rings and he tells me he is looking for parking. After a couple of minutes I go into the hallway to wait for him. I immediately spot Rudy coming through the main entrance. He looks sharp. He is wearing a tan silk shirt with DJ imprints, creased khaki pants, and light brown suede Timberlands. His cornrows look new, tight, and neat.

Though Rudy is not very tall, his presence is huge. I instantly picture the way he described his father's personality because, when he steps into the classroom, everyone immediately quiets down. Without hesitation, or my introduction, he walks swiftly to the podium. From my seat on the side I try to interject a few comments about Rudy, but I see that he is raring to speak.

Rudy begins by speaking about "that Man upstairs" and says that all he does is because of and for the Lord. I am a bit surprised by his tone because I have never seen him speak so explicitly in public about his spiritual beliefs. I wonder if the church-like ambiance moves him. Then, as if reading my thoughts, he asks, "Are we in a church? You know, it's an interesting classroom." He takes a moment to look up at the colorful ceiling. When his eyes re-focus on the class, his demeanor is unmistakably tough.

Staring at the room of teachers he says, "I'm not here to judge nobody. I'm not here to tell nobody what to do. I'm merely here just to give off some information maybe that you could utilize in the field. The battlefield working with youngstas." His ideas flow passionately: "The biggest battlefield today to me is dealing with the minds of the youth of today . . . the generation that we are dealing with now is from the crack cocaine era. All the way from the year 1985 all the way to right now, that's 20 years." Rudy provides the teachers a glimpse into his work. "The kids that I'm working with now in that area from 20 and down, a lot of them are going through the crack syndromes and going through situations that a lot of people can't deal with. You know? And me being a recovering drug dealer and a recovering drug addict, it allows me to deal with that process better." The strength of Rudy's voice and the conviction of his words creates an uncanny silence in the room. I watch my students watch Rudy, their eyes fixed on his every word and motion.

"Whoever controls the mind of the youth of today is going to control the future." He explains to us that youth—and little children—can "recite a whole album of 50 Cent" but, at the same time, "when you handing them homework, they can't submit it." A number of teachers nod their heads. "These kids that we workin with, you know, they got ADD, they can't listen, somethin wrong with em or somethin ain't right." A few teachers continue to nod. Rudy looks directly at these particular educators: "I don't think that's it, not that." With certainty he clarifies, "I think a lot of these kids, how they say they lost, I think actually a lot of these kids that we work with today are being misled." Part of what is misleading youth, he contends, is the education system.

The education system is set up for "our peoples to fail" because "the things that the kids are being taught today are not the truth." Rudy urges the teachers in the room to create lessons that are relevant to the lives of their students. "As far as things in life, know your truth. Know your history. Know who you are. Know why the poor is gettin poorer. Why there's enough money and food in this world but it's not being relinquished over to a lot of other people. And that's what I'm thinking. A lot of kids are getting the wrong information." He explains that the youth he works with need teachers who can "talk about the crack epidemic . . . talk about man, food! Police brutality![4] Talk about shit that we know! About killings! You know what I mean? How do you deal with stuff like that!" His voice cuts through the silence. Some of my students look a bit shocked and scared by the sheer force of his convictions.

Perhaps Rudy recognizes their bewilderment because he calms down and his tone softens. "If you guys are the ones that are gonna be working in the battlefield in that population, we got to have tactics in how to deal with the youngsters today." According to Rudy, more often than not, kids today tune teachers out. He draws an analogy: "You got Channel 2 all the way to 500. And you watchin 2, you don't like it, you going to flip to 4, you going to 5, 6 . . . you going to go through all them til you find something you like. That's how the kids is today. They sit in class and you trying to educate them, you try to teach them and you not telling them what they want to hear, and they going to turn the channel on you. And then you going to wonder why they always talk in the back or they ain't trying to hear you." In order to engage students, Rudy believes the content must "relate to what's going on." However, Rudy recognizes that many teachers do not know or understand what is really going on in the lives of their students.

"Y'all know Hunters Point, right?" Hunters Point, commonly called HP, is a predominantly African-American community. Though it is home to many family businesses, community organizations, recording studios, mosques, and churches, it is also an extremely marginalized area. It neighbors toxic waste sites, and has both a 30% unemployment rate and a reputation for extreme violence. The statistics on violence in the city are startling: although African-Americans make up fewer than 8% of the population of San Francisco, in 2005 they constituted 63% of the homicide victims.[5]

Rudy shares with the class a personal story about HP. "I used to stay up in Hunters Point. Seen a lot of the murders. Seventy-five, 80 percent of them murders are not being solved, and it's not by coincident, accident, they not being solved. The police will come to us and say: 'We know who did the murders and I know y'all know who did the murders, but we not gonna solve the homicide rate unless you tell and let us know who's doing the killing.'" Even though the cops know who committed the crime, they need witnesses to come forward and testify in order to strengthen each case. Rudy provides a personal example about why this does not work. He tells us that his sister-in-law was in the car when his cousin "got smoked." She decided she would testify against the killers as long as she was put into a witness protection program. The police moved his sister-in-law from Double Rock, a project in HP, to the nearby Potrero Hill projects. "Before two days, they done shot her house up. That's the witness protection program."

Rudy connects this personal story back to the work of teachers. "This is how it fits into what you're doing. A lot of the kids that you guys gonna be working with are comin from the neighborhoods that a lot of these murders occurring from. So they comin with that frustration, that stress. Cause when somebody gets killed, off top a hundred people are affected by it. You guys understand about post-traumatic stress disorder? And it's not even post. It's present that we dealing with." How can teachers educate students dealing with these types of trauma?

Rudy explains that most teachers are afraid of their students because they do not understand them. Exacerbating this situation, most educators have no idea what is going on in their students' neighborhoods. They would have this information, he insists, if they knew their students. He urges the teachers in my class to "be a ear hustler, pull up an ear." This not only gives them a glimpse into their students' lives but will, perhaps more importantly, show students that "you on they side" and "you ain't just here to educate em" but genuinely care. When real-life issues arise for the class, he contends, teachers need to be flexible with their curriculum. "If you got a game plan that you got for today, it might not work for yo math class that day cause half the class is trippin on somebody who done got killed . . . And maybe before you even start talking about math, wait and have a little discussion about what's goin on so they can get it up off they chest." Finally, Rudy urges teachers to be prepared to have community resources at their disposal so that, if something does happen, they know who can offer support.

Although Rudy wants teachers to learn how to create a safe, supportive space for their students, he is cautious about the extent to which they should intervene. For example, "If you ain't bang and you want to talk to the kids about gang banging, it's not going to equate. You got to get someone that, you know, man, that can relate to these kids and to pop at em so they can really relate and they can generate the information that's being given." Rudy makes an important point that parallels his work at Balboa. In order to reach and teach young people—particularly those from violence-ridden areas—teachers and community-based educators must work together. He advocates for my students to use community resources in a comprehensive way in order to build stronger connections between schools and the streets. He invites them to attend a UP meeting or to call him ("only seven digits away, and the digits work") if problems arise at their schools.

Even though Rudy's invitation is genuine, an alliance between school-teachers and community-based educators can be difficult to forge. It is not necessarily a natural connection and Rudy has questioned the motives of many teachers over the years. "There's a lot of teachers I'd done seen in my life, I ain't going to lie . . . Balboa was one of the most notorious schools back in the days. Teachers would come in and they would sit in the class. Before the day is over they would get up and walk out the class while students were still sitting down." My class looks baffled at Rudy's depiction. I suspect they do not believe they would ever walk out on their students. But it does happen and according to Rudy, even with the best of intentions, it could happen to them. Rudy explains this is because most teachers cannot handle the "pressure that a lot of kids who are coming to the classes ain't trying to hear about English or they not trying to hear about math, because they just came from an area, man, that's really a war zone. And they coming from areas where they done seen people, man, get smashed on or they would see people with heads gettin blown off their shoulders."

Rudy reaches into his bag and pulls out an 8.5″ × 11″ photograph of a young man sprawled out on the concrete with his head blown off. I hear a few gasps. Rudy passes the picture around the room. People stare at the photograph and someone asks if it is real. "Hell yeah. This man right here was a snitch." He wants all of us to realize what particular communities are living through. After stepping over this body, "you expect them to go ahead and do 45 plus 45 and who met Johnny at the corner. Ain't trying to hear that, man. You got to understand the complex behind it." In order to be effective, he advises, "when you a teacher in there, you not only teachin one thing. You a social worker, you a counselor, you a mental health worker, you in there dealing with so many different dynamics of the game." A few people in the class begin to cry. Rudy speaks slowly: "Everybody is not meant to be teachers" but, if you decide to go "into that battlefield," then "you got to prepare yourself and use and utilize your resources that you have—cause you can't do it alone."

Rudy connects the critical work of teachers to a larger movement for social justice. "Do you guys know how much it cost to keep one person in YA for a year?" Silence. Then a white woman asks, "What's YA?" I am surprised that many of the teachers I work with, and educators in general, are unaware of the criminal (in)justice system, especially when it is such an overbearing presence in the lives of many youth they teach. CYA is the California Youth Authority, an incarceration center for youth aged 16 to 19. Rudy tells them that it costs on average $80,000 per year to incarcerate a young person. He contends, "you prolly could send like five or six people to a good college off of $80,000."

Rudy believes that the poor are incarcerated by design. Prisons are so popular because they are profitable. It is precisely "because they makin things like this, right here!" Rudy lifts up one of our desks, slams it down, and then pounds his fist on it. He continues with rage, even "the chair that you guys are sittin on! That's modern-day slavery . . . It's like plantations!" His voice echoes into the silence of the classroom.

"The system is designed for our peoples to fail," he then whispers, as if telling us a secret. It is not an accident that so many youth "love this thug life." He explains, "A lot of the youngstas that I deal with up in juvenile hall are kids who you guys are going to be working with." Even though the teenagers are relatively young, some of them have already experienced and participated in "murder beefs, rapes, and car jackins. They will come to these neighborhoods right here and do the damn thing and do it and wouldn't have no conscience or remorse about what they doing. They not knowing, man, that that thug life is going to send you to one of those penahoochies [penitentiaries] or is gonna send you six feet under." Too many young people are on a path to self-destruction; they are, in Rudy's definition, misled.

Consequently, classroom teachers have a unique opportunity. "It's yo job and it's yo challenge as our future educators to get at em and get into they minds. It's yo chance and yo opportunity to make that transition so they don't have to go there because a lot of people think that's all they got. They little block or they little set, that's their paradox, and they don't know nothin outside that box except when they go to school." He looks around the room. "A lot of cats go to school just for a safe haven. Or a lot of the kids come to school high on whatever just to escape the reality that they comin from. And then the cold part about it is after school is over, then they got to go right back." Essentially, many students go from a war zone in their neighborhoods to school and then right back into the war.

Because of this dynamic, "today's education is more bigger," and teachers need to take heed. "If you're chosen to be here," Rudy preaches, "don't make it a job for you, man, make it yo life. And go all out. Expect sacrifices. Just continue, man, to know that the odds is against us. The odds is always against us in this field. You'll meet a lot of resistance. But just continue, man, to fight that battle on the battlefield. The kids that we have now, it's our responsibility and our duties, man, to guide them to the right direction. They are our present. Everything that we have right now is in front of us, those are tools that we need to use." He mentions that even hip-hop can be a way to connect with students. Regardless of the particular strategy, Rudy is convinced that "we're dealing with the most interesting generation that we need to deal with and work with right now with everything we know and we got. We just got to know how to utilize it right. You're built for this field if your passion, if your motives are more than just money. Or just teachin math and English." He repeats, "Today's education is more bigger than that. The arena is more open."

Rudy reinforces to the class of teachers: "Not everybody is meant for this field. Not everybody, man, is meant to do this." Who is meant to do this kind of work? What are the attributes of an effective educator? "First of all, you guys got to want to do this job. You got to want to have the passion and the commitment to make it." Second, he urges teachers to get to know their students and be open and honest about themselves because if teachers "front" students will see right through their façade and "you'll see people walkin out your classes." Third, "find out some of the people who are in your classes, the kids that you know that's up there, that's a big influence in the class, to work with them to get everybody else settled." Fourth, when you have students who are "up in the back who's wilding out, those are prolly some of the students you should get at because those the ones who is eager to learn but they don't know how to get it." Fifth, show them "you not scared of them" by being diligent and stable, and holding your ground. Sixth, "find out what programs they got on school campuses. Find out who are there from the community that these kids are coming from." Seventh, "have a lot of love, love, love." He shrugs. "See, those are little tactics just to get up there and teach your class."

He concludes, "Like I said, I'm not here to judge nobody. I might never see you again for the rest of my life. But I know that the information I give out is important." He grins. "I just want to say one thing before y'all leave. One of the greatest poets was a Caucasian man. His name was Popeye the Sailor. You remember what he said? 'I am what I am, and I am what I am, and that's all I am.' Boom, be yourself. That's it." These final words bring a roar of laughs from my students. The class started off somber, somewhat intimidated, and ended full of smiles and a few tears. When I dismiss the class, many of the students do not leave, but stay to talk one-on-one with Rudy.

Class runs later than I expect and it is nearly 10:30 p.m. when I leave the building. As I drive back to the East Bay I keep replaying over in my mind Rudy's talk and my students' reactions. I cannot get the photo of the murdered young man out of my mind. Rudy believes that when one person is killed at least 100 people are affected—and a simple photograph affected my students and me. Because of tonight's talk I suspect many of these first-year teachers got a glimpse into a different world. Rudy dispelled any ignorance my students could possibly have about street violence. Moreover, he told them that the teenagers in their classes might not be able to do their work because they are dealing with "present-traumatic stress disorder." This was an important message for the teachers to hear. However, I am reminded of the way that, as a student, Dereca would lean on her drama in order to get out of schoolwork. I think it is relatively easy for us as teachers to hear about gunfire and suddenly feel sorry for our students, suddenly lower our expectations. A fine line exists between teachers becoming aware of urban strife and teachers becoming guilt-ridden. Teachers need to have a clear understanding of their students' realities coupled with high expectations. High expectations are a critical point

for Dereca, but not as much for Rudy. Nevertheless, as teachers, it is important
to become attuned to the urban reality. Rudy not only understands the streets,
but also gives students the opportunity to create solutions.

What We Gonna Do

Peanut, this year's UP president, walks in with a stern face and tells us who got
shot and died. A few heads nod in agreement as if to say, "we've already heard."
The 40-plus youth and adults sit silent for the next few minutes. Peanut looks
around the room, "What we gonna do about this!?!" Participants speak candidly about how the family is devastated and, in addition, cannot afford to
pay for the cost of the funeral. The youth begin strategizing about how they
can help. They decide to give some of their "emergency funds" to the victim's
mother to help pay for the funeral.

UP's car washes, bake sales, and other school activities are not organized
to help pay for a trip to Washington, DC, or raise money for the debate club.
Students in United Playaz raise funds so they have cash available to help those
in need. In extreme cases the students use these funds to help a peer or might
even buy a grieving grandmother a bag of groceries.

If United Playaz never existed, most of these teenagers would still know
far too many people who died. The difference is, with UP, they have a place
to react, respond, and heal. Having UP on a high school campus is extraordinary because Rudy is able to create a necessary bridge between the streets
and school. In his 25 years on the police force, Officer Bardoni has "been in
contact with a lot of people" trying to make a positive difference for youth.
Without wavering he says that Rudy is "number one" because he relates to
youth who "don't feel they got alternatives—they feel like they're going to be
dead by 18 anyway" and shows them "there's another world." In many cases,
Rudy is able to involve students, like Xavier, who would otherwise choose the
streets as their only viable option. How does he do this?

Like Dereca, Rudy believes that choice is critical. He cannot control or
judge the way anyone decides to live his or her life and he does not try to.
What he offers are lessons he learned along the way, coupled with activities
that can broaden a student's imagination. During the year, Rudy will take
groups of students to San Quentin State Penitentiary to sit down and talk
with inmates. He will also take them to the welfare office, other social service
agencies, and even mortuaries. Rudy is clear that this is not a scared-straight
approach. Rather, he just wants youth—particularly those who view the streets
as their only choice—to see the direction their life will probably lead: prison
and/or death. At the other end of the spectrum, he spends an equal amount
of time taking UP students on college tours. He also has them visit the San
Francisco business district, and has taken them to conferences in Los Angeles,
New York, and Chicago. These activities are strategic: "To me those are not

field trips, those are educational. We try to hit every dynamic where they get to see the reality; that's an eye-opener."

In addition to these eye-opening excursions, Rudy wants UP participants to be able to "kick it as a family." They have taken trips to Disneyland, and have gone camping, canoeing, and river rafting. Local, fun activities such as bowling and ice-skating are also integral parts of their year. Even these light-hearted events have a deeper purpose because "you'll see the kids be kids." Then, at least momentarily, "the mask" will come off. Taking off the mask is crucial, because it gives youth the opportunity to see themselves differently; through UP, they start to see themselves as leaders.

Students in United Playaz make many kinds of decisions. For instance, when DeShawn Dawson, a UP student at Bal, was murdered, the students had to respond. They began working with Vellie Williams, the first UP president (who is still involved), to write a play on youth violence. As Evangela explains, the storyline is about Tyra, a "ghetto thug girl," and her twin brother Tyrell, a high-achieving student. At the end of the play both of them get shot and their mother is left all alone to grieve. Following this scene the students play one of Tupac's ballads and pictures of murdered youth are shown on the large screen. Afterwards, the UP students step out of character and facilitate a discussion with the audience about violence. For the past 2 years UP students have performed this play at middle and high schools throughout the city. Courtney is always amazed at how many people recognize the pictures they show. She looks out at the audience and "I see everybody cryin." This form of peer education reaches a vast array of students in the city and she surmises that, like most UP activities, it "saves lives."

It Takes a Thug to Save a Thug

Rudy believes the best teacher of a youth is a peer. Similarly, he recognizes that the best gang-prevention expert is a former gang-banger. He uses a metaphor to explain his strategy: "If you knew somebody had a toothache, you wouldn't go up there and dig in his mouth and take it out. You would call somebody who knows how to deal with the toothache. I mean, temporarily you can run to the store and get some Orajel or something, but if you ultimately want to get it out you got to call somebody who knows how to deal with that situation." As Rudy explains this allegory to me, my mind wanders to the first time I grasped this characteristic of United Playaz.

In my field notes I describe one particular UP meeting: "There are 65 people crammed into this classroom. There are OGs [Original Gangstas] with braids and tattoos, and a soft-spoken Latino brother who just got out of the penitentiary after 25 years of lock-up. The oldest person looks well over 60 while the youngest is Mookie, who is now 3. The high school students come in and talk candidly with the adults present. They speak of the drama on the streets, what they're learning in school, a bit about their families or an upcoming UP event." I then pause, lean back on the couch, and put down my pen. Though I have been to countless youth organizations, something about UP feels different. What is it? I try to describe this dynamic. "It takes a thug to save a thug," I write in my notebook. In this moment, I fully appreciate that the best people to deal with youth who are "with da shit" are those who have genuinely struggled in these streets. As illustrated in his story about needing a dentist, Rudy's quintessential tactic is that the people most qualified to work effectively with high-risk youth are those who have had similar life experiences.

I bring up this observation—it takes a thug to save a thug—with Rudy. He leans forward, nods his head: "That's real talk." He explains how his life experiences shape the way he reaches youth because "most of the kids that I deal with are myself when I was younger." He reflects on when he was thugged out: "I know what it's like to struggle. I know what it feel like to get my ass whupped. I know what it feel like to be whuppin a mothafucka's ass. And I know what it is like to walk down the street with two pistols in my pocket ready to jack somebody." These first-hand experiences give him insight into how many of the youth he works with are feeling. He knows all too well what it feels like to be an addict to money, drugs, and the life. This thug mentality can be a hard place to get people out of ("the biggest institution is yo mind, homie") so he tries to empathize with them.

Rudy's life experiences shape his teaching style. Reflecting on his past, Rudy knows that "if somebody had come up to me and was like, you know young brotha let me tell you about God or let me tell you about the struggle, I'd be like, 'I ain't trying to hear that shit. That ain't my everyday reality.' If you comin to me and talkin about how to make some money or about some shit I could relate to, then I'll listen." Consequently, Rudy consciously uses the language and culture of the street as a way to communicate and get students' attention. I have watched him use profanity because he understands that "if that's the communication that I have to use to get to them, then by all means, that's what I gonna use." His teaching tactics are simple and straightforward: whatever it takes.

In terms of content, Rudy always has "a hook," that is, "something they can relate to." For instance, "when I meet the kids [in] juvenile I do not talk to them like, 'check this out—why we are poor,' I don't get at em like that cause a lot of them get turned off. I would come at em about some shit that we can relate to. Whether it has to do with music, or it has to do with even a video game or the shit that happen recently 'you know that muthafucka that got shot?' And then once they start feelin me, most of em'll ask 'you used to be in that shit man' and I'm like, 'yeah.' Then I start tellin em what I do and what they think about it. And that's when I start openin their eyes and the ears really start listenin because I'm still bangin. I'm just bangin for a purpose now. And they like damn, 'I ain't thought of it that way.' And it works. Trust me."

Teaching youth to think about "bangin in a different way" is powerful. Rudy awakens students to their agency by discussing social justice for the streets. For Dereca, the emphasis is on African history and popular culture. Whichever the approach, Rudy is clear: often it is the "hardest of the hardest kids—kids who are killers" who deeply understand the message, or as Rudy says, "smell the coffee while it's perkin." The "most powerful tools that you can have is them youngstas who has walked through Baghdad barefoot and been through the grid iron. Those are the kids who we need to get on the frontlines if we going to ever stop what's going on with our communities; to get out there and relate cause like the saying is, like you told me, only thugs can save thugs." Rudy does not just run a program; he is, in many ways, building a movement of young hardcore activists.

This method works for Rudy. But would it work for me? A white woman in her late twenties with all the right intentions? According to Rudy, one of the main reasons that his style works is that he is sincere. "I think the best way to connect with kids is to be real" and "don't try to be nothin that you not." Could any class train teachers "to be real?" Even if we are "real," what if we still cannot connect with our students because of our limited life experiences? Is that even the role of the teacher? But even Rudy cannot always have direct first-hand knowledge. In these instances, he does not "front." Instead, he finds the dentist—the expert.

A case in point: Rudy wants to teach UP students about the pitfalls of the pimp–ho lifestyle. As I described in Dereca's portrait, when she taught about pimps and hos she critiqued the ways "pimps are predators" and drew a clear connection to the ways corporations abuse particular communities with their products. Her analogy linking a street hustle to the larger dynamics of capitalism was fascinating; it clearly excited and informed her students. This approach works for her. Rudy's strategy is very different. Rudy works with many young men and women who are involved in, or at least glorify, being a pimp or prostitute. Therefore he decided to bring Fillmore Slim, the "world-wide known pimp that everybody knows—got him on books, records, TVs," to this year's Playaz Ball.

Fillmore Slim stands at the microphone at the Playaz Ball looking bright and fly in his pimp outfit, his work suit. Youth and adults rush toward the stage to meet this notorious man. Although he might fit the stereotypical image of a pimp in his long coat, hat, and snakeskin shoes, his words are atypical. Rudy recalls, "He came down to speak to the kids about *not* pimpin, how you don't glorify that lifestyle, how that's not the life to live." His talk was so pertinent, says Rudy, precisely because the message came from a "true-life pimp."

Rudy orchestrated the evening because he understands the best way to teach is through the wisdom of people who have had a similar experience. "I brought somebody who was really bout it. I could have spoke on pimpin but what do I know? I never pimped. I wanted to get somebody in livin color, the baddest of the baddest muthafuckas." This tactic is unique and effective. Through Rudy's personal networks on the street, he is able to connect with hardcore pimps, gang-bangers, and others who have first-hand advice about the destructive lifestyle.

Traditional schoolteachers, for the most part, do not have associations like this. Consequently, when educators encounter students who live and/or glorify the streets, they tend to have few (if any) tools to deal with it. They are, for the most part, not equipped to help students believe in viable, practical, real alternatives. According to Rudy, teachers in schools cannot do it alone. "That's why it's very important to use the resources that you have in the community or have people that you know that's in the field to directly deal with those issues." Educators desperately need partners from the community as allies and co-teachers because, as Ms. Gray confirms, "Rudy is teaching."

What does Rudy teach? Courtney and Evangela provide me with keen insights in a conversation after school one day. When asked the initial question, Courtney repeats Rudy's popular mantra: "if you're goin to bang, bang for your community, bang for what's right." And, she adds, "to always be yourself." Evangela laughs just thinking about what she is about to say: "He taught me we got to come together as butt cheeks. The stuff he say, it be funny, but it's real. Come together as butt cheeks means even if you don't know somebody, get to know em." He has given her other lessons. For instance, "It's bigger than just me and you or bigger than just a couple of us. It's a bigger and better world out there and that's what we need to see." And once a person's eyes are opened, they become responsible to "make sure this government is not holding us down for too much longer." Courtney and Evangela continue to talk back and forth. I ask them how Rudy's lessons are similar to or different from those of their teachers at Balboa. "Schoolteachers try and get you a diploma," explains Courtney, "and as for Rudy, it's more like your life. You know, like real stuff. I mean, school is very important too, but his teachings is like what you need to do in your life, make your smart decisions and everything for you to succeed."

Rudy's lessons for success are steeped in everyday reality—his curriculum is life. Furthermore, the content comes from his personal experiences. United Playaz students, in the broad sense, receive an education. But this type of education is distinct from the common, narrow conception of school that takes place in a building. For him, learning needs to connect directly to the needs of the people. This is, quintessentially, a *pedagogy of community*. Education in this milieu is not a noun, but a verb.

A Real Warrior

I've been examining the work of Rudy Corpuz for almost 3 years. During this time, I almost got accustomed to hearing students talk matter-of-factly about shootings. At UP meetings, moments of silence are as much a part of the agenda as Rudy's comments about people's grades. What happens, I wondered, to the students who make it? Rudy works ceaselessly to save lives, but what kind of lives do students lead once they are rescued? Who do they become? In our final interview I learned precisely what success means to Rudy.

Rudy teaches people "how to give back" and has many stories about what this looks like. "There's one young lady who started our program, 1994, was off the hook, gang-bangin Samoan girl. She is currently runnin her own youth program in Visitacion Valley. Doing what she learned back then. Going to schools, working with youngstas, running a program, hiring people from the hood. Cats who's comin from the hood, hookin them up with jobs, putting money in they pocket, feedin they families." Rudy highlights this person for a number of reasons. She used what she learned in UP as a catalyst to develop her own program. At her site, she hires people from the community. This is the clear domino effect of Rudy's work. Teaching people to "bang to save our neighborhoods" is his achievement.

Rudy tells me about another young woman who was a United Playaz participant but still got into trouble and ended up in juvenile hall. Rudy and the UP family never gave up on her and eventually "she got her thing together." She graduated from UCLA, came back, and is workin with the youngstas—givin back!" Rudy is excited about his student's accomplishments. Another story comes to mind about a young man who was "in and out the joint—straight up hardcore gang-banger. Got him hired, workin the population with the kids now. Now he's bangin like we bangin." Although Rudy sounds proud as he tells me about these individuals, he is quick to mention how much more needs to be done. The last eight funerals he went to were for people under the age of 24.

Taking into consideration his work at Balboa and his concept of success, I ask Rudy, "What do you consider yourself?" He does not tell me, like Ms. Gray and his colleagues, that he is a teacher, though he admits, "we have to be teachers." I suspect teaching means something different to him because without a moment's hesitation he looks at me seriously: "A freedom fighter."

Perhaps Rudy is a teacher, but he is foremost an activist. The lessons he imparts to youth revolve around life skills, leadership development, and giving back—all of which connect to a larger movement for social justice. I remember the pictures of the Black Panthers hanging in his house and in the UP classroom. For Rudy, today's Black Panthers are misled youth. He teaches me that "The sleeping giant is them cats out there who's thuggin it." And when this sleeping giant awakes, change is not only possible; it is inevitable.

Rudy relates his vision to the work of Tupac. "Tupac was so smart because he wasn't born as a thug. He was born into a revolutionary family. But he did his homework and said the sleeping giant is the street cats. How can I reach those youngstas? Well, let me be thugged out. Let me go ahead and spit the ra-ra and get out there man and talk about guns, pistols n hos n drugs n bitches n money—that'll catch they attention. And once I get they attention and they start feelin it and listenin to it, let me drop this real shit on em . . . If you listen to Tupac when he really speaks . . . he would spit about the revolution." Like Tupac, Rudy's goal is to build a movement with the so-called unreachable and unteachable. He is convinced that these particular youth have insight and wisdom *because* of their struggles. It is their battle scars that make them, like Rudy, exceptionally qualified to reach, teach, and lead.

Rudy asserts that high-risk youth are not, as the media portrays them, a menace to society. He contends that they are the reverse: menaced *by* society. In many ways "the system" is to blame; equally harmful are adults who consciously and unconsciously "mislead" today's youth. I wonder: *Are young people responsible for anything? What about personal responsibility?* "The system is designed for our people to fail," says Rudy. "The only way for change to come about," he contends, "is from the bottom, it is from us. I think the solution is us, our own peoples." Here, Rudy reinforces points from the literature (e.g., Ginwright et al., 2006) as he describes the importance of awakening agency to overcome oppression.

Rudy is convinced that the people "who's done been through it" are the solution. "The ministers, the deacons, the preachers, the teachers, the counselors—they couldn't do it. They couldn't do it! They can't save, man, our peoples in the hood. The only people who could save our people in the hood, is our people. You can't depend on the government. You can't depend on that city hall or the state to keep fundin us with money." I push Rudy and further question his perspective: "So the government should not be held accountable because 'the people' are responsible?" He responds, "It's like how Pac said, man. There's enough money and food on the other side of the door for everybody to be content. But they not goin to share it wid us. They never have and they never will, and they don't want to. So the only way we can do it, man, is start gettin with our own peoples and start doin it on our own." Rudy recognizes that "there's a lot of obstacles and potholes in our path that detours us from gettin to where we need to go, whether it's the white man, it's the system that's boggling, that all contributes." But, he emphasizes, "it never stop a *real* warrior."

Rudy's call to awaken and organize the "real warriors" inspires me. I realize this is so much bigger than school. However, the fact that UP exists on high school campuses is significant. As I explained earlier, school remains one of the safest places for youth, especially for teenagers of color living in poverty. Advocates of critical pedagogy argue that, while schools are safe, they could be so much more. Schools have the potential to be cornerstones of justice. Thus learning should be deeply connected to personal and community transformation. In order for this to occur, teachers need a clear understanding of their students' realities and needs, as Rudy shows so clearly.

Evangela reinforces that Rudy bridges various contexts. In junior high she kept hearing, "UP crack, UP crack, whoo, whoo." She was curious about the program and, as soon as she got to Balboa as a freshman, she went to check out UP. When she first entered the room, the first thing she noticed was the picture on the wall of her cousin who died in 1995. She felt an immediate connection and became involved. Four years later, Evangela is a force within the group. Becoming a leader within UP also helped her excel in her classes at Balboa. She is the first member of her family to graduate from high school.

Courtney is also an active UP member, but she did not have the same type of immediate connection. When Courtney first saw Rudy in the quad one day during lunchtime she was "kinda scared to go approach him" because of his "style." He came up to her and her friends and asked if they wanted to buy a Gambisi CD and she realized he was "very welcoming." Rudy explained that everyone is accepted at UP and urged Courtney to "check us out." Courtney has been a United Playa ever since and is the group's official historian ("it's just to be in charge of all the pictures and the times that we're in the media").

Even though Rudy is a link between students, teachers, and the streets, he does not have the same appeal to everyone. As much as his street style attracts some people, it repels others. Unfortunately, teachers often do not respect or appreciate his approach. Half the teachers at Balboa feel "intimidated by the work that I do because of me being an ex-felon and somebody who doesn't dress like the normal teacher or speak like the normal teacher. They feel threatened because their students flock to me." This is a problem because teachers and community-based educators are thought to be on the same team. As I demonstrated in the introduction this is not always the case. How can this alliance between teachers and community-based educators be forged? I remember the way Rudy told my students at USF that teachers, more often than not, mislead today's youth. What type of information does it take to redirect them? The answer comes during our final interview.

I Love Education

I listened intently to the advice Rudy gave my USF students. He spoke about the need to educate youth about "some real shit." I also recognize that Rudy was on a destructive path and that working with youth made him want to change his life. But I still want to know who woke him up. Who gave him his political fervor? He says, "That's a real good question."

Rudy explains to me that his real teachers were the men "behind them walls." When he was incarcerated, he learned about his history. "When I was in the pen, I ain't going to lie, I had a group of dudes that would sit me down, they would tell me what's going on, how a .45 gun was created, you know, things that I knew about." Rudy could relate to this topic, he chuckles, because he used to carry "two pistols: for suckas on the left, and suckas on the right."

The elders in the pen taught Rudy that "back when the Filipinos had the war gainst the Americans, the Filipinos used to tie the bark around their body from the tree and they used to chew on certain leaves to make them more energized. And we used to have bolo knives. So when we would come at them, the Americans only had their .38s. That was all that was created. Well, pop, pop, and [they] would reload. By the time they reload, we'd get up and come with a knife and, boom, chop they head off. So for every one Filipino, we was killing three Americans. So they said what do we have to do to lay they ass out? Let's go create a more powerful gun, the .45. Went back to the lab and they made a gun called the cannon, what the kids call on the streets right now the cannon."

When Rudy learned about this history, it "kinda turned me on" and ignited his interest in social change. Rudy started coming to these guys regularly. "They would start telling me about the struggles and then they would start telling me about how crack cocaine got in the neighborhood. And they would tell me about why we are in these conditions, and they would tell me about the struggle that our peoples going through, why the rich gettin richer and the poor is gettin poorer. Why they got mo money for wars and how they not feeding the poor. Those are things that I could relate to. And I was like, man, I ain't never heard of this. I love education!" These lessons sparked Rudy's desire to learn because they were culturally relevant and connected to larger issues of equity.

If Rudy's teachers at Mission High School had utilized a culturally relevant curriculum, would he have been able to engage in school? "One of the things that I think teachers could have did to kept me in class" was to "have really came at [me] with things that I could relate to . . . Like history, I hated history. I could not relate to that. I would argue with the teachas. 'How the hell you talk about Europeans findin America when there was already people there? So how did they discover it?' And they wouldn't give me answers that was right. So it kind of turned me off." It is a shame that Rudy was turned off by school and had to wait until he was locked up to receive an education. The topics that stimulated Rudy revolved around his people, oppression, and resistance.

Now Rudy is in a position to teach students about organizations such as the Young Lords, Brown Berets, and other youth groups that sought social justice. But, even more than that, he wants them to experience that giving back is "gold. That's real diamonds. That's the real oil. That's the real medication." As youth become leaders in their communities, they receive, Courtney exclaims, an education in "empowerment."

A relevant curriculum is a vital part of reaching students, but it is not that simple. Rudy has other, larger critiques of the school system that are beyond the control of classroom educators. For instance, one reason why Rudy was able to fall through the cracks at Mission is simple numbers: the teacher was trying to deal with too many students. Classes should have been smaller or, at the very least, teachers needed to have assistants. Because of these circumstances, Rudy convinced himself that his teachers did not care ("they ain't trippin off us") and that he had no reason to even try. Hence, the student-to-teacher ratio is important. Even in his work, Rudy finds that "you can't catch these kids when they [even] like five deep, it's gotta be more a one-on-one or a one-on-two for them to really catch and grasp that message." Although teachers cannot change the number of students in their classes, it is worthwhile to try to meet with them individually, especially those who are at risk. This should not be a matter of detention or punishment but rather, as Dereca mentioned, about building strong relationships.

Rudy's style is unique because he is so street tough. Rudy accepts, at times seems to romanticize, everything "gutter." I often heard Rudy say, "we're from the gutter, we stay gutter." When I ask him about this phrase I am taken aback by his response. "I think when I say we're from the gutter, I actually mean God's people. Cause God worked with the bottom of the barrel. He stuck with the pimps, the prostitutes, and the killers and the poor, and that's what we are. So don't be ashamed of who we are and what you about. We live this shit. We are some of the strongest people on this planet . . . We could live in better conditions but it's on us to go ahead and get it." His tone is forceful, yet calm, and his stare piercing. I am looking at what Tupac called a thug-angel.

Rudy Corpuz, Jr., founder of United Playaz, glorifies the hood—he loves the street. "I stay on the streets. That's my office. I stay grindin on the streets. I stay hustlin." Even when he needs to relax and rejuvenate he goes to the corner to "just hang with my patnas." Rudy embraces the hustle of the street, loves the gold teeth, pieces, and rhythm of "the people." And he abhors the destruction. But Rudy does not try to change the young people he works with. This is unique to UP; many students who enter programs go through a metamorphosis and become square, so to speak, in order to excel. At UP, youth are completely accepted, and even applauded, for their dreadlocks, tattoos, and white tees—and this is no accident. Even though Rudy transformed himself, he never abandoned the gutter that raised him. He models this lesson to youngsters and even announces it on the new UP t-shirt: "It takes the hood to save the hood."

Our interview comes to a close. Rudy is rushing out the door to a speaking engagement for social workers at San Francisco State University. The back of his black-and-white jersey reads thug-angel.

Victor Damian is a young Filipino man working with troubled teenagers. This is perhaps one of the only things he has in common with Rudy. In contrast to Rudy, Victor's approach is creative and compassionate. Even though he does not have first-hand experiences with the street, Victor is able to reach and teach young people whose lives and belief systems are drastically different from his own. His ability to create connection is the focus of the following chapter.

4

VICTOR DAMIAN

Pedagogy of Compassion

Few people have heard of the Youth Task Force (YTF), but those who have speak about it as a transformative force in young people's lives. In the same breath, they brag about the coordinator of the group, Victor Damian. I am told he is "powerful, energetic, passionate" and that he "challenges his youth to do more and become more." I learn that the young people he works with are incarcerated or in foster care, receive mental health services, and/ or are in special education. In fact, to be part of the YTF, youth must have experience in two or more of these systems. As Victor will later tell me, this means that some of the teenagers he works with "have seen so much that they have attempted suicide six or seven times." This includes youth who have been ordered into "residential placements for substance abuse . . . crack babies . . . their fathers had put guns to their head . . . been former prostitutes . . . really high-risk. High-risk meaning they just been through so much stuff that it's hard to work with them because they don't know what to do cause nothing's working." He insists: "Those are the youth that I need. If they're youth that are cool and never had anything go wrong in their lives, those aren't the youth that I'm looking for. Even if it's a young person that wants to change the system but has never been in it, I don't work with those youth. Those youth are just hopefuls, they can find other programs. I have a specific base of young people, young people where nothing else is working and then they choose me."

I wonder why.

I find a possible indication in the program's mission statement. It declares that these youth are to become "agents of change" within the system so that services become, for instance, "more youth friendly." At the outset, I am impressed with some of the goals of the YTF. But what does this program look like on the ground, day to day? Who is Victor and what makes his particular group so successful? When I contact Victor, he is very easy to reach. I am struck by his exuberant tone over the phone. He seems genuinely excited about my research topic and open to further discussions.

A few days later, I take BART (Bay Area Rapid Transit) to San Francisco to attend my first Youth Task Force meeting. It is the fall of 2004. The group meets once a week from 4:00 to 6:00 p.m. at the downtown office of Legal Services for Children. Unable to find the building, I stride up and down the 1200 block of Market Street on this cold, windy day. Finally, out of the corner of my eye, I notice someone opening a thick metal door. On this anonymous-looking door I discover a tiny piece of paper with the words Legal Services. I try to pry the door open. It is absurdly heavy so I use both arms to open it wide enough to get inside. Once off the street, I find myself in a dark corridor. I walk up a flight of stairs, past a vacant second floor, and continue on until I hear voices on the third floor. In stark contrast to the entrance, the office is bright, with fluorescent lights. I hear rap music coming from the conference room so I walk right in.

Four young people sit around a large table and there is no adult present. One of the girls nods her head to the beat and sings every song. I sit down and try to make eye contact, but none of them look in my direction. However, as soon as I look away I hear, "Who is you?" I can feel this student's mug (that is, her disgusted expression), so I say matter-of-factly: "A visitor. Victor know I'm coming." The young woman rolls her eyes and smacks her lips, "Oh."

Minutes later, Victor enters. He seems to bounce into the space, beaming. He puts a bucket of Kentucky Fried Chicken on the table. While the youth dig in, he walks over to me, and puts out his hand. As we shake hands, he explains that he is going to let the students eat, "chill for a minute," and then start the meeting. Two more students stroll in and sit down. While eating, the group talks casually about someone who got shot over the weekend, and about a dysfunctional caseworker. The topic of conversation does not shock me, but I am surprised by the nonchalant tone: how normal a recent death seems to be, and in the same breath with a complaint about a caseworker.

Altogether six youth sit at the table. The Youth Task Force is relatively small compared with the large meetings I am used to at United Playaz. But here, the intimacy feels important. Perhaps the small number of students is strategic. I look around the table; it's as if we're a family sitting around a large dinner table at the end of the day. As I will later learn, the YTF is the closest thing many of these students have to a family unit.

At 4:30 Victor sits down at the table for a check-in, asking, "What's your weather like today?" He goes first: "My forecast is real sunny" and talks momentarily about his day. He then mentions that over the weekend Bonnie, one of the Youth Task Force members, "spit on the mic, blew it up!" Victor almost jumps out of his chair when he tells us about Bonnie's exceptional skills. I watch him make eye contact with every person at the table. Victor's eyes sparkle and radiate joy, whereas the students' eyes are melancholic, almost expressionless. The contrast is profound. I write in my notebook: he seems to be trying, quite literally, to pull their energy up.

Victor turns to his right and we go in a circle talking about our forecasts. At times, the forecast descriptions meander into elaborate stories about a movie someone just saw or a depressing saga about visiting a parent in jail. The students seem very interested in each other's words and comment compassionately on each other's lives. For instance, an older teen advises a younger girl: "You are really beautiful and you have to have higher expectations of yourself." As these conversations continue, Victor gets up and quietly walks around the table. He sets a piece of paper in front of each of us. He sits back down, waits for our talking to turn into silence, and then tells us to flip our papers over. In a forceful tone he reads:

> Your children are not your children.
> They are the sons and daughters of Life's longing for itself.
> They come through you but not from you,
> And though they are with you, yet they belong not to you.
> You may give them your love but not your thoughts.
> For they have their own thoughts.
> You may house their bodies but not their souls,
> For their souls dwell in the house of tomorrow, which you
>   cannot visit, not even in your dreams.
> You may strive to be like them, but seek not to make them like
>   you.
> For life goes not backward nor tarries with yesterday.
> You are the bows from which your children as living arrows
>   are sent forth.
> The archer sees the mark upon the path of the infinite, and He
>   bends you with His might that his arrows may go swift and
>   far.
> Let your bending in the archer's hand be for gladness;
> For even as He loves the arrow that flies, so He loves also the
>   bow that is stable.

The room is quiet. Without a word, Victor passes out paper and pencils, and tells us to write. The students appear familiar with the exercise. He explains that we can write our own prayer for children, a personal affirmation, or a response to the poem. Victor sits down to write, and I follow his lead. Everyone at the table is writing. The only sound in the room is of pencils on paper. When the sound of writing starts to slow down and cease, Victor asks us to share.

Sonia raises her hand. "But I don't want to read it aloud," she quickly tells us. "Are you nervous?" asks Victor. "I just don't want to read it." "All right," says Victor, and he agrees to read it for her. She has written: "As you see others do, still follow your own path. As you hear of drugs and pain, don't follow the hidden path. Follow your heart and not always your mind. Trust your instincts and not those of others to please them. Show your mythical side, don't hide. Trust the air in which you breathe. Bathe in the sun before it sets. Allow yourself to love and be loved. Don't make yourself fall if no one is there to catch you. You are yourself no matter the view. Push yourself no matter the distance, and don't let go, if you're going to regret. Love yourself, for you are and always will be loved in return." Victor lets out a long exhalation, "It's so good." The other students nod in agreement. "Wow," I comment.

Mark reads his next. "Dream of a place that I never seen. Haunting memories that seem to haunt me with steam . . . just because you can't hear what I'm saying doesn't mean that I'm not praying. I look towards you when times get rough. I lost my courage so I'm cold in the buff. With no clothes, I'll still strive forward. Happiness is what I'm trying to move towards. Scrambled brains mixed with a mangled heart shall guide you to the light from the dark." Mark shrugs his shoulders, "That's it." "That's really nice," Victor comments. After Victor and two other teens read, the students *command* me to share.

I feel on the spot, insecure. But I know that this is part of building trust and that I must put myself out there because this is what I want them to do with me. I ask, "It's all love, right?" No response. So I just begin: "Arrows not able to fly free through the air towards a natural destination cause we're guided in despair and earthly indignation. Conceive of life mandated by blocks and glocks sends arrows back upon ourselves. We are our own worst nightmare. Unable to wake up from a manmade reality that has stopped our soul from being able to breathe. Allowing us, forcing us, to forget our natural destiny. We are born here, but not of here. We come to this earth to fly free, no matter what. We are arrows meant to soar in our own direction, without limits—now this is true immaculate conception."

Without hesitation another student, Cloteal, exclaims "I want to go next!" She reads, "Today is the day of appreciation . . . you will find a positive influence today . . . you will love you when nobody else does. You will love everything about you, even your flaws . . . People might not understand who you are and who you are getting ready to become . . . [but] the world wouldn't be what it is without you."

Cloteal's poem makes me consider who these youth "are getting ready to become." Amidst all of the chaos in their lives, they commit to be part of this particular group. Why? Through this short writing exercise, I glimpse their feelings, dreams, and needs. In so many ways, their masks came off as they sat reading and writing their poetry. The tough fronts I encountered when I first walked in are no longer prominent. Instead, I now see young people trying to discover who they are.

Victor thanks everyone for sharing and tells us to use the pieces we wrote for encouragement and guidance. He explains that the author of the poem we read was Kahlil Gibran and that his trials and tribulations shaped the beauty of his art. Victor, paraphrasing Gibran, tells us, "All knowledge is half asleep within us . . . it's not an external thing, it's not something that only certain people could own. It's within every young person, every being could always become better." I sense that he is trying to draw a correlation between Gibran and the youth. Similar to Gibran, their struggles can spur greatness in unique and important ways.

Victor sits down next to Rose, giving her his full attention. With Victor so preoccupied, everyone else starts talking and one student turns up the radio. Cloteal tells Ronald that this particular "Bananas" song has "everyone at the club going crazy." Laughing, we all start singing out the lyrics and they are surprised I know the words. By 6:00 p.m. the youth start packing up and say goodbye to Victor. He tells them their paychecks will be available next week.

"They get paid for this?" I ask. Victor and I sit back down at the table and he gives me an overview of the YTF. The YTF is a group of five to ten students between the ages of 14 and 21. The number of participants is always in flux because the students' lives are always in flux; in the middle of the year, for instance, a youth might be transferred to a different group home. Notwithstanding this level of inconsistency, the primary responsibility of the YTF is to make policy recommendations so that youth-serving agencies become more effective.

The majority of YTF members are recommended by caseworkers and judges, although some hear about it from their friends. The students receive $10 per hour for participating and Victor concedes that the money is usually what entices them to join. A student will later corroborate this: "My social worker recommended me to the program. I was like ten dollars an hour, I'm there!" Though the pay rate is good, the hours are minimal. Typically, the youth receive $20 to $30 a week. Victor realizes that this is not enough and works hard to give them other opportunities to make money. One way students can earn extra hours is by speaking at conferences. As I will learn, these young people realize that telling their story is a form of healing and a form of activism. Storytelling is an integral component of Victor's ability to reach and teach.

Everyone Has Stories

When Victor and I schedule our first interview, he asks if we can do it at my place. Since we both live in the East Bay, it is definitely the most convenient. Victor is the only person in this study to come to my home. Even more than being a research participant, he tries to be my friend; this tells me a great deal about Victor's personality. On the questionnaire, YTF members all described

Victor as their *friend*: "a best friend" and "a friend even when he doesn't know exactly what to do."

Victor does not always know how to advise his students because their world can seem so different from his own. He is not familiar with the street like Dereca and Rudy. He does not know, for instance, what it is like to have a mother on drugs or how to boil cocaine into crack. Yet he is still able to connect with youth who have these first-hand experiences. As I watch him interact with young people, I realize that being from the street is not indispensable. Victor is effective in remarkable ways; his style works for him and the youth he serves. His tactics are deeply connected to his own quest for awakening.

We sit down on my living room couch. "My full name is Victor Alexander Damian. I was in born in 1978," he begins. Victor is the youngest of three children. Since his sister and brother were both born by cesarean section, the doctor advised his parents not to have any more children, but they did. Victor was born prematurely, by cesarean, and weighed only 3 pounds. His parents called him Victor because "I kind of won" and beat the odds.

However, even after a miraculous birth his woes continued. Victor did not feel like he had won because "everything was a battle and everything was a struggle." In Victor's deepest moments he reflects, "I'm not supposed to be here." As a young child he was "allergic to everything . . . I couldn't have wheat, I couldn't have my mother's milk." Whenever Victor ate, he got severe rashes. In order to stop him from itching, "my parents would duct tape my hands and feet together and throw me in front of the TV because I'd itch my face so much it would bleed all the time." Victor does not talk about this memory with sorrow; instead he reasons, "I always knew I was a fighter." A smile spreads across his face as he tells me what is was like "fighting my hands free and my legs free just so I could itch my face. Or I'd itch my face on the carpet and there would be blood stains on the carpet." Though this image is a bit grotesque, Victor is proud of his innate ability to overcome adversities.

I inquire about Victor's parents. They are both from the Philippines but met in New York City. Soon after, they settled in Rochester, New York, and started a family. They lived in a small two-bedroom house with several other relatives. At times up to nine people—aunts, uncles, and grandparents—were all living under one roof. Victor appreciated having a large family, though space was a serious issue; he and his sister shared a large closet as their bedroom. Moreover, although his home was full of Filipinos, he did not have ethnic pride because "my parents were taught that assimilation was the answer. To be American, you're not Filipino. They never talked to me too much in Tagalog even though they spoke it." Victor felt he did not quite belong at home; unfortunately, he did not have a sense of belonging in his neighborhood or at school either.

Victor's community was predominantly African-American and Puerto Rican. "Everyone made fun of me. They called me Chinese Nigger . . . Spic."

School was also difficult, but in a different way. For 12 years Victor attended a strict Catholic school that was overwhelmingly white. Consequently, in each arena of his life—home, community, and school—Victor struggled to find his way.

When I ask him what school was like, his face becomes drawn, reflective, almost depressed. I am struck by his shift in tone because the Victor I see at the YTF meetings is so positive; he is the cheerleader. Now there are no smiles. He shrugs. "I was never really good at school" and was "always questioning" Catholicism. Attending a Protestant Sunday school only added to his confusion. "A lot of church stuff," he says with dismay.

Victor admits that he tends to sugarcoat things. Seemingly exuberant and confident, he knows underneath that "it was really tough growing up and really hard dealing with identity." He leans forward. "A lot of times I wished I was white because it seemed like they had it all . . . the big lunches with lots of snacks . . . they're just the most privileged and I kind of wanted that." Victor wanted the innate privileges that whiteness brings, but his skin color would never change its hue; he had to search inside himself for an identity. As he sits across from me on the couch, I reckon that he now has a clearer sense of self. I cannot help but notice the juxtaposition between his comments about whiteness and the man I see in front of me wearing a black shirt with bold yellow letters that read: Kultural Guerilla. The shirt celebrates a Filipino band of "social revolutionaries" who use music to build community. I comment that his shirt appears to announce pride and ask, "So what happened? When did you start celebrating the fact that you're Filipino?"

In high school Victor started learning Filipino martial arts, "the only martial art that was used in warfare." He also began to understand his people's history. He straightens his back and looks right at me: "Learning how to be Filipino was great . . . Learning that [the United States] built the .45 caliber bullet to kill a Filipino." Throughout the Spanish–American War, American troops "had to wear collars made out of leather and metal so that they wouldn't get their heads chopped off." With a serious look he claims, "That made me proud!" Victor's ancestors were fierce, remarkable warriors. When the bolo battalion fought the Japanese, they wiped them out. Each warrior would have "over 200 murders to their name." This history, this type of education, "gave me strength." Victor no longer looked at white people with admiration. Rather, he became impressed by his lineage and inspired by his ancestors.

While Victor talks, I cannot help but think about Rudy. Very similar experiences also sparked Rudy and gave him a greater sense of self. However, hearing Rudy talk about the .45 did not seem out of place during our interview because guns were a big part of his lifestyle. Sitting here with Victor, I am a bit shocked by his excitement that Filipino warriors had "200 murders to their name." I think of Victor as calm, peaceful, and a bit hippie-ish, so I am surprised to hear him speak so jubilantly about murder. He seems to pick up on my bewilderment. He leans forward and explains in a calm, soothing tone: "The difference between a soldier and a warrior is a soldier just follows orders; a warrior follows his heart." I smile and nod.

"As I got older," Victor continues, "I started wanting to know more about my culture, know about being Filipino, and that started to give me identity." Victor realized that his family was implicitly teaching him about his culture through their stories; he started to acknowledge that he was always learning about his ethnicity. "The best things about my life were my parents' stories, my grandparents' stories about growing up." The lessons he found in these stories helped him learn about "the beauties of my culture" and became his foundation. Years later, as a spoken word artist, storytelling became his form of expression. Now, at the YTF, he insists that the teenagers tell their stories.

"Everyone has stories," he says, and in many cultures lessons are passed down through oral tradition. Stories are "probably the most important thing" elders can pass on to us. For example, Victor learned how to work with young people by listening to his grandmother. She told him about a bridge back in the Philippines that she had to cross every day. As people walked across they would call out to each other, "watch out over here . . . there's a gap you can get your foot in." She related this practice to Victor's work: always show youth their options and warn them. "Point out where things are good or bad so that they don't have to step into it. But if they choose to do it, that's fine, that's up to them." Her advice continued, "Don't ever argue with your youth, they've been through enough. Who cares if you're right or wrong? Just don't argue with them because they've just been through it and they just need you there to listen." His grandmother's words guide his daily interactions. First and foremost, he listens to the youth in YTF and then tries to direct them "across the bridge" toward success. His emphasis on listening reminds me of Dereca and Rudy. But, for Victor, listening is related to storytelling.

According to Victor, his family's stories formed his education and spurred a lifelong journey to learn about his culture. However, it was his paternal grandfather who sparked his deep quest for spirituality. He "just had this presence and I always knew that he had this energy that I needed to have." When Victor's grandfather would walk down the street, animals would come toward him. Victor was mesmerized by his energy. "I just knew that he knew things."

Victor's grandfather was part of an esoteric society that studied alchemy, "changing something that wasn't so good into something more positive." Accordingly, he always tried to make things positive because he was a "really spiritual, mystical person." One day Victor found one of his grandfather's books. He vividly remembers the content: have knowledge of self and realize the God within. His grandfather emphasized, "You really can't know anyone unless you know yourself. There is a higher power and that higher power doesn't change but your understanding of it does."

As a young adult, Victor took his grandfather's wisdom to heart and made some critical decisions. He did not want to end up like his father, who was addicted to gambling and filed for bankruptcy twice. Nor did he want to end up like his mother, who served as a doormat for his abusive father. I ponder, for a moment, the stark contrast, and yet the eerie similarity, between Rudy and Victor. Rudy's father emphasized structure whereas Victor lived in the storm of abuse. So Victor consciously created his own rules and discipline for success: "Having so much bullshit happen to you and so much arguing [at home] . . . you find these beliefs that you guard with fierceness and you say you're never going to do that." He avows: "I've never gotten drunk. I never smoked weed . . . I never gambled because those were the things I thought would make me a lesser man." Like Rudy, he believes that "all the hardships and trials and tribulations that I've been through have definitely stretched my heart enough to feel a huger capacity . . . I just want to jump over the local personal drama and work on harder, deeper issues for the bigger community."

Victor's desire to build community relates to his decision to work with troubled young people. But this decision did not come overnight. Victor graduated from the University of Pittsburgh with a degree in Cultural Anthropology and Religious Studies. At this time, he was on a personal quest and, after seeing the movie *Slam*, decided to become a spoken word artist. Before Victor made his poetic debut, he was afraid of public speaking. But this endeavor helped him discover his voice. Victor's gift "with the word," coupled with his storytelling skills, launched him into the spoken word community in critical ways. He quickly became popular. "I just slammed. I was Pittsburgh slam champion . . . I got on NPR [National Public Radio]." He shakes his head, "I got a lot of awards." But Victor did not wallow in this success. On the contrary, "I realized at that moment that performance for competition was not where it was at; I need performance for the people."

At 24, Victor had just toured with the Pittsburgh National Poetry Team. His life revolved around spoken word. Concurrently, he was working for AmeriCorps at an environmental non-profit organization that told him to educate "urban youth about the environment." In this position, he did his best to offer training to "low-income youth, people of color" in "leadership development, civic engagement, and community service." But it "wasn't successful at all." Victor was frustrated with his position and wanted to move out west. He saw an advertisement on Craigslist for a program director in San Francisco. The ad sought a person who had a master's degree in social work or therapy, or extensive experience working with incarcerated youth. Victor had none of those credentials or expertise. What he did have was "imagination" and "creativity." And he had his mind set on this particular position. Though he did not have the job, he packed up and moved to the Bay Area. Fortunately, he got an interview.

The interview panel consisted of social workers and lawyers. During the interview "I just kept giving my spiel: I'm here to follow my heart, I can make this happen, just give me one chance and I'll prove to you that it's going to work. Leadership isn't about position, it's about action. I'm here to do it!" Victor's enthusiasm and confidence won them over ("they loved it"). When the interview was over, he took BART back to the East Bay. As soon as he got off the train, his phone rang and they offered him the position. "Can you come and start work on Monday?" That was in March 2002.

The following Monday, the Youth Task Force had its very first meeting and it was "horrendous." Ten young people showed up: "they were all little hoodlums" and "some of them were smelling like weed." Moreover, they virtually ignored the adults and focused on facing each other. Since they were from different areas of the city, "they were just mashing and clashing" because of turf drama. Even though Victor was "very animated" and had a "positive can-do attitude," he was not prepared and felt disconnected from them because "I'm not from the community." Victor knew the meeting was out of control but he did not know what to do. A lawyer and a social worker sat in on the meeting but, according to Victor, "they were scared" and never came to another YTF gathering. I cannot help but think about Rudy and what he would have done in this situation given his tough street-savvy approach. At first all Victor saw were "little hoodlums," whereas Rudy sees himself.

Victor continues and tells me that in the following weeks it was still "bad, bad, bad." But he remained "unbreakable" and kept meeting anger and hostility with "positivity." Despite the vast differences he felt between the teens and himself, he was determined to create connections. His first step was to engage them with the "powerful stories that I know to tell" from his own life, alongside "warm-up activities [and] ice breakers" he had learned through AmeriCorps. As the students became more comfortable, they began to open up.

Victor explains his approach with youth: "Anyone that loves their life has a moment where things just click. You see that in our youth, too. They can be the worst people that we deal with until one day they're like *I'm just sick of this, I'm going to really invest and I'm going to start doing this.* They have to come to that on their own, but how do you help push them a little bit faster and how to you help guide em to make those decisions?" I concur that those are critical questions. I ask, "How do you feel like you do that?" Victor understands that there is not one particular way to reach young people because they are so different. Accordingly, he uses a variety of tactics—but they are all rooted in the same philosophy. He *always* tells them "how important they are." He "always reminds them in subtle ways that this is a job and that they're here to make positive progressive change in the systems." Optimism is key. Like Dereca and Rudy, Victor wants each of his students to know that he believes in them and their abilities to create change.

Change Is Possible

Victor tries to have a consistent, encouraging message, though he has moments when he has to "get in someone's face" and be tough. He told one young man, "You're a statistic . . . you are going to fuck up and like everything says that you're not going to make it so how do you prove that this isn't going to be you?" Victor has learned that sometimes he has to be harsh in order to get through to his students. Although this style seems natural for Dereca and Rudy, it does not come easy to Victor. However, he realizes that this confrontational approach is sometimes necessary because youth in crisis have a lot to overcome.

At one point Victor kicked a student out of the program because of severe bad behavior and theft. This was a very hard decision because "I love the kid." So he told him, "I can't keep you in the program but I can keep you in my life. I'll go one-on-one with you on our own time. I'm going to meet with you once a week and we're going to talk to each other a lot more than we ever talked before." Once the young man committed to this first step, then "I had to hold him accountable." In this teenager's entire life, the only consistent relationship he had with an adult was with his parole officer because it was court mandated. Working with him, Victor sighs, continues to be "a long process" but "he's starting to make conscious changes."

Victor tries to get "my youth" (as he likes to say) to believe they can succeed. "Oftentimes they don't know that it's okay to be more successful than their parents or that they don't have to live a life that they're living because they don't know anyone that's living a better life." At times students will defend inadequacy because that is all they know. Unfortunately, "nothing tells them that it's okay to [be] successful, they could be rich, they can make it, they can fight and make it happen." These youth "don't hear those stories as much as they should. They don't know that exists. They don't know that's real." Recognizing these drastic limitations, Victor remains a pragmatic optimist.

If nothing else, Victor wants to insure that these young people recognize alternatives. One student reinforces this idea. Victor taught her that "even though you been through this or that, you could still accomplish things, you could still go places . . . I think if not for knowing Victor and his group I wouldn't have thought there was any other way."

Like Rudy, Victor focuses on providing young people with new opportunities, not just berating them for their bad choices. He does this by providing them with responsibilities that encourage their leadership potential. Victor had a profound realization about youth leadership. When his teenagers were speaking in front of therapists and social workers, they were "professional" and gifted "motivational speakers." Moreover, after they spoke, Victor noticed a drastic change in behavior. As they told their stories, they gained a sense of identity, belonging, and felt empowerment, some for the first time. "It was very powerful for the providers and for them." Another student echoes these sentiments and tells me about the first time she spoke at a conference. "We really had people sittin there cryin and just clappin. It seemed they would not stop clappin. We were sittin down, they were still clappin!" As she reflects on this moment, she beams with accomplishment right before my eyes.

Another of Victor's students, Cloteal, made a drastic shift in her lifestyle. When she began the YTF, she had dropped out of high school. During the YTF meetings, she would lecture younger students about the importance of school. She vividly remembers what Victor told her: "How you gonna tell these kids that they need to go to school and school is important, if you not getting your high school diploma?" This motivated her to return to school. Since her outlook on life had changed and she had a newfound commitment to education, she "knocked it out quick." The same was true for Scid at Leadership Excellence. Cloteal credits Victor and the YTF for her transformation. "I rarely went to school before I started goin to the YTF . . . I went from rarely goin to school, or goin to school and not doin the work, to graduating with a 3.95." Her accomplishment exemplifies the necessary link between reaching *and* teaching. Once she was reached, her academic abilities took over and she excelled.

Cloteal's success story is inspirational. Unfortunately, it is not the norm. Some students in the program are trying to get their GED, some are stuck (literally) in special education, and others refuse to even go to school. However, they may have other indicators of accomplishment, such as not picking up a pistol when they get angry or being able to face their mother for the first time in 10 years.

When Victor began this work, he set clear goals for each of his students. He wanted them to go to high school, graduate from college, and make a positive impact on the world. His objectives changed when he learned about the complexities of their lives. He no longer tries to superimpose his version of success onto them. "My only goal for them is that whatever time they're with me, if it's one minute, it's one hour, it's one week to ten years, I want to know that in that moment their time with me or in my program was worthwhile." For Victor, success is when young people are "a little bit more at peace within themselves" and can "look themselves in the mirror and say *I love you*." Victor does not believe he has lowered his expectations; rather, he has become clearer about the process. Victor asserts, "If they first find the love in themselves . . . then everything else will fall into place." Similar to Dereca, Victor wants his students to be triumphant, but recognizes that he is not "in control" of their lives or "the choices they make." He cannot foresee their future but he can shape his interactions with them.

Victor wants all of his interactions with people to be meaningful. He is on a quest, both personally and professionally, to build a conscious community. "How do I find connections with people and how do I make them deeper than just like hey, what's up? . . . How do I find out their story, their lives, and really build a deep community with people." I grin and agree.

Moved by his commitment, I ask him how this philosophy relates to the Youth Task Force. He says he tries to get his students to the point where they are open and willing to share with the group. He facilitates this process: he asks the right questions, gets the food, provides the stereo, insures they get paid, and organizes the activities. But the real magic comes from the students. Storytelling is integral to this development; when they hear each other's accounts, they recognize similarities and become each other's allies. "They're the most empathetic and they're the best listeners, because they listen to each other's stories with so much passion because they find themselves in those stories." As students listen to the wisdom of each other, change occurs. "Some really deep truths surface through our poetry workshops and activities," Victor states. Students find their inner voice, speak from their conscience, and become guides to one another. This is peer-to-peer transformation, where Victor is only the "coach" and "guide." Inevitably, he cannot create community for the YTF because the youth must create it for themselves.

Learn to Grow

It is a breezy day in August and I am in another YTF meeting. After a short warm-up activity, Victor hands us a sheet of paper with questions and asks us to answer each one. The paper reads:

> Why are you here on this earth?
> Is there life on other planets?
> Do you believe in a God?
> What happens after you die?
> Why do we exist?
> Have you seen ghosts?
> What is the meaning of life?
> Is there life after death?

As we sit reading the questions to ourselves, Victor bellows, "This [takes] some serious thought." The room gets even quieter, but it is not silent because of the low murmur of rap music coming from the boom box. I am taken aback by the irony of the lyrics. The rapper Too Short speaks, "What's my favorite word? Bitch! Why they gotta say it like Short? Bitch! You know they can't play on my court. Can't hang with the big dogs." Why is Victor allowing music like this to play while we write? He does not seem to notice that the radio is still on. He repeats, "Put some serious thought into this . . . If you don't know just think, think, think, think. Squeeze your brain as much as possible."

We are writing furiously. Minutes pass. Victor says, "Y'all ready for the bonus question?" A few youth nod so Victor proceeds, "What is love?" A female speaks up: "That's [a] hard question." Then everyone starts speaking at once. "Write it down!" Victor declares in a loud, deep authoritative voice. We refocus our attention and are still writing when Victor tells us we only have one more minute.

"Let's go around. Let's just open it up. Let's just talk. Why do you guys believe you're here on this earth?" The responses trickle out. "God's angels," "Cause of a higher being," "For a reason," "To enjoy life," and "Cause of my mom n dad." Victor proceeds, "Who's ever thought about that on their own time?" Every person at the table admits it is something they have wondered about at some point. Victor goes over the rest of the questions. The answers turn into conversations about the purpose of life and the students share personal beliefs about ghosts and God.

"Okay," smiles Victor, "Before we go into our last bonus question, which you all know about, I'm thinking of a number from 1 to 7 . . . everyone close your eyes." One of the students opens her eyes and asks if the number is 7. Victor responds, "It was 7." A few students gasp and everyone starts laughing. This feels a bit hokey to me, but I must admit, it really works for Victor. He has created a beautiful, sincere moment. It makes me happy to hear the students laugh and see their excitement to talk. For the first time I write in my notebook: *they look like children—joyful, innocent children.* I am impressed and moved by the way Victor was able to change the energy in the room, to change sorrowful faces and mean mugs into bright, heart-full smiles.

Victor asks the group, "Why do you think I put *these* questions for you to answer or attempt to answer?" Salim quickly replies, "To open up our minds." Victor challenges the students to always question what they are taught and what they perceive as real. Though the questions he posed were relatively esoteric, he encourages us to think on a very "practical level. Think about all the influences that tell you about what it's like if you're in the system or what it's like if you're Black or what it's like if you're Latino." He looks around the table, "What kind of pressures force you to come up with these ideas?" The room erupts with conversation. Victor directs students to "Clap three times if you hear me." He takes a few comments from the group and then continues, "I want you guys to really think about all the influences that are happening. If it's rap videos to like Mac Dre to like what you see on the streets to like all these influences that [the] media has telling you what young people are . . . what the system is . . . You feel me so far?" I do not know if Victor intentionally left the music on, but the backdrop of rap lyrics during this activity now seems extremely apropos.

A young woman takes the conversation to another level. Sharply critical, she questions the power of the governor who, with the stroke of a pen, can shut down schools. She juxtaposes his position of authority to that of her oppressed community. Even though they fight tirelessly, they cannot keep their schools open. Victor uses her statement to remind the students about an upcoming conference in Sacramento. Involving the Youth Task Force in critical dialogue *and* activism engages them on multiple levels.

Victor concludes the lesson: "You're here to learn to grow cause no one is gonna do this for you. No one is gonna grow for you. No one is gonna make you an adult. Y'all in the system. Y'all defined a certain way." He stands up. With conviction he tries to convince them to "rise" and "resist." He tells the students to write a piece for the upcoming conference. I see a few nods. "You guys feel me?" The teenagers smile and appear to get it. "All right," grins Victor, "clean up and take off."

The students pack up their stuff and leave. As is customary, Victor and I talk about the meeting. I ask why he chose to leave the music on and he says it is simply because it is part of their lives. I also ask why he chose to have us answer such introspective questions. "A lot of times we just focus on behavior but really, you can't change behavior if you don't change belief systems." I concur. For all of the community-based educators, it is critical that they help young people see themselves differently. Often, this requires a dramatic paradigm shift.

Victor and I walk out of the room, go down the elevator, and continue our conversation. I understand that Victor wants his students to look critically at the ways "the system" and "the media" try to define them. But how does Victor see them? I ask him this question. He stops walking, turns to face me, and explains that they are all "hurt in many different ways. Personally in their community and institutionally, they're all hurt." Over the years the majority of YTF participants have been people of color—Latinos, Pacific Islanders, and mostly African-Americans. Regardless of ethnicity, explains Victor, "they all come from poverty, they all were hurt in some way or another, they've all been shit on by these systems that they're in, and they're struggling, and they're scared." He recognizes that "most of em don't know long-term relationships with anything or anyone." Victor acknowledges the strife that these youth have experienced. When he looks at them, however, he also sees their strengths.

"I really feel like these young people are probably the wisest, bravest, most experienced youth that know the deep meanings of life . . . these young people are the most powerful beings ever." His voice is soft, yet piercing. He leans forward, looks deep into my eyes, holds my hand and says, "I learn so much from them. They're my teachers. They're my friends. They're the true alchemists." I remember how Victor spoke about his grandfather, the alchemist. Victor tries to carry on the tradition of the alchemist in his interactions with young people. I understand the depth of his work as incredibly spiritual and transforming, and not just for the young people. He too has been changed. "They really take things that I could never imagine ever going through, and they can still smile and they can still laugh." Victor is their guide, and they are his inspiration.

I walk Victor to his motorcycle. He gives me a hug goodbye and tells me to drive safely. This afternoon's meeting and subsequent conversation with Victor have energized me. I realize the YTF is successful on multiple levels: for the student, the teacher, the group, and the larger community. Victor does not have his students write their narratives, share their lives, and develop their opinions in isolation. One tactical reason he encourages students to write, reflect, and speak is so they will gain the courage and confidence to act. He contends that their criticisms can create change, and that their stories can change the world. That is why they go to Sacramento, speak at board meetings, organize in-service activities for social workers, and make a CD for national distribution.

In 2003 the YTF members embarked on an intensive task, compiling their poems, raps, and letters into a pulsating CD entitled *I Am That Youth*. On the back cover, I read: "The members of the Youth Task Force use their voices and experiences to reach out into the community. In doing so, they are able to create partnerships between agencies, act as liaisons between providers and other youth in need, and most importantly, empower themselves." The album received the nationally recognized ECCO Award.

On the way home, I listen to Rose's story on that CD. Rose has been a YTF member for a few years and is now 15 years old. In her poem she describes a haunting memory. And, she says, once she voiced her pain, she felt release and, for the first time in many years, could breathe and dream of a future with herself in it. On this track, she and Victor go back and forth in poetic conversation. The following is an excerpt.

Victor: If young people's voices are not heard and no one listens
      Their stories do not exist.

Rose: It was the social worker's decision
      Suggestion
      To move all of my eight brothers and sisters
      All in foster care
      To the Philippines
      It was the social worker's decision

      There was one young child
      Age 10
      Raped by first cousin
      Late night
      Asleep

Nearly died in the morning when she awoke
Deadly fever
Deadly threats from family members to be silent
Rape
Repeated
Day after day
Until finally her siblings were to suspect what was going on
Like little mice peeping from a hole

Victor: There are secrets that only the wind knows
There are stories that must be known
There are stories that must be heard
Why is the wind the only one that listens?

Rose: Pregnancy at the age of 10 going on 11 in the year of 1997
2 months late
brought an abortion
messed up her system
not able to have any children

Victor: A child age 10 going on 11
The year 1997

Rose: It was the decision of the social worker
Who messed up a child's past and future

Victor: Is it the person or the system?
Who is to blame?
Child welfare
Child providers
We are dealing with lives
This is not a game

[Victor continues in a commanding tone.]

I do not want to hear about the one success story of a foster youth who survived the system. The one foster youth who emancipated out and transitioned into adulthood with ease. Who found a job, a home, a career, furthered her education. I want all foster youth to be success stories. I want to hear all foster youth say *I love this system. It helped me succeed in life.* Foster youth need to succeed. They don't have family to fall back on. Once they are out of the system, they have nowhere to go. I cannot have my young people be in a system that is set up for failure. If one young person did not make it out, then the whole system needs to be changed. Would you send your children on a plane where there is a 50% chance of survival? You are not dealing with your caseload. You are dealing with people and their future.

Rose: My success is my survival.
          My survival is my success.

I play this track over and over again as I drive home across the Bay Bridge. Rose's experiences pierce through aloof policies or irrelevant political agendas. For her, the call to improve the system is deeply personal and powerfully poetic. Victor provides input between her words, urging providers to honor the humanity of foster youth. He declares that their stories must be acknowledged. I continue to want to know: *How does Victor get young people, such as Rose, to open up? How does he get them to the point where they want to share their wisdom and woes on a CD for national distribution?* This is the focus of our next conversation.

Listen

It is a warm day in June 2005 and I have been collecting data on the YTF for nearly 2 years. I am on my way to meet Victor in his new office in Bayview Hunters Point. Sitting in bumper-to-bumper traffic between the East Bay and San Francisco, I reflect on how much has changed since our last interview.

The YTF is no longer associated with Legal Services for Children; now it is part of the San Francisco Department of Public Health Community Behavioral Health Services. This promotion occurred when Sai-Ling Chan-Sew became director of the department. Instead of simply funding the group, she wanted the Department of Public Health to take notice of this effective program and replicate it. Now, youth voice is an integral component of all youth-based services in San Francisco.

Victor agreed to this transition. He believed that this move would enable youth to make a greater impact on the systems—juvenile justice, special education, mental health, and foster care—by acting as a partner within these government services. Victor made this change as smooth as possible for the young people, for example by keeping meeting times the same. Being aligned with the Department of Public Health has been extremely worthwhile for the YTF, both locally and nationally.

This shift in Victor's job, however, made his responsibilities more significant than he ever envisioned. The YTF became federally funded by Substance Abuse and Mental Health Services Administration (SAMHSA) and, when reviewed, was recognized as a model program for young people. This recognition is powerful, with ramifications for any program under SAMHSA. As a result of this exemplary evaluation, every SAMHSA grant recipient must now have a youth coordinator. Victor is extremely proud of this accomplishment: "Now there's a youth coordinator in Guam, Hawaii, Minnesota." This system-wide change is part of a larger movement to involve teenagers as decision-makers "in the process of their own change" and development.

Victor also wanted to allow this changeover to be an opportunity for improvement. During this time, he reflected on the YTF and wrote me the following email. "My new focus will be recruiting new youth who are in intensive care management, . . . educate myself on more social issues, build a sturdier curriculum, more concrete guidelines for the youth, find ways for the leadership to move more into their hands, maybe even have them rename the group, basically building the foundation all over again." He also planned to review the training manuals that SOUL (School of Unity and Liberation) designs and uses in workshops, to support the growing youth sector of the social justice movement.

Even though Victor received a promotion, he did not allow himself to become complacent. In fact, he became even more motivated to strengthen the YTF. To do so, he constantly asks himself: What more could I be doing? How can I make it even better? In this vein, he is always open to learning new curriculum and seeks out new approaches. Victor, the youngest community-based educator in my study, has been running the YTF for only 3 years. His email reveals his reflective praxis and ambitious nature, as well as some programmatic insecurities.

Victor's new office is near the Bayview Plaza and across from City College. When I enter the building, a serious, middle-aged Asian woman asks me whom I am here to see. She rings Victor to tell him he has a visitor. I am struck by the formality. At Legal Services, the setting was extremely casual. This office space is much larger and more organized, and houses all the children and youth services within the San Francisco Department of Public Health.

Told that Victor is ready for me, I walk along a line of gray cubicles, turn a corner, and see Victor's corner station. As usual, he practically leaps out of his chair to give me a hug. He is wearing a long red-and-orange Indian shirt, jeans, and flip-flops. His clean-shaven head and ebony eyes glisten under the fluorescent lights. I am wearing boots, and feel enormous standing next to him. I realize he is probably 5′ 5″ tall. While he finishes up emails on the computer, I glance around his office space.

The walls are decorated with artwork and various newspaper articles on the YTF. A bright oil painting of a woman's coming of age ceremony focuses my attention. Victor tells me one of his students painted it for him as a gift. Interspersed with these pieces are numerous awards honoring Victor and the group. While these are the images on his wall, everything at his desk seems more personal. For instance, Victor keeps a photograph of the Dalai Lama close to him because it represents a "higher expression of compassion." There is a postcard of the American flag but in the place of the stars is a brown, clenched fist. Instead of the red and white stripes, there are different colored bandanas. The caption reads, "To the cops we all look the same . . . Why fight each other? Fight for Justice."

While Victor checks on something down the hall, I examine the knick-knacks and quotations surrounding his workspace. On top of Victor's computer sits the "hear no evil, see no evil, speak no evil" statue of three little monkeys—one holding his ears, one his eyes, and the third his mouth. I also notice a poem by Nikki Giovanni that reminds me of Victor. It reads: "And if I ever touched a life I hope that life knows that I know that touching was and still is and will always be the true revolution." The poem illuminates Victor's approach: create authentic, real, and deep connections with others, especially troubled young people. Dereca is a revolutionary (introspective and interpersonal) in much the same way.

Victor returns to the cubicle and I ask him if there is an enclosed office we can go to. We walk down the hall and enter the childcare room. Sitting at a short table designed for toddlers, I take out the tape recorder. When everything is set up, Victor smiles and says with a wink, "Let's communicate."

Over the last couple of years, I have attended dozens of YTF meetings. I know the setup: music, food, check-in, activity, check-out. During this interview, I aim to get a clearer sense of *why* Victor does these things, that is, the strategies behind his actions. "Music is a medicine for young people," he tells me, "and so is food." He uses these comforts to make "them feel safe." Victor always starts with a check-in because "their world is in constant flux and constant change." Based on what they say, "I know that I need to adapt to that and understand where young people are right now at the moment." Even when a student has behaved badly, Victor tries to "keep my mind open and not take things personally."

After every meeting Victor takes time for reflection. He considers "why are they coming in late, why are they coming in early, why do they keep acting up?" The answers give him the ability to respond with empathy. Their behavior, good and bad, provides him with a starting point to "explore their feelings more and try to find ways so that they can open up and talk."

However, this was not always the case. When Victor first started this work he would get "jumpy" when a student walked in late before he realized "that's what they want." Youth might come in late just to see his reaction because "they know how to test adults, they know how to test providers. Sometimes the only healthy thing they know is to argue and create drama and create conflict because it's giving them attention." Once he recognized this pattern, Victor was able to shift *his* behavior. He now tries to have extensive one-on-one time with each student because many of them need that level of attention.

During these moments, Victor gauges where and to what extent they need him. He then tries to be realistic about what he can and cannot do for them.

Developing honest dialogue is paramount for Dereca and Victor. And for Victor it can be a real challenge. In rare cases, a young person opens up during their first meeting, but for others it might take months, or even years. Victor is always patient because he understands that "everything's a process." Since he directs his own program, he has great flexibility. This is drastically different from teachers, who must meet stringent standards such as those surrounding No Child Left Behind. In the YTF, Victor does not have to accommodate any imposed expectations. Consequently, he develops the program based on the individual needs of each person in the group.

"Once I realize that a certain young person will need something, I'll try to find ways for them to get it," even to the extent of taking money out of his own pocket. When one student was having trouble with therapy but showed an interest in rock climbing, he got her a membership to a climbing club. Another was interested in art, so Victor talked to people in various systems and got him free art supplies. He has even gotten them bank accounts. Victor thinks "outside the box" and realizes "those little things make a difference." He is keenly aware of the reciprocity: "Whenever they invest in opening up to me and I can understand what they need, then I could go and try to be there for them and support them in a different way."

Meanwhile, Victor recognizes that there are degrees and limitations in his ability to help. "There's layers of historical oppression and guilt and feeling like they're bad or not believing in themselves that need to be addressed." Dereca addresses this predicament with intense history lessons. Although Victor's approach is different, the underlying philosophies are the same.

Victor explains that, for young people to be "advocates or youth leaders or like create change in the system, they need to first believe in themselves." In order to inspire confidence, he must convince them that their "life isn't destined for failure" even if they were "born in jail because their mom was on drugs and their dad left them." During moments of reflection, many of Victor's students confess that they do not believe they are capable of traditional forms of achievement. At the last meeting two young people stated matter-of-factly, "I don't believe in myself. I don't believe I'm going to make it." Recalling this exchange, Victor points out that it is important for them to be able to admit their fears. It can be "very painful," but "once you realize their world and their truth and their reality, then I can work from it."

For example, Victor encourages self-reliance by having the teenagers write letters to themselves. In these letters, he asks them to describe their current situation. "I try not to get them into thinking about the future but anywhere from the past up to the present. To see where are you in your life right now and then they seal it, and in about six months, I'll give it back to them and they see where they've gone." This journal activity helps students reflect on their lives, giving them the opportunity to "manifest something different." Victor partakes in all of these introspective activities; sharing himself is a way to build trust. He never asks the young people to do something he is unwilling to do himself, which I witnessed during the Khalil Gibran poetry exercise and at every subsequent meeting. In everything, he participates instead of dictates.

Victor employs many other tactics. Since he has a genuine friendship with the students, they stay in contact long after the Youth Task Force. "I've kept in contact with every young person that's ever been in my program. If they went out to college . . . got their high school degrees, even if they're in county jail, they still call me and we still work on different levels." I inquire, "Why do you think they see you as such an important person in their lives?" "Because I listen," he responds. From Victor's perspective, listening *is* effectiveness.

Listening to young people is imperative and is a repetitive theme. Victor gets frustrated with most adults who work with teenagers because they fail to hear their students' ideas. He argues passionately, "We always want to tell our young people what we want them to do. We always want to tell our young people what's best for them. We always want to tell young people that we know the answers . . . But we really don't understand what's going on in a young person's life." He declares: "We're not listening to them!"

Every educator in my study proclaims the importance of listening, or, as Rudy put it, "ear hustlin." This seems as if it should be obvious. Without listening to and learning from students, teachers are less likely to build the bridge of understanding. Without this basic tool of communication, little reaching or teaching is possible. Victor emphasizes this. "How do we listen to them and listen to them and listen to them and feel what they're saying, feel what their reality is, feel what their truth is?" He says, "The real process is how do we just listen to them." Once a young person trusts to open up, then "sometimes you can throw in something that will make them shift their perspective a little bit more." As educators, "you just got to keep shedding as much light as you can. And it's not by talk, it's by example."

In his example, Victor leads by "going through the dirt" with them and "being there for them" in a real, sometimes hard way. When one of his students had a meeting with all of her service providers, she asked Victor to attend. When Victor arrived, the other adults (schoolteachers, a social worker, and therapist) were badgering the student, telling her what to do. Victor intervened, and "it felt like me and [the student] against the world." This incident showed the young person that she is not alone and, according to Victor, that is exactly what she needed. The other adults in the room were unable to grasp this because, at the bare minimum, they never even listened attentively to what she had to say. So their efforts were futile.

I can understand the significance of this defining moment for this particular teenager and believe Victor has her lifelong development in mind, but what about the other adults in the room? They were sidelined from the process because it basically became Victor and the student against them. Instead of creating an us–them dichotomy, how can Victor communicate his effective model to other adults? During the in-service training for providers, for instance, how is Victor able to teach practitioners?

Again, Victor stresses the critical theme of listening. To do this, he amplifies the voices of young people. At the annual YTF conference, students take center stage. On average, 300 practitioners attend and experience this daylong event. At one point, the youth sit on a panel talking about their experiences in juvenile justice, foster care, special education, and mental health. Adults listen attentively to their stories of maltreatment and pain. The teenagers explain that they often feel more like a case number than a person. I am close to tears by the end of their presentation. Their stories are heart-wrenching and, as I look around the room, many people are drying their eyes. Victor says this event is vital: "It just opened up the providers' minds and their hearts enough to just realize maybe they're going at it the wrong way, maybe they need to listen." As adults hear young people's stories, Victor hopes it "will bring them back to why they even started working in this field" and remind them "why we love" and "why we care" about these students. I smile and nod. This is as much about emotion as it is about cognition, as much about art as it is about science.

I'll Help You

It is an overcast January afternoon when I next head over to San Francisco to attend a YTF meeting. I take the elevator to the fourth floor of the Department of Public Health building at 1380 Howard Street and make my way to the large conference room. When I enter, students are sitting around the table having a heated discussion about ankle monitors. Victor brings in a platter full of burritos and requests that the music be turned down. After our normal check-in, Victor takes out a board game. We all look skeptical. What are we about to do?

"It's called Abundant River," Victor says excitedly. He explains that the game was invented in the Bay Area by a group of "very spiritual people" who use positive affirmations to become successful. The purpose of the game is to delve into the deeper purpose of our daily acts. Victor hands out playing pieces to each of us.

"My name is not *Christ*," a male student roars with exaggeration. Victor completely ignores his outburst and tells him to put his piece at the starting point. He instructs us calmly: each of us will get a turn to roll the dice. If we land on yellow we take a yellow card; on orange, an orange card; on blue a Sage card. And if we land on white we have to laugh as a group for 1 minute. Frances, one of the students, rolls her neck and says sarcastically, "Laugh for one minute!?!"

The first person lands on a Sage square and picks up the card. A look of confusion crosses his face. Victor jumps in, "You want me to read it for you?" The teenager responds, "Do you want to read it?" Victor takes the card and reads, "What a person thinks, he becomes . . . Consider that everything happening around you is a reflection of what is going on inside of us. Share with the other players an action you could take that would create an experience of peace." With a calm self-assuredness, the young man responds matter-of-factly: "Being happy."

Another student, Shariff, rolls next and again Victor steps in, "Try to read it out loud and I'll help you." The young man starts to read, but has a stutter so the words come out slowly. "We should take care not to make the . . ." He pauses on the word "intellect" and Victor glances over his shoulder to read the card.

This pattern continues as young people pick up cards and Victor jumps in to rescue his students from having to read. As a teacher, this is extremely hard for me to watch. How will they ever learn to read if someone is always reading for them? I try to see the situation from Victor's perspective: maybe he wants the game to go quickly or perhaps he is worried about his student's insecurities. I try to rationalize his behavior. But I do not know why he is reading for them. Since I do not want my frustrations to brew, I take a deep breath, lean back in the chair, and try to enjoy the game. I decide I will bring this up in a subsequent conversation with Victor.

The cards offer inspirational words of advice or suggest activities. Cloteal picks up a "river guide" that tells her to turn right and look into her neighbor's eyes for 3 minutes. She stares at a younger YTF member. Surprisingly, they take the directive quite seriously. I go next, and land on a white square, so we all have to laugh for 1 minute.

We play the game for the next 30 minutes. In the middle of someone's turn, an older student feels moved to speak: "I'm not really into Church and not so much as to the religion but just spirituality itself. I've had a lot of bad things happen in my life, and I always try to focus on the positive things that I want to have or the way that I would see myself becoming. I've been taking a lot of time and say when I get real, real frustrated or real mad . . . breathe. Think about what made you mad, don't swing first, think first, breathe again." This statement brings the game to a close because students begin discussing their interpretation of the game and what they got out of it. The River Guides activity is thematic of Victor's approach since it pushed us to talk about ourselves and created a genuine bond among group members.

Later I ask Victor why he had read for the youth. He explains, quite simply, that he knows his students, whereas I do not. He feels attuned to what is going on with them, knowing when to push or pull back. I am not impressed by his answer. I am convinced that his "reading for them" strategy shows low expectations.

One month later, during a YTF meeting, Shariff stands up in front of the group and reads to us an intimate, personal letter he wrote to his father who had abused and abandoned him. Though he still stutters, his voice is strong and fills the room. I am amazed. I can hardly believe his drastic change in behavior. I can hardly believe he is sharing so much of himself with us. I can hardly believe how well he is *reading*. Though Victor's tactics are different from mine, he seemed to move Shariff to a remarkable place both personally and academically.

Shariff tells me that the YTF "changed me a lot . . . I used to stutter a lot. Hopefully I'm not stuttering on this tape right now. I just kinda used to feel bad about it and Victor told me to go talk in front of the mirror" and just practice. He says confidently, "I started getting better and better." His speaking ability got so strong that Victor told him to write a letter to an important person in his life and, when he was ready, share it with the group. As mentioned, Shariff chose his father.

Victor recognizes that the Youth Task Force is relatively small, but acknowledges the significant impact it has on young people. Agreeing, every student told me, both in person and on my survey, that without the YTF they would probably be "at a corner smokin" or "hoin and/or hustlin, pregnant" or "in jail without a high school diploma." Victor attests that these teenagers have learned that they *can* make a difference and *are* making a difference. Bonnie exemplifies this positive impact.

Bonnie is white and 19 and has been participating in the YTF for almost 4 years. She is 9 months pregnant and, at the start of our interview, asks me questions about giving birth. She chuckles as I tell her the stories of my children's delivery. Her dirty-blonde hair is pulled back into a ponytail. She has pale skin and rosy cheeks, and looks a bit warn and tired. At the same time, she has that beautiful, motherly glow. When I begin asking her questions—even simple ones such as her name—her eyes scan the room and she does not make eye contact with me. She seems a bit nervous with the interview process, a bit scared about being a new mother with no support, and smiles, almost nervously, when she tells me about her pain.

Bonnie grew up in the foster care system and has lived in Hunters Point most of her life; she currently lives next to the infamous Double Rock housing project. The only family member she has contact with is her little brother, who has been AWOL, a runaway, since he was 13. Sadly, he is now a drug addict. At one point she was able to get him involved in the YTF, but he dropped out. Bonnie considered leaving the group when her brother did, but she decided to stay involved so that she could be an advocate for other young people.

Bonnie has a lot to say about the system, and is especially critical of special education. "The whole time I was in high school I was in special education" because of "bad behavior." Bonnie has immense disdain for this type of tracking because "it really slowed down my learning." She explains that she would be given worksheets with cartoon characters and could not believe it: "this is really insultin my intelligence!" By eleventh grade, Bonnie dropped out of school. She is clear that "I didn't drop out because I didn't like school . . . I dropped out because it wasn't challenging!"

I am enraged by Bonnie's experiences in school. What were her teachers thinking? Why didn't they help her? Although these thoughts surface for me, I do not voice them. Instead, I heed Victor's advice and just listen. She continues, talking about the inadequacies of most of her teachers. The exception was one teacher who tried to get her into an advanced placement (AP) history class because she loved the subject. However, despite this teacher's best efforts, she was never allowed to take interesting classes.

Bonnie felt her life was destined for failure and underachievement until she got involved in the YTF. I probe to get a clearer understanding of how this program changed her outlook and behavior. She elucidates: "I been in therapy for almost 12 years" and "it doesn't even compare to" what she has "learned in the past four years from bein in the Youth Task Force. Anybody can tell you ever since I got involved with the Youth Task Force I turned into a whole different person. I'm still me but I'm me in a more intelligent type. Just a more mature person." The YTF has influenced Bonnie in remarkable ways.

Victor gave Bonnie the opportunity to do something she had never done before: critique the system that raised her. She speaks with pride about reforming one part of foster care. As Bonnie tells it, when she was young and wanted to spend the night at a friend's house, the home had to be inspected by a social worker. This step in the process was usually too much for her friends' parents and so she rarely got to stay the night at anyone else's house. Bonnie and the other YTF students changed this policy; now foster care youth are no longer singled out and can, like their peers, go have a sleepover.

Bonnie is proud that she advocates for youth in the system. She affirms that her lifelong experiences have made her an expert. It is a revelation to her that, when she expresses her opinion, people listen, and change happens. Other young people I interviewed shared similar experiences.

Cloteal is another person who exemplifies the type of positive changes that can come from YTF activities. When I first met Cloteal about 3 years ago, she was a mature, but smart-mouthed, 19-year-old. I remember one instance when I touched her shoulder to greet her. She reacted, "Scuse you! Don't you touch me, I'm eatin!" She carries a strong, powerhouse attitude, but over the years I have learned that she has another side. For example, one day she let me tape record her reading a poem because "I got love for you, Vajra." Whether Cloteal is befriending someone or checking the group, she is a force to contend with.

When Cloteal first began attending the YTF she admits that she was "a jerk. I was stubborn. I was hardheaded. I was well beyond feisty." There are reasons for this. "I had a lot of rage . . . from all the different things that I've encountered in my life." Cloteal has faced immense tragedy in her relatively short existence. Of her six siblings, four have been murdered. She advises people who come into contact with her: "Don't be sympathetic for me, be empathetic for me . . . Don't be havin no pity party cause I'm not gonna join in wid you. I got too much to do on a day-to-day basis than to be sittin around tryin to feel sorry for myself." Cloteal has overcome tremendous calamity.

Victor recognizes this, but can also see her leadership potential. Noting her ability to check others, he challenged her to use her persuasive voice to be a spokesperson on behalf of the community. Cloteal was skeptical about this advice until one day she felt that her voice really did matter. A conversation about turf violence with District Supervisor Sophie Maxwell led to her being nominated, months later, for a youth achievement award. Cloteal called me the day of the event and told me I *had* to come. I can still remember her childlike excitement and I promised I would not miss it. When she received the award, she was beaming, and Victor and I were cheering. Even with the grief in her life, Cloteal has been able to triumph.

Cloteal does not sugarcoat anything, so I want her honest opinion about Victor's pedagogy. Does she consider Victor's approach to be effective? Without hesitation she says, "I do. I do." She elaborates: "Even if the young people don't stay in the program, they still get the opportunity to learn that people can show you love even without knowing you. And there are people that do care about your well-bein even if you don't care about it yourself." It is clear that she wants me to grasp (even though I have been observing the YTF for several years) that Victor has "really intense work," that he "is still young," and "he still learning a lot. His program still kinda four years fresh."

I concur, but she still seems wary that I do not fully comprehend Victor's fierce challenges. "It's not an easy job to have because he's dealin with what they call the high-risk youth," she emphasizes. The youth he interacts with might be "on probation and they done got into a fight or they done tore up their mama house or they done tore up a group home or a foster home or they was homeless in the beginnin and now you can't find em cause they movin from place to place. They don't know where they goin so therefore you don't know where they goin or they done got wrapped up and in the system so they locked up now. Or they somewhere pregnant or somewhere on drugs and I mean like smokin crack, not smokin no weed. Young kids. They bein pimped, they bein raped, they bein molested. They bein motivated to drop out of school instead of continuin."

Cloteal believes the reason Victor succeeds in these circumstances is that "he never gives up," has "compassion," and is "patient." Compared with other community-based educators she has had contact with, Victor is "more humble, not necessarily passive though, but more humble." She leans back, looks up at the ceiling and grins, "Victor got the heart!" As Cloteal speaks, I realize that Victor embodies a *pedagogy of compassion*.

The Same Results Every Time

In May 2006, I have my last interview with Victor. In this final conversation, I hope to clarify what he might recommend for teachers working with disenfranchised youth. When I reach his cubicle, he is waiting for me and, as usual, has a mesmerizing smile. I am excited to talk with him and feel a bit sad that I will no longer have the privilege of participating in dynamic YTF meetings, or have any "official" reason to carve out 2 hours just to sit and speak with Victor. Alas, this is the research process.

While getting organized for the interview, Victor and I talk casually about themes that emerged during our last conversation. Once we are settled, he is raring to go. I turn on the recorder and transition our conversation from the community to schools. Victor thinks of himself "as an educator, as a teacher" because "my work really consists of finding extreme amounts of creativity and imagination to engage a young person." Although he does not teach traditional courses (e.g., reading, writing, and math), he has a curriculum revolving around "knowledge of self." Victor hopes that teachers would have a similar goal of "self-empowerment" for their students.

However, Victor acknowledges that teachers do have very difficult jobs and are under great pressure to perform to stringent standards. Despite many restrictions in the current school environment, he urges teachers to attempt to spend one-on-one time with their students. As Victor puts it: "Get down at their level, kneel down at the seat and be like, hey, I wanna be here for you. I wanna listen. Tell me what you need to make this class work for you." This is Victor's caring style. "If the teacher could do that to everyone in the class, which is pretty impossible, then I think things would get better," he advises. When teachers do not know "the whole story of every youth," they fall back on their authority when problems arise ("You're bad, go the principal's office") to perpetuate a lose–lose situation. As a result of this dysfunctional process, the student and the teacher both fail, and the ideals of education are left behind.

Once a teacher understands a student's reality, Victor suggests that they need to make the curriculum engaging. Education must relate to students' lives so students "can identify with it" and teachers can "build on it." Anyone working with young people—especially those who are disenfranchised—must have "a lot of creativity" for any chance of success. As an example, Victor points to one of his students who is a "great rapper" and knows "every Mac Dre song," yet cannot concentrate in his special education class. Creativity and imagination are important tools, without which "you're going to get the same results every time." (Victor supports this with a quote from Albert Einstein: "The definition of insanity is doing the same thing over and over again and expecting different results.") He wants teachers to consider alternatives. Creative lesson plans that include students' interests (such as hip-hop) could benefit even classes such as math and reading.

Victor is always trying new tactics to break through barriers and reach students, pushing himself to think outside the box. "You got to see where a young person's at all the time. You can't be like, oh, I have the formula, this always works," he says. "If it works one way and doesn't work the same way next time, I'll try a different way." Victor does not let valuable strategies become stagnant, but is constantly reflecting on his methods. Stay away from "very mechanical ways to do it," he warns; every single encounter has significance and presents an opportunity to form an authentic bond. The first step is "to realize this person is a human being and some way you and this other person magically met and there's a reason for that." Even without the mystical perspective that Victor seems to exude, the reality of the relationship formed must be acknowledged. "Once you get the connection," he says, "then everything could open up. But if you don't get that connection with a young person, then it's not going to work."

In order to create an authentic connection, Victor continually refines his responsive style of teaching, looking for new points of entry. Victor insists, "I'm not going to be another person doing the same stupid shit." Effective tactics must be dynamic, not dictatorial. From his experience, he states forthrightly that he is "not going to tell [youth] what to do any more." Instead he implements what I underscore as his main strategy: "I'm going to support them and listen to them and be there for them, and then make them feel safe because they've never felt safe in their whole lives. I'm going to be there giving them food, making them laugh, having em tell their story, make them feel valued, making them feel like they're somebody and realize that all that experience could be turned into some kind of teachable expression or they could be the professors when they teach providers what the hell is really goin on." His is a very personal, humanistic approach, not unlike the role of a caring parent.

Does it work? Does he change people's lives? Victor is clear that his tactics allow young people to be leaders, teachers, and healers. He shares: "This one youth was on five or six different meds and manic," he demonstrates with a particular example. "He was drunk at six and smoked weed at eight and snorting coke most of his life." Victor gave him a chance to speak at a conference and the young man "spoke about everything to substance abuse providers, mental health providers. He just shined. He was really the expert. We call him professor. It was beautiful. It gave him a chance." The conference audience "heard his story . . . and people went up to him. When people clapped after he spoke, it was huge. He felt like he was worth a million bucks. All the stuff that he talked about was stuff that brought his self-esteem lower, made him feel small. But he used that to make it be his light. This is my assets. This is my grains of sand that turned into diamonds." The point is not just to have high expectations for youth; it is to give opportunity for individual expression and achievement. Without opportunity, there can be no accomplishment.

When I ask Victor how he would apply lessons from the YTF to mainstream classrooms, he responds, "I wish there was a formula," and returns to his theme of adapting and listening. "I wish there was a recipe where if you add these certain things, then it can make a provider very successful. I wish I knew. I think it's a calling; like this is what you were born to do. Your heart's there. I think honestly, it's being an active listener," he says. And "be compassionate. To imagine as if this young person is like your niece that just broke her ankle and you're like, *oh my God, what can I do for you?* Nothing else matters" at that moment—"that kind of attention." Teachers may already know, but he says anyway, "curriculums don't work sometimes when someone is crying." He urges, "Keep your ears open because everyone can be a teacher. Anything can be a teacher. Teachable moments have to happen."

Sadly, sometimes these teachable moments, these opportunities to connect, happen when a tragedy occurs in the environment associated with high-risk teenagers. "A lot of our youth, especially in Bayview Hunters Point, deal with post-traumatic stress," Victor says, echoing Rudy's exact sentiments. Victor continues, "A lot of their family members and friends are getting killed all the time. The last thing they want to do is Algebra or Geometry or U.S. History when they can't even think about anything else." This is a serious dilemma for urban educators. But teenagers under severe stress sometimes "don't even know why they're acting out." When a schoolteacher notices a young person is hurt, Victor wants them to respond thoughtfully and sensitively. To emphasize the importance of this, I recall my interview with Salim—sweet Salim—who nearly beat his teacher to death.

Salim is small, outspoken, and charismatic. One day Salim was sitting in class when his teacher told him it was his turn to read out of the textbook. Salim did not want to read and the exchange became confrontational because the teacher kept forcing the issue. Salim became enraged, ripped the phone off the wall, and beat his teacher unconscious. I am shocked to hear about this incident because, like Rudy, I am a teacher who tends to confront uncooperative students head-on. I suspect I could have been that teacher, and sympathize with the difficulty of getting to know students. I presume it all comes back to having already established an authentic connection. If the teacher had a clearer understanding of Salim, would he have pushed him to this extreme?

After this violent encounter, Salim's social worker recommended him to the YTF. When I inquire about Victor's understanding of this incident he tells me, "the teacher got mad at him and confronted him and he was like don't come any closer. And the teacher, being egotistical and not listening or being soft, came closer." Because of Victor's humble approach, Salim has had an "extreme" turnaround, recounts his caseworker. Victor "really changed his life."

In our interview, Salim talks about his personal transformation. "I was kinda really lost until I found the Youth Task Force. I just think I was getting in trouble, hitting teachers, just gettin suspended from school, cuttin school.

And then Victor kinda changed my way of thinking. The Youth Task Force kinda changed it. Now I'm doin kinda better." I ask Victor what he did. "It wasn't like don't go to the hall, don't do bad things. It was just like show him that he's loved, man, like show him that someone cares about him and that if he needs somebody, then somebody will be there for him . . . and all the rest will fall into place."

I still feel unsettled. Victor tends to protect the student to the detriment of the teacher. What about Salim's responsibility for his outrage? I hear little blame of Salim from Victor because, from my observations, he does not criticize or judge his students. Though this seems too soft for me, his positive turnarounds are persuasive.

Today, Salim is an active participant in the YTF and is excited by the idea of improving the system. Salim used to think that he "ain't goin to change nothin. I just thought, nobody goin to listen to us. But as [Victor] kept talking and people have done stuff in the past, I'm just like maybe I can change it too." This activism engages Salim. This is part of what Victor calls "the youth movement"; which he believes will be led by troubled teenagers. "The youth movement could really change the world on a huge scale," he proclaims. "I look at all the heroes that I look up to in my life and they all come from really terrible pasts, I can't believe they went through it. I'm working with all those youth now. They could be the Mahatma Ghandis, they could all be the Nelson Mandelas, they could all be the powerful political leaders or just the really good fathers that they never had."

Jerome Johnson, a case manager for over 16 years, confirms that students in the YTF experience transformation. "I can assure you that at least two of my kids have shown extremely, I use the word extremely—not to dramatize it, but to really emphatically say—that they have really changed their lives." Jerome wants me to understand "what clients we deal with" and explains, "we're talkin about kids who are suicidal, low self-esteem. A lot of em are caught up in the jail system. Lot a broken homes. So just a myriad of issues that the youth have to deal with." Given these dynamics, Jerome is highly impressed with Victor's effectiveness. "To have Victor come in here and at least change two of my teenage boys' lives around, I won't say it's a miracle, but darn near close to it. We go in there not knowin if we're goin to be successful or not and nine times out of ten we're not successful. This gives you an idea of how high-risk the youth are" and how powerful the YTF is.

Jerome believes Victor has succeeded because he "got them to talk about their lives, got them to recognize that they're not the only one with issues. To me what's successful is really gettin the youth to use their voice—that's huge when you look at youth that cuss and swear at you on the drop of a dime to come to the point where they're talkin to you on a mutual respect level." Jerome underscores Victor's ability to use spoken word poetry to build community.

Yet Victor's overall philosophy is not spoken word. Rather, his approach is to show each student "that he's loved." I prod Victor to clarify what he means and provide me with some specifics. But Victor is such an artist, such a poet, that he can only give me a compelling metaphor: "If you're a seed, what nourishment do you need? Each seed is different and individual so we need to know exactly what the young person needs."

A moment of silence comes between us. I look down at my interview questions and am ready to move us forward. But Victor wants me to see, feel, and fully grasp this notion of educating like a gardener. With a gleam in his eye he tells me: "I think every young person is a beautiful seed of divinity that needs the right nourishment. Unfortunately some of em are just buried deeper into the soil and they have a harder way to push out from but I know that with us or without us they'll make it. I have to believe that." Victor recognizes that the youth he works with have a remarkable array of assets; they are all "very creative" and have "imagination that's way more important than knowledge. If you just support them and nourish that seed in the right way, so much could happen."

Victor does the heart-wrenching work of the YTF gladly. One of his colleagues puts it this way: Victor "seems to just get jazzed up about helpin people." He feels privileged to work with high-risk youth, and I notice his enthusiasm at every meeting. Marlene Matarese, the Youth Involvement Resource Specialist at the national level with SAMHSA, says that, of all the youth workers with whom she comes into contact, Victor is extraordinary: "He exudes genuine love to all people which is something so many youth need. He is truly a gift to this world . . . He is a true leader who leads with compassion." Victor is grounded in the daily reality of the YTF teenagers. He does not try to "escape" from the harshness of their lives, but tries "to live that world and make the world artistic, make the world poetry, make the world art." Through storytelling and dialogue Victor shares himself with the YTF members and encourages them to use their own voices as a tool for empowerment. Each utterance can be a bullet to change the world—an expression in the discovery of self and purpose. I agree with Marlene, who characterizes Victor as a "gentle warrior."

After our final interview, Victor hands me his new CD of his own artistic endeavor, *When Thoughts Manifest*. His spoken word echoes through my car as I speed home across the Bay Bridge.

> My young people are trying to be heard, so nod your head
>   when cars pull up
> to thumping speakers and get lost in the revolution of spree
>   well rims
> and the roar of Chevy big block engines
> You see, even skid marks tell stories

. . . I just wanted to say that my life can't get better than this,
Than fighting for something you believe in
Giving to a cause bigger than yourself
And how stupid I was for believing that I could change the
     world
I only want to change their world.

★★★

Thus far, all the community-based educators have been people of color, and relatively young. Next, I examine Jack Jacqua, who is older and white. He is co-founder of the Omega Boys Club and teaches inside detention centers and prisons throughout the Bay Area. He is a provocative—Afrocentric—teacher. Jack is a powerful ally of the oppressed and his commitment to the streets is unparalleled. He is the focus of the last portrait.

5

JACK JACQUA

Pedagogy of Commitment

Jack Jacqua is famous on the streets of San Francisco, in detention centers, and in penitentiaries throughout the country. He is described as "the one and only" and "to the left of Malcolm X." Jack is unique, an anomaly, a personality rarely found elsewhere.

Now in his early seventies, Jack has been working with youth for over four decades. He is co-founder of the famous Omega Boys Club in San Francisco, whose mission is to "keep people alive and unharmed by violence and free from incarceration." Omega strives to "provide youth with opportunity and support to build positive lives for themselves." I read these words inside the Spring 2003 issue of Omega's *Street Soldiers Magazine*. The 28-page glossy color magazine exudes class and prestige, and seems so far removed from the man I met.

The Jack I know is a bit disheveled. In fact, his colleague, Dr. Joseph Marshall Jr., describes him as a "prematurely gray, hippie-haired, wild-bearded, three-day-jeans-wearing white man" (Marshall, 1996, p. 39).[1] Though Dr. Marshall, a charismatic African-American, is the Executive Director and face of Omega, the program would not exist without Jack's deep commitment and connections to the community.

The story of the club's origin is noteworthy. By 1987, Dr. Marshall had been teaching in public schools for nearly 20 years. He started his career eager to infuse his curriculum with relevance and consciousness. Though his ambitions were clear, he could not make a substantial impact. "The more deeply involved I became, the more clearly I could see that the school system was failing the young people of the city. The teachers simply couldn't do enough for them" (p. 36). His frustrations became painfully clear when a former student, an obvious crackhead, approached him on the street and told him he was the best teacher he ever had. Marshall could not accept this compliment and began to question his effectiveness as a traditional schoolteacher—"if I'm so damn good why is this boy strung out on dope?" (ibid.).

Marshall did not know what to do. Around this time, he began venting his frustrations to Jack, a colleague at Potrero Hill Middle School. While Marshall was teaching math, Jack was "part coach, part counselor, part aide, and primarily a free agent able to somehow circumvent his official role" (p. 39). Marshall was impressed with Jack because he had "created a niche in which he served more or less as the students' faculty advocate. He was like their family representative on campus, the father figure, or big brother or uncle—whatever the situation called for—who understood their special situations and took it upon himself to steer them through the daunting, sometimes treacherous corridors of middle school" (ibid.). Although Jack and Marshall respected each other, they did not immediately take to each other. They both cared about the students—that was their point of connection—but they had little else in common.

Marshall, quite frankly, was skeptical of this white man who "railed untiringly against the shortcomings and evils of the school system" (p. 40). It took Marshall some time to understand and appreciate Jack's sense of service: "even a man like Jack Jacqua, who is white and has no children of his own, recognizes, through reason and open eyes, that the urban youth problem is very much his problem because it's his city's problem and America's problem and humanity's problem" (p. 4). Marshall was inspired by Jack's relentless dedication to the struggle. Furthermore, Jack had something Marshall did not: a rare relationship with the community. Jack knew the neighborhood, the families, and details about the students.

Jack had this repertoire because he helped students both inside the school and at the local community center. After school ended, he would go to the Potrero Hill Neighborhood House and help kids with their homework. His eagerness to help, even then, was non-stop and all-encompassing. Jack reinforces this point when he tells me that he was "doing the work" long before the Omega Boys Club began. However, he knew that something more needed to be done. "I basically just got the idea that it was important that we do something other than just teach" and that "the usual work the teachers do day in and day out" needed to be expanded upon in order to really help the neediest of students.

With some trepidation, Marshall and Jack decided to join forces and start a club that was academically oriented, drug-free, and non-athletic. Even with Jack's reputation on the street and Marshall's status in the school, they were skeptical: would any youth participate? Still, they took the chance.

On a Thursday night—February 26, 1987, to be exact—more than 30 young people arrived at the inaugural Omega Boys Club meeting. Jack and Marshall led the students through an overview of the club, explained that it would be very serious, lectured a bit about African-American history, showed the documentary *The Vanishing Black Family,* and finished the night with one of Jack's famous, nondenominational, pulsating prayers.

Jack and Marshall realized something powerful that night. They discovered that the young people were as "interested in turning their lives around," writes Marshall (p. 49), "as we were in helping them do it." This magic—from the students—gave Jack and Marshall new energy. The momentum created that night was so strong that they both decided to dedicate their lives to building and sustaining the Omega Boys Club.

Two decades later, the club serves over 12,000 students through presentations at schools, colleges, and detention centers. Dr. Marshall also hosts a nationally syndicated radio show on Sunday nights, which reaches over 300,000 listeners. Omega has its own community center in San Francisco and offers a myriad of classes to male and female students through its Leadership Academy. On Tuesdays they have math and science from 5:00 to 6:30 p.m., followed by literature and English from 6:30 to 8:00, and family meetings from 8:00 to 10:00 p.m.; College Preparation Courses take place on Thursdays from 5:00 to 7:30 p.m. All classes are free and open to the public. In addition, Jack provides individual counseling to inmates and offers Omega classes inside incarceration centers throughout the Bay Area. The Omega Training Institute is offered once a year to practitioners (teachers, parole officers, etc.) who are interested in combating violence in their communities. Taken together, these programs change young people's lives.

As one example of this change, Omega has sent over 200 students to college on full scholarships. This is momentous: many of these teenagers have literally gone from the jailhouse to the schoolhouse.

Demadre Lockett explains, "If not for Omega, I'd be 6 feet under or in the penitentiary. My dad was in and out of jail. My mom was 17 when she had me. I could barely read when I got out of high school. But my life got turned around. I went from juvenile hall to the University of Memphis . . . by way of Omega."

Another young man, Charles Robinson, puts it this way: "At 14 I'm in prison for blowing up my neighbor's house with six sticks of dynamite. My mom is a crackhead. My pop walks away from my 10 sisters and 6 brothers . . . Omega helps kids like me. Omega is people talking to kids whose souls are crying out. They helped me. I'm at Jackson State University now. My goal is to teach."

Finally, Sakari Lyons reinforces Omega's effectiveness: "My dad would steal tooth-fairy money from under my pillow when I was 5. Both my parents were crackheads. By age 7 I knew what crack cocaine smelled like . . . Omega was a shelter for me. They listened to my rage . . . taught me it was OK to be angry and helped me believe I could do something despite my sorry home situation. I attend Howard University. I get straight A's."[2]

These testimonies demonstrate the harshness of these young people's lives and the ways the people at Omega listened, helped them heal, encouraged them to learn, and supported them through higher education. These achievements are compelling and, for the core group of Omega students, such transformations are the norm. Although I am touched by these stories, I am more interested in the process. How does a student go from incarceration to a college education? Jack is credited with making this happen, but how? I am eager to have Jack participate in this study.

Freedom Train

On December 1, 2005, after weeks of trying, I finally reach Jack. I talk nervously about my research project and he rebuts: "To tell you the truth I ain't into this kind of . . . research stuff. Someone needs to write a paper or something and I'm not into all that. I don't have anything against it . . . it's just not me. I do the work. I'm out there dealin with folks locked up, thugs 4 life." I can feel my heart sinking; he is not going to participate. I do not know what to say.

Perhaps Jack senses my disappointment because he continues, "It's not my style to say yes to this but you sold me on your personality. I don't know, it seems to me you're really down for the people. We'll see . . . we'll work together." I thank him profusely. He then asks what institution my research is associated with. "Harvard," I respond. He reacts slowly: "I heard that. That's really interesting." Jack quickly rambles off a few upcoming events and tells me about the days he teaches at juvenile hall. I am still writing down the information when he says he has to get off the phone. "Peace," he says, and hangs up.

A few days later, at 6:30 p.m., I receive a message from Jack. He explains on my answering machine that at 7:15 everyone is meeting in front of the Youth Guidance Center (called YGC, it is San Francisco's juvenile detention facility). In a panic, I look at the clock, breastfeed my newborn daughter, explain to my 3-year-old son that mama has to go out, tell my husband when I will be home—and I'm out the door running.

I cross the Bay Bridge, exit at Duboce, make my way through the hectic San Francisco streets, and finally crawl up the steep, windy hill, toward Twin Peaks. At the top of the hill I spot the detention center: a gray, concrete, three-story building. It looks so anonymous that I imagine many people drive right past it and have no idea what it is. I park in the adjacent lot and dash up a flight of steps to the main entrance.

As soon as I enter, the guard motions for me to go through the metal detector. I take off my jewelry and belt, place my keys and cell phone in the plastic container, and ask where I can find Jack. He rambles off the directions. I walk down a silent, sterile hallway, and up another flight of stairs. I reach a locked door, get buzzed in, go through another metal detector, and make my way to the B-4 unit at YGC. A guard opens the door for me and I walk, as quietly as I possibly can, toward the program area.

The teenagers sit in a circle. They are attentive and still. All of them are wearing green sweatshirts, khaki pants, white socks, and plastic khaki sandals. These uniforms look dirty and worn, as if they've been used for generations. There are approximately 30 male students who range in age from 14 to 17. The vast majority are African-Americans, with a few Latinos and Asians. Amidst this diversity, Jack and I are the only white people in the space. The guest speakers are all African-American.

A young man, John Henry, stands at the center of the circle. He talks about growing up in the hall. "I was you. I sat right where you are sitting 20 to 25 times. I was in the life. Then the message overtook me." The "message" John Henry alludes to came from Jack and the crew of people who accompany him into juvenile hall. Twice a week these people, who range in age from youth to elders, speak with the incarcerated teenagers. The topics range from personal stories to radical social critiques. The overarching message, in Jack's words, is that the teenagers need to "wake the fuck up" and realize that a criminal lifestyle will lead them to the pen, 6 feet under, or both. Jack teaches that youth have the power to free themselves—physically, emotionally, and mentally. The lessons Jack presents are symbolic of what he calls "the freedom train." This train is for everyone and even if "the wheels fall off," a student will later tell me, "or the track breaks, we'll get off and walk with you to freedom . . . cause that's where we goin." Jack's message is straightforward and relevant; I can even hear his call to "stay alive and free" reiterated in the sentiments of everyone speaking.

John Henry continues, telling us about his journey from a lifestyle of captivity to freedom. When he was incarcerated at YGC, Jack would visit him during the day, and on Monday and Wednesday nights, Jack, along with the Omega crew, would re-educate him. These lessons sparked something inside John Henry: for the first time in his life, he believed he had a future. As his belief system changed, his behavior improved. The last time he got out of "juvi," he was a new man. He joined the Job Corps, worked "nasty jobs" at fast food chains, and just tried to build his résumé. Once he completed his Job Corps program, he was able to get a steady job for $10 an hour fixing air conditioners.

John Henry then beams with excitement, and a wide grin, which seems uncontrollable, takes over his face. He tells us that a few weeks ago Dr. Harry, an affiliate of Omega, informed him about an opening for a Senior Air Conditioning Technician at the University of California, San Francisco (UCSF). John Henry applied, was hired, and today was his first day of work.

"I'm making $95,000 per year plus the super called me in there and gave me a $5,000 signing bonus because my references were so strong! I have insurance! I have 40 plus days of vacation! I get days that I get paid even if I'm sick!" John Henry's joy is contagious. Aunty Marsha, one of Jack's colleagues, says, "That's right baby!" The students seem shocked by the amount of money John Henry is making; they hang onto his every word. He continues, "on the streets, cats like to say, *I do what I gotta do*. Me too! I do what I gotta do!" He advises the students to dress professional ("no saggin pants") and speak professional, so opportunities materialize. "I just changed that negative mentality into a positive . . . If this is what I gotta do to live phat, eat phat, this is what I'm gonna do." He grabs the UCSF identification card hanging around his neck: "I wear my ID like it's a gold chain!" With passion, he literally jumps back into his chair.

One of the students asks John Henry if he went to college in order to make that much money. John Henry shakes his head, "No." Jack jumps in, "Life is not all about the money. It's not all about money." Though Jack encourages the students to get their lives together and be successful, even if that means in the material sense, he urges them to have a commitment to the struggle. He proclaims, "The more you know, the more you owe!"

The next speaker is Rob. Rob stands up but does not move to the center. Instead he stays close to his chair and begins to talk about the perils of his life. Rob is 44 years old and just got out of the penitentiary after 20 years. After sharing his life story, he mentions that he has seven children by six different women. He used to believe that having a lot of women made him a man. Rob is just starting to realize the ways his previous thoughts and belief systems were misguided. He looks over to Jack, who sits on the outskirts of the group, and then back at the students. He tells us that his street mentality led him to the penitentiary. And in the pen the most he was able to make was 20 cents an hour. Rob juxtaposes his circumstance to that of John Henry and insists that the young men in the room take heed of the message being given.

Jack walks over to the circle and puts his hand on the shoulder of a student. "Lee, will you lead us in the prayer tonight?" I watch everyone's heads lower. In unison, eyes close. In a tranquil tone, Lee says, "I ask God to keep us safe and allow the wise words to enter our hearts and guide our direction." Aunty Marsha follows in right after him. In her low, raspy voice, she pronounces that "God loves it when we sing n shout praises to His name so I'm gonna sing *Have Mercy on Us*." As Marsha sings this hymn, the young men in the room join in. The deep sounds of the melody fill this concrete space. The sanctified energy is palpable; I feel hope.

A few counselors stand on the periphery, interrupt, and tell Jack they need to take the students back into their rooms. In a loud authoritarian voice a woman orders them to stay seated until their block is called. As the young men leave the program area, they hug Jack and Aunty Marsha and thank the speakers for sharing.

I sit watching the way students hug Jack as if they do not want to let go. And even though I did not see Jack teach tonight, I got a feel for his style. From my first impressions, I think Jack prioritizes the voices of people in the struggle. Jack insures that people, such as Rob, teach alongside him about the pitfalls of a thug life. Furthermore, he seems to encourage peer-to-peer education, by having young people who were incarcerated, such as John Henry, share their experiences with the students. He also goes a step further and prompts the incarcerated students to speak up, as Lee did, about the ways they are trying to reinvent themselves. The other striking feature of Jack's strategy is prayer. Although people call out various names of God, his approach is rooted in the spiritual. But these are just my initial thoughts. I have a lot of questions for Jack.

When all the students have left, Jack asks everyone to come together and he introduces me to his comrades. "This is Vajra . . . she got a real good spirit." Despite the introduction, I feel that a few of the guest speakers are skeptical of me. On our way out to the parking lot one of them questions my motives: "What do you do? Is this work in vain?" As the young man asks me this, his stare is so bold and piercing that I step back. I piece together some sort of response about my previous experiences and say that inevitably "time will tell." Looking unimpressed with my answer he shrugs, "We'll see," and begins a conversation with someone else.

As I drive home, I cannot get the young man's questions out of my mind. His suspicions about my intent make me feel insecure and unworthy. Compared with Jack's legacy, I am not doing enough for the cause, am not as dedicated, and am not as real. Do I walk the walk? No. I type. Later on Jack will advise me, "Don't sit at a computer all day. We ready to blow ourselves up, I mean, human life." Because of this urgency, "one of the best things we can do," he says, "is reach out."

I wonder if my research will reach out in any way. Will it make any difference? Or will it sit, in vain, on a shelf—useless? I fear that this might happen and all the years I spent collecting data will be purposeless. Even for Jack to take an hour out of his day to talk with me seems like a waste of time; he views it as a waste and, on some level, so do I. Instead he could be doing something more important, more hands-on. I suspect that if this book impacts people and shapes the way they reach and teach, then, and only then, will Jack consider his time with me worthwhile. Until then, in Jack's eyes, my research process is futile. Just as Rudy said, the only way to fully grasp effectiveness is to be effective—and this requires action. I must, as Jack says, get on board the freedom train.

Ain't Nothin Wrong with You

One night, after I have attended the Omega classes at the hall for a couple of months, Jack suddenly tells me that I will be teaching. I recognize that he is still feeling me out and that, before we can set up an interview, he needs to see me in action.

Jack, Aunty Marsha, and I walk down the hall, pass the girls' unit, turn the corner, and arrive at the door of B-4. Jack takes out his keys and uses them to bang on the door. A guard quickly opens it and greets Jack with a big smile and a pat on the back. I walk in behind Jack. His light blue jeans hang low on his waist and the curly ends of his one long dreadlock poke out from underneath his purple Omega windbreaker. On the street they call him the Wizard.

In addition to the youth I met in previous sessions, tonight there are two new Ethiopian boys, a young man from India, and a white teenager. The youth sit at tables throughout the room, playing such games as checkers, cards, and dominoes. As we approach, the counselor tells them to put everything away and get ready for Omega. A few more youth arrive from another unit; an adult leads them in, single file and silent. The counselor orders the students to sit down and wait for class to start. When everyone is settled, Aunty Marsha and I go around the room and shake hands with each person. Jack is at the back station checking in with the counselors and security personnel.

As I wait for class to start, I think about the stark differences between some of the YGC counselors and Jack's crew. Whereas some of the YGC adults order the youth around and keep their distance, Aunty Marsha and Jack always try to create an authentic connection: they check in with each student, shake their hands, and even give them hugs. These Omega meetings, inside juvenile hall, have a family feeling. But the hall itself is a void. Even the hallways are bare, impersonal, uninspiring.

Jack walks to the center of the room and says to everyone, "We're about to get started." He then leans up against the wall and just starts talking, almost mid-sentence, about a graduation ceremony he attended at Downtown High School. He speaks about a young man who did not have his mother or other family members present for the big day. "It's a damn shame," he says, "because if that kid was shot I'd bet they'd be at the funeral . . . but you see, the priorities aren't right." He continues, "Some of the youth I saw graduate today were sitting in these same seats—just like you." He emphasizes that the young men can all change their lives; they can all graduate from high school. But, he teaches, in order for this to happen, they need to get a "check-up from the neck up" because "you believe you're special ed, you believe what they told you. That somethin's wrong with you. Ain't nothin wrong with you!" Jack pounds his chest, looks around the room, and says, "Quit making excuses!" Like Dereca and Victor, Jack desperately wants each of his students to realize their innate potential.

Jack carries on about the commencement ceremony. He tells us about the father of one of the graduating students. Jack knew this man "back in the day" because he used to be "in and out" of prison and was "one of the most feared brothers in SF, a real shooter." However, this man completely turned his life around and now works as a painter for the city of San Francisco. The father told Jack, "You know, you were at my graduation, and now you're at my daughter's graduation. That's somethin special." Jack uses this fact to reinforce the power of Omega and the gravity of the situation. I am equally impressed with Jack's intergenerational presence in the community. "This stuff we doin here," he urges, "it's real serious."

Jack then shares a story about his good friend, a lifer at San Quentin State Penitentiary. This particular man, Jack explains, is a well-respected inmate who embodies redemption. When he went up for parole, everyone on the panel agreed that he deserved to be released. He was set to get out and the only person with the power to overturn the board's decision was the "Governator" Arnold Schwarzenegger. Schwarzenegger had 150 days to overturn the verdict. On the 150th day, which was a Saturday, Jack was sitting with his friend at San Quentin when the letter was hand delivered. It stated that Schwarzenegger had stopped his release and that in 3 years he could appeal. Jack was frustrated, but when he looked over at his friend, he became inspired. This particular inmate did not get angry but calmly told Jack it would be okay; he would attempt freedom in the years to come. Jack's friend exemplifies peace, patience, and perseverance. According to Jack, "he's my hero."

Jack stares at the students and shakes his head: "I know you've had it hard. Some of you had it real hard. Been molested, abandoned, watch your mama get beat. But whatever it is, you got to deal with that anger. You got to deal with that shit." He declares, "your public pretender don't give a fuck about you. Your boys on the block don't really give a fuck about you. Where are they now? Your girl, or whatever, she don't give a fuck about you. Cause where are you? You ain't wit her. You're here!" He asks them point blank: "Are you afraid to succeed? Are you afraid of success? Afraid to get your shit together?" He insists, "Here, tonight, man, nobody's gonna die. You safe, relatively. Five people have been shot in the last couple of days, but not you. There ain't no bullshit here." He puts his fist to his heart. "This is what we got for you: love, love, and more love!" He takes a deep breath, coughs, and then turns to Marsha, "Okay, I'm done now."

Marsha stays seated, straightens her back, and proclaims, "Obedience to God." The youth respond in unison, "Obedience to God." Aunty's health is poor so she gets up very slowly and walks, in her slippers, to the center of the circle. "I could be with my grandbabies right now but I'm here cause I love y'all. I don't want to bury y'all like I buried my son." As soon as she starts talking, her energy picks up. For the next 20 minutes I watch her shout, pray, cry, cuss, use slang, talk about the latest drugs on the street ("thrax, tt, and them damn pills"), and straight-up clown the teenagers into changing their lives.

With a sense of urgency, Marsha tells them their lives are sacred. And the students sit straight, all eyes on her. At times they laugh, nod their heads, and drop their jaws in disbelief over something wild she says. Aunty knows the streets, lives the struggle, and understands how to hustle. She uses her experiences to connect with and heal these young men. She sees this work as deeply spiritual. Toward the end of her talk, she says, "The devil can scare you but only God can take your life. Only God can snatch you away from the devil. Only God can save you really. The devil can't take your life. The devil can only scare you into doin the wrong things. God snatched me up." She sits back down, leans back, takes out a roll of lifesavers, and offers me one.

Moments before Marsha sits down, Jack puts his hand on my shoulder and tells me I am going next. I look around at the young men—some of them just boys—sitting quiet and sober, looking so humble. They appear so innocent and yet are charged with being so guilty. This observation shapes my talk with them.

"All of you are lookin real nice tonight—young, handsome." I go on to share with them about "this fine ass brotha" who used to stay across the street from me on 63rd in North Oakland. When we were in high school, he was incredibly popular. In tenth grade he dropped out and the streets—selling dope, shooting people, and pimping—consumed his life. I remember when his apartment got shot up. A couple of years ago I was driving through my old neighborhood and I looked over at his unit. The windows were missing and garbage bags were taped onto the window frames; three bullet holes pierced the front door. I almost did not recognize him, but he was standing on the corner near his building. I parked the car and went over to greet him. Though he was barely 30 years old, he looked nearly 50 because his face was so worn and he had gained a lot of weight. He had an extra-tall can of beer in his hand and explained to me that he's an alcoholic and cannot get his life together. I told him I wished he could tell that to these youth out here who romanticize the streets. I asked him, "Where you think you'd be if you didn't drop out?" "Not like this," he shrugged. "Maybe playin ball. I don't know."

I look at the students at YGC. "You see, everyone think that this shit won't happen to em but how many grown-ass-gangstas do you know who are free, never did no time, and ballin?" A few of them shake their heads. "My friend went from bein fine to hella grimy in a couple of years. If you keep livin this life, glorifyin this shit," I bellow, "what the fuck you think gonna happen?!" The students are absolutely silent. I take a deep breath and calm down. "You are young," I tell them, "you have so many opportunities and I believe in you. We all do."

A large gentleman stands on the periphery of the circle with his hands folded. He nods as I speak and, as soon as I sit down, he slides into the center and introduces himself as Sam. "This here is the freedom train," he begins, "and the freedom train stays movin. This is like the Underground Railroad established by Harriet Tubman." He provides a brief description of Tubman and then explains that he will prove to us tonight that incarceration is the newest incarnation of slavery and that "this right here is a plantation."

Sam starts his history lesson in 1492 and goes on to discuss details of the middle passage. "Sharks would congregate near boats because there was so much blood in the water from bodies bein thrown overboard." He continues, "The 13th amendment is a loophole. Though no longer race-based, the constitution does allow for indentured servitude for people who are quote unquote criminals." I immediately think of Rob, who told us the most he was able to make in the pen was 20 cents an hour. "This is modern-day slavery," Sam says.

Sam reaches into his pocket and pulls out a pair of shiny silver handcuffs. "We all know these," he chuckles. "Now what I'm about to show you I got blessed to have in my possession just so I could teach y'all something tonight. You can't touch what I'm about to show you and don't be asking too many questions cause then I'll think you a snitch." His face is stern and motionless. He looks at the students but says nothing. Slowly, Sam reaches into his coat pocket and pulls out a white plastic bag. He unwraps a pair of 6-pound, rusty-brown handcuffs. He roars, "Where are these from?" He reads the engraving on the side: "The Georgetown Plantation Police . . . for use on Negroe women and children." A dead silence fills the room; I get goose bumps and I swear the room gets colder.

As Sam holds the contemporary handcuffs next to the slave shackles, the similarity is haunting. A student turns to Aunty Marsha, and says, "That was like made for you." Tears begin to trickle down Aunty's face. She tells us, "I used to be a slave. I used to be out there doin all kinda stuff. But now I'm free. I'm free and it feels good. I'm so thankful. I just want to thank you for sharing that with us tonight." Sam nods and in a serious tone tells us about the moment he knew he had to get free: when he was unable to fully stretch out his arms because his cell was so small. In that instant, he realized he was being treated like a caged animal and that, once he was released, he would not go back to prison. He laughs: "If I'm ever locked up again it will be because I'm a political prisoner." He will not, like most of the youth in the room, get arrested "doin some bullshit" but rather "cause I did somethin real for the people." He glances over to Jack who has a wide smile on his face. Jack nods and Sam brings his lesson to a close.

Sam's bold, informative lecture tied together history and the present-day police state. The facts were impressive and so were the group dynamics. This class of ethnically diverse teenagers was captivated by Sam's message; the energy in the space became surreal and even these prison walls felt momentarily transcendent.

When the Omega class is over, we all walk out of the building and into the parking lot. Jack gives me a hug good-bye and says, "I knew you'd be good, but I didn't know you'd be that good." I'm elated by the compliment. However, after I teach a few more times, Jack says bluntly: "You talk too long. Say what you got to say and sit down." This is Jack: straight up, no nonsense. As the youth say, "he keeps it real."

Driving home, I think about Sam's lesson on slavery. Though Jack did not teach it per se, he orchestrated the evening. In fact, Sam was once a student in

Jack's classes at YGC. In the years since, Sam grew up, and equally important to Jack, Sam grew in consciousness. Sam attributes his life change to his father, who is, he says, Jack Jacqua.

Patronizing Pedagogy

Though I have participated in countless meetings at YGC and a few Omega events, I can barely raise the courage to ask Jack for an interview. When I began this study he agreed to be interviewed, but that was nearly a year ago. I have a number of burning questions and need his answers to clearly understand his strategies. With trepidation, I tell him we need to talk.

On a brisk day in 2006, I meet Jack at the Potrero Hill Neighborhood House[3] in San Francisco. Designed by Julia Morgan, it is an architectural gem. As I wait for Jack, I look around the community center. Expansive windows bring in natural light along with an amazing view of the city. When Jack arrives he says "waz up" and then asks me where I want to have the interview. We can sit outside, he tells me, or go downstairs to the recreation area. "Either way," I tell him. "This is your thing," he responds curtly, "you got to tell me where you want to go." I shrug: "All right, downstairs."

After months of anticipation, the interview is about to start. Jack folds his arms and grunts, "How much time do you want? I mean, seriously, you scare me with an hour cause I don't have a clue what you could be asking me for an hour." I show him that I have a sheet of questions and that we can skip whichever ones he does not want to answer. "Fine," he retorts.

I begin. "Last night when we were coming out of YGC you told me most of the students in the group are mislabeled special ed and ADHD [attention deficit hyperactivity disorder] but are able to sit still, quiet, and attentive for over 2 hours during the Omega class. Why is that?"

Jack's answer comes in the form of a criticism of the system. The purpose of school is to perpetuate oppression, he explains. "School is about controlling the minds and hearts of young people, controlling folks, telling them there's something wrong with them. It's a business, it's an industry," especially the "special education business." He says that these tracks make money off of "poor children" and "young Black males" in particular. These students are told there is something wrong with them (e.g., anger issues, ADHD) and they are "put into positions where they feel like they're definitely second class." This form of oppression, under the guise of public education, "enforces an already bad self-esteem that many have coming out of the hoods of America." He leans forward and proclaims, "These youngsters *can* sit still." Unfortunately, they are often lulled into mediocrity with "ice cream and cookies" and a patronizing pedagogy that says "there's something wrong with you."

In stark contrast, at YGC, Jack "runs a tight ship" and the students understand that they must adhere to the agenda because Jack treats every teenager "normal and according to the rules of the game." This means that during class the students cannot use the restroom, talk to each other, or fidget (e.g., twist their locks). "Because you are strict," I clarify, "that's why the students are attentive?" Not quite. Jack believes the crux of good teaching, at juvenile hall or in any classroom, is "all about expectations." This is an important point for him and is similar to something Dereca told me. "If you expect certain things and you have certain standards and you have a certain commitment and make it very clear what you're doing and you have a consistency day in and day out, day out and day in, then it's going to be fine."

Jack explains the difference between the hall and school: in the Omega classes at YGC the vast majority of students ("65 to 75 percent" in a class of 30) have been "diagnosed" and continuously told by "IEP's and psychologists that they have these disabilities."[4] However, Jack does not follow these labels because they produce low expectations. Most teachers believe that "it's okay," for instance, to let youth with ADHD "go to the bathroom every 20 minutes. It's okay to coddle them and not be too harsh on them." Jack coughs, clears his throat, and tells me, "It's just part of the genocide. It's the liberals' contributions, one of their many contributions, to the genocide." But, he clarifies, teachers do not have to perpetuate the problem.

The real key to being successful with young people, he proclaims, is simple: listen. "You have to listen to these youngsters. Adults don't listen. Adults have a very bad habit of not listening to young people. And then they get mixed up when I say listen to young people, cause somehow they think that that's agreeing with them. It's not agreeing with them, it's listening to their pain. Listening to what they're saying. Just listen." He continues, "Preachers don't listen. Police don't listen. Politicians don't listen. Mamas don't listen. Nobody listenin. So it's important to listen." Every community-based educator in this study has emphasized this exact point.

According to Jack listening is essential, and so is asking the right questions. He believes that there is usually an underlying reason for bad behavior, a reason for aggression, and a rationale for the mask. Unfortunately, many adults are afraid to find out what it is.

"Why is that child late to school?" Jack asks. "Why is that child not payin attention to his work and not focused? Why does that child seem to have different personalities on different days? There's a reason." He advises adults never to disregard the student's answer. For instance, to the question, "Why is that youngster angry?" a myriad of responses are possible. Maybe the student says he is angry with his mom. From Jack's experience, many adults will say, "Well, I don't know why you're angry, you have such a nice mother." Jack disagrees with this approach. In this situation Jack would acknowledge that the student's "mama is working and trying to do the best she can" but he never discredits a young person's feelings. He warns, "you can't act like the anger shouldn't be there or somehow it's manufactured. It's real anger!" He puts his hands down on the table and pauses before continuing, "Sometimes we don't want to deal with that because if we don't have our own shit together, that youngster might come up with somethin that affects our life. We don't really want to go there. Cause we supposed to be the one sitting above the class and tellin the kid." Therefore, "if we get on some sort of same level, we can't, a lot of times, handle that as adults."

Jack believes that adults who do this kind of work, and want to do it right, must delve into the real, hard, and deep personal issues that are often the reason for a student's severe misbehavior. But many teachers do not have these types of conversations with their students. Jack is clear: "Teachers, people who work with youth, do not listen because of our own issues. We don't pay any attention to their conversation because you may have the same anger problem. You've been denyin your own anger, and especially the source of your anger in your passive role that you created in your professional life." To Jack, many teachers deny their students' pain because they deny their own pain. As a result, they often replace listening and dialogue with silence and control. This trend perpetuates bad behavior and does not help the student or the teacher.

Jack acknowledges two types of good teachers. The first is committed to the cause and teaches for social justice. The second is also committed, not necessarily to the process of liberation, but to doing a professional job. Jack says, "They're both acceptable to me." He is clear that, whichever type a teacher chooses to be, they must have pride in their profession and do it to the best of their ability because "these kids deserve the best."

When it comes to school, Jack has clear critiques, but also suggestions. Jack advocates for full-service schools that are institutions of learning as well as community centers. He continues, "Tonight they're going to make some ridiculous decisions in closing schools down in San Francisco. We need to use these schools for families, for counseling, for jobs, for food, for tutoring, for recreation. Schools need to be open. Maybe they should close at midnight, as we take the last of the folks home and make sure they get home safely. We open again at six in the morning for childcare. And have them in our communities. Educate our own, that's extremely important." Though Jack is skeptical of the oppressive school system, he recognizes that schools can serve as a site for neighborhood revitalization. He argues, like Warren (2005), that schools can succeed if they provide wrap-around services in needy communities.

Jack has a clear vision for schools and clear-cut suggestions for people who want to work with urban youth. He believes that adults can be effective if they listen to young people, ask the right (sometimes hard) questions, and never discredit their answers. And teachers, in particular, must have rules in their classrooms, hold to high expectations, and be consistent. Taken together, these attributes will make well-intentioned good-hearted teachers part of the solution instead of cogs in the crisis.

Whatever Jack's recommendations, he says none of his advice will matter unless teachers take a good look at themselves. His recommendation to teachers is similar to those of the other community-based educators: "Look at yourself; know who you are." This sounds simple enough, but how do we train educators to have knowledge of self? Again, explains Jack, it's about introspection. Each person should ask themselves why they want to work with youth and what they want to accomplish. The answers need to be based on a deep commitment to helping young people improve their lives. This dedication must be real, he proclaims, and so genuine that, when problems arise or a student is disrespectful, the teacher does not take "stuff personal." This perspective reminds me of Dereca, Rudy, and Victor. "It's not a personal thing," Jack declares. Teachers whose "feelings are that fragile . . . get burned out early"; that is because they were "never burned on in the first place."

Jack leans forward and his beady blue eyes sparkle under his thick dark-rimmed glasses. He tugs on his long white beard and shares with me that "you can't make it if you can't handle the fact of a young man you spoke to yesterday was hit and killed today." This has been Jack's reality too many times. Teachers who work in a war zone "must prepare themselves spiritually and always keep their mind on the bigger picture." A look of confusion crosses my face. Jack explains that one of his students decided to change his lifestyle after his friend was murdered. Even a death, as sad as it is, can serve as a catalyst for change. "Miracles happen every day. There's so many miracles that are happening out here along with all the devastation and the hopelessness."

In order to succeed in the long run adults need to know "what your mission really is in your heart." This is not about having a job; it is about having a calling. "If you're real," Jack says matter-of-factly, "it's not about teachin from eight to three and thinkin you're going to forget about it." He shakes his head and looks right at me. The type of work he does requires around-the-clock perseverance. This is his life.

As Jack talks about this level of commitment, I am reminded of Rudy's approach. Rudy and Misha have four children of their own, but their family activities include UP youth; this is one of the ways Rudy is able to constantly be of service. Jack's situation is a bit different. He is single with no children and this allows him absolute flexibility. I do not know if his reasoning and requirements are realistic for teachers. Then again, I presume it all depends on how effective we want to be.

Jack's perspective is staunch, his advice so straightforward. I cannot help but think about my own situation. I am not always able to make it to the YGC meetings, for instance, because I have two small children. I feel compelled to ask Jack, "Does that mean my efforts will be futile?" He tells me, "Of course your own family is always first but you have to be able to basically want to teach these children the same way you're teaching your children. So it's all just one commitment. Seven days a week. You might have to do somethin Saturday for somebody or on a Sunday you might have to go to somebody's church when they're bein baptized. It's just what you got to do I feel, to integrate it." This is exactly what Jack does: he attends everything from christenings to graduation ceremonies to funerals.

Shifting the conversation, I ask Jack if incarcerating youth can help them in any way. Whereas I expect to hear him rant about the criminal (in)justice system, as he did about school, his answer is surprising. "It can," he tells me, but YGC must be "tougher." The first time young people are locked up they do not know what to expect. Therefore, it is important to treat YGC like a real prison so that youth do not want to come back. Instead, YGC is run like a recreation center in which the teenagers "watch movies and play games, they get attention," and even "get sweet snacks." As a result, some of the youth "really feel like it's cool." Jack believes YGC is "not taken seriously [by] the folks in charge" because they are afraid of damaging the children. "Rather than worry about how do we *repair* the damage . . . we are so worried about lawsuits and complaints that we try to be as easy and as loose as we can be." For Jack, this is a major problem.

Jack wants teenagers to get a message: incarceration is no way to live. He does not want students to be allowed "out of their room much." And when they come out, "they should have mandatory counseling." If they watch films, "they ought to be films on redemption and victimization" and on the "realities of the prison system that's ahead." "I mean," Jack says, with a hint of frustration, "they ought to be watching films on their story as opposed to his-story." These tactics would "awaken some" of them. Unfortunately, these days, juvenile hall is a set-up because "kids get out and don't care if they come back." Jack says these young people have tremendous possibility; YGC could really help them.

Jack believes the "most highly intelligent of the young brothers . . . wind up in trouble because they see the hopelessness." Like the Hallway Hangers in MacLeod's (1995) study, Jack has found that many troubled youth are keenly aware of the farce of equal opportunity and do not believe in the rhetoric of meritocracy. Because of their outlook, these teenagers embrace the streets instead of school. Yet even though "they don't go to school," many of them "have college-level skills." Just think "if they'd ever get involved on some other levels." Jack smiles.

For example, one of his students (a "young brotha") on a murder charge resembled Malcolm X. Like Malcolm, when he entered prison, he could not read. Jack explains to me that the lawyer planned to argue that the teenager was "basically retarded" because he "couldn't even hardly write his own name" and "had a first grade reading level." After spending "over 2 years in juvenile hall on this homicide case," he was acquitted. When he was released, they retested his literacy. He scored as high as a sophomore in college. Though he had "never really been to school," he was highly capable. "You know, this wasn't something I read in a book about a great historical figure, this occurred. He decided that he wanted to read. He was not retarded, never was. So, it's up to the individual to decide that they don't hold themselves back." Jack's role in this process is to "shine the light" and "give them the information. You got to give em the blessings. Make sure you tell em they're okay."

Jack wants young people to recognize their own agency. He tries to awaken his students to see that they are powerful. He teaches them that the reason they cannot find success is that they do not understand their potential. "It lies within them not understanding what they can be and who they can be and what they can do. And how they do have a voice." But their voices are often drowning because their pain is too deep.

Understanding this dilemma, Jack gives one-on-one time to youth and in these sessions he tries to address their pain. He goes "eyeball-to-eyeball" and asks personal questions such as "Why are you so angry?" These interactions are intense. He tries to get them to talk through the pain—whether that's because a young man did not have a father, was molested, or "cause you watched a man beatin your mama" and are now "16 but have never dealt with that anger." Jack says emphatically, "So deal with it! Realize the truth and it will set you free!"

In order to heal, the students need to be able to speak about the secrets that are eating them up inside. Dereca relies on controversial questions, Victor uses storytelling, and Jack relies on confessions, but for all of them the process is similar: dialogue. Though these sessions are reflective in nature, Jack, in particular, is steadfast in his critique of the system; he desperately wants them to understand the structures of oppression that impede their choices. Once students have a critical analysis of the system, they will be in a better position to make new decisions. Jack's lessons have a layered purpose: introspection, agency, and empowerment.

Soul Shaker

I want to interview someone close to Jack, and no one fits this description better than Aunty Marsha. Aunty Marsha is one of Jack's comrades. She has known him for over 35 years and has tremendous insight into his character and teaching ability.

It is a 90-degree day in June when I arrive at her apartment. As soon as I park, I notice that Aunty is waiting for me outside. As we walk to her apartment, she introduces me to a few people in her complex and a couple of kids follow us into her home. She serves them each a scoop of vanilla ice cream and then shoos them out so we can talk. We sit down on her couch. A poster-size picture of her son hangs above us and a medical bed takes up most of her living room.

Marsha tells me that she is excited to talk about Jack and that this project is "real important" to her. However, first she wants me to understand that I am "lucky" that Jack is part of my study because "all kinds of people from all across the country always wanna interview Jack but he doesn't mess with fake people. He only messes with people he thinks is real. He won't just let anyone come up into juvenile hall to talk to his kids." She warns me to not "take this opportunity for granted in any way." Jack is weary of "people who might write about his kids in a book just to make lots of money." She looks at me seriously and says, "He's seen people make degrees off the struggle and that's a form of abuse so don't abuse your privilege." I respond: "Yes Aunty, I know." She smiles and nods. Since we are clear, she is ready to begin. According to Aunty Marsha, Jack has never changed: "He's a great person then, he's a great person now." I ask her to clarify what exactly makes him so great.

Aunty Marsha started accompanying Jack to juvenile hall when her son was locked up. She asked Jack to speak to him because "I didn't have no daddy in his life. I didn't have no daddy in my life." Jack spoke with Marsha's son, but first, he talked matter-of-factly to her: "He ask me was I plannin on moving out of the neighborhood. I told him no. He told him my son has a sickness." Marsha was confused by Jack's statement. "A sickness?" Jack explained to her, "your son got the hood sickness." Jack spent one-on-one time with her son and when I ask Marsha what they talked about she is clear: "I can't even tell you some of the things that he said directly to him . . . Jack not goin to repeat that confidential information. But whatever it was," she shakes her head, "it was working." After her son got out of YGC, Jack got him a summer job. Unfortunately, soon after, he died in a car accident.

Aunty Marsha leans forward, stares into me, and says, "Jack's a miracle worker. He's a soul shaker." Though many people pontificate about social change, only a handful of people, she finds, are "for-real for-real." Anyone who knows Jack understands that he "walks the walk." He is not like some people at Omega who just "talk" about the community. Rather, Jack is in the community.

In order to be effective, asserts Aunty Marsha, a person must collaborate directly with the people, not just lecture about them. Though she has never heard Jack complain about Dr. Marshall or "talk bad" about him, she adamantly believes "Jack *is* Omega." He is the one who is in the trenches and works closely with the "kids in the struggle right now" who are "fighting to stay alive." When Marshall, for instance, gets on the radio each week, she feels his message is completely out of touch with the hood. Her voice deepens. "We're losin our kids on a daily basis." I nod and look up at the picture of her son. She repeats, "On a daily basis. I never thought I'd have to say that. But it's happenin." Because of this urgency, she cannot fathom why anyone would sit behind a desk all day, complacent about the immediate crisis among inner-city youth. For her, Jack's way is the only way because it works. Speaking quickly, she asserts, "If you know Jack, that's Omega enough, right there."

I empathize with Aunty Marsha's perspective and I must admit that the *Street Soldiers* radio show is basically irrelevant to most of today's youth. Still, I am not so quick to cast Dr. Marshall aside. I think he too plays a critical role.

I agree that Jack is the one who gets young people off the corner and into Omega, but it is Marshall who oversees the math and college classes. He is also the one who secures funding for scholarships, goes to conferences, and networks with funders. As Jack will later tell me, he and Marshall are still on the same freedom train, just in different cars.

Marshall is square and Jack is radical, but this distinction does not matter because, at the end of the day, they are "family." This family bond can, and does, withstand critique. To onlookers such as Marsha and many others, Jack does not receive the credit he deserves. Perhaps more importantly, they believe that Jack's strategy is imperative because he is in the neighborhood, stopping street wars, whereas Marshall's traditional role as executive director is outdated and pointless. I recognize this tension. In fact, my colleagues at the university pointed to Dr. Marshall as someone to participate in this study but, when I talked to community members and youth, their opinions were clear. In terms of effectiveness, says Aunty Marsha, "you're on the right track by knowin Jack," and her smile glows in my direction.

She then shifts a bit in her chair and reinforces her point: though Jack does "all these things," Marsha is convinced that "he's gettin paid hardly nothin." This surprises me, but she says convincingly, "Oh, no, no, no. Hardly noth . . ." She pauses mid-sentence and acknowledges Jack's perspective. "All the kids that Jack's worked with, he doesn't get the money for that" but, more importantly, "he gets rewarded in his heart." She declares, "There's nobody better as far as the street soldier is concerned. I'm African-American and Seminole Indian. I seen all these different people on the street, mother so-and-so in Oakland feedin the homeless; mother so-and-so over here in San Francisco feedin the homeless. What street worker do you know for free and from his heart and works as hard as Jack and knows all these youth?"

Jack genuinely knows these hardcore kids, "knows all of them and their families and can remember them by name." "There's no one better," she urges, "you've met the best of the best." I understand that Aunty loves Jack. But I am still trying to understand what exactly makes him so effective. Is it because he is in the community? Is it his forthright, no-nonsense style?

Aunty Marsha thinks the main reason is actually that "he's been in this business longer than anybody." A young woman I spoke with in Hunters Point said something similar: "Jack's an institution around here." But there must be more to it than his years of experience. Marsha thinks the other element that makes him stand out is that he treats the kids as if they're his own. "They're his children too." This is also a recurring theme.

It is clear that Jack is a father figure throughout various turfs in San Francisco. I speculate, *about how many young people has he helped?* "Oh, girl, you can't put a number on that. These children have changed their lives. Jack has really turned a lot of these kids around." Jack participates in every step: "He sees em before so there's prevention. He sees them during the time they're in juvenile hall, if they go to juvenile hall . . . he's doing prevention, treatment, and aftercare. I don't care if they graduating from trade school, Jack's there." Jack believes his students are his family; as a result, his approach is encompassing and never stops, no matter how old they get. This relates to Aunty Marsha too, but on a very personal level.

Though Marsha loves and admires Jack, they have not always stayed close. After Marsha's son died, she wallowed in her grief. She relied on drugs to get her through and isolated herself from everyone, especially Jack. One day she bumped into him in the grocery store and he went straight up to her and began asking her personal questions. "What's the matter? Are you still grieving about your son dying? You did your best." Marsha's response was to tell Jack the doctor had her on morphine and codeine. Even though they were standing in the middle of the aisle, Jack roared, "Don't let nobody give you that! What are you taking it for?" Marsha started to respond but Jack interrupted, "Nah, you don't need that stuff. You don't need nothin. You need to come back and do what you do best! Give back what you owe! You don't know how great you are!" This memory is still tender for Marsha and she begins to cry. "It was a wake-up call. It hit me hard."

In the months that followed, Jack persistently told Marsha that she was "better than just snortin cocaine, rippin and runnin. I raised my kids and I should be better than this. I should think better than this. Simple as that." He encouraged her to start speaking again at YGC. Each time Marsha reached out and spoke to the youth, she could feel herself healing, gradually.

Jack's constant tough love brought Aunty Marsha out of her grief and addiction. She tells me he's "been a great friend, mentor, counselor, everything. He helped me, as old as I am." "Next to God," she proclaims, "he's my best friend." She straightens her back and nods, "I changed my life and I know that I've changed. I could be shot, I could be dead, anything." With pride and purpose she tells me she rides "the freedom train" and is not ready to get off even though the doctor said she has "16 months to live." She beams, "I'm on my nineteenth month" and "ain't even countin no months no more."

Aunty Marsha recently held her annual "Stop the Violence" barbecue. This cookout is not part of any program; she does it simply out of the goodness of her heart. It takes place "right here in the projects" on the lawn outside her apartment. Everyone in the neighborhood donates "food" or "money" and the "kids come out in droves." She says, "you ought to see em comin . . . Girl, you think we don't have a good time. We cook all day . . . we have big pots of collard greens and I fry corn bread—it take me all night for pattin out that corn bread and fryin it." Though "watermelon, macaroni and cheese, and ribs" might not sound like a path to peace, part of stopping violence is creating community, which is essentially bringing people together in harmony. This event does just that.

The ripple effect of the extended family model is impressive. Jack explains, "This is not anything one does alone. This thing has become so big and magnificent" that now the Omega "family base is very large and very powerful. So this healing, this knowledge, this love, occurs in many different directions each and every hour." Aunty Marsha's efforts are a clear example of Jack's statement. This theme is crystallized when I attend the Omega Boys Club center. Once youth are released from the detention facility and are on their road to recovery, Jack invites them to receive tutoring and social support from Omega's other teachers. This is the next step in the process of rehabilitation, transformation, and social justice.

Extended Family

Jack invites me to the Tuesday night math class and family meeting at the Omega Boys Club center on Tennessee Street in Potrero Hill. The center is in the middle of an industrial area, yet the immediate block is full of houses. I drive up and down the street looking for a sign that says Omega Boys Club, but see no such thing. I then notice a group of young African-American women sitting on the front steps of one home and decide to park so I can ask them where the club is. "Where's Omega at?" I ask. Responding in unison, they say, "Right here!"

From the outside the center looks like a home, but inside it definitely feels like a community center. The space is packed with people coming and going in different directions. I enter into the large multi-purpose room. White boards hang along the main wall, a number of long tables take up the center, and chairs are everywhere. Several visitors are present as part of Marshall's Omega Training Institute; I sit with them on the periphery, waiting for the upcoming math class to start. I ask one of them how long the class is and a gentleman responds, "On the board it says it's 2 hours but that can't be right." I smile, nod, and get out my notebook.

In the next 10 minutes, the room fills up with 18 African-American students. There are as many young women as men; the youngest student is a sixth grader and the oldest is 19. The teacher looks as if she is in her mid-twenties and is also African-American. Though she is dressed in casual and trendy clothes, her face is stern and her directives clear. She relies on a call-and-response teaching method. For example, she asks the group, "Is 1 the same as nothing?" A short silence sets in so she asks again, "Got $1, is that the same as nothing?" The students giggle and a few say "No." She repeats the question until everyone is saying, in unison, "No!"

A young man sits twisting his locks and is not paying attention to the teacher. He says under his breath, "I don't like math." She quickly responds in a vociferous tone, "You don't like math? What do you like?" He turns to her,

"I like money!" She smirks, "What is money?" "Paper," he tells us. She asks again, "What is money?" He says, "Numbers." She nods, "Exactly. Math is money. Math is numbers." With this statement, the class is refocused.

As I watch these interactions, I am reminded of something a student told me; the math class is a relatively new program at Omega. It was developed because a number of Omega students struggled in their math courses in college. To fix this problem, the adults at Omega recruited students who had done well in math, and asked them to become Omega math instructors. The benefits of this approach are clear and students are doing much better in their classes. The teenager assured me that Omega students "crushed a lot of the stereotypes that the system had enforced on us." These thoughts are ever-present as I watch the students learn Algebra.

The teacher writes various problems on the board and then demonstrates how to do the first one. For the next 20 minutes the youth sit quietly and work independently. During this time, the teacher walks around the room. And just when I think she is going to give us a break, she tells the students to simplify an equation:

$$\frac{x^{-5}y^{6}z}{z^{-3}y^{2}x}$$

Without a moment's hesitation the students flip their papers over and begin copying the equation from the board. Then they work in teams to solve it. Subsequently, a student is chosen to present the answer. The teacher nods, implying that it is correct, then announces, "I want all my exponents negative. What do I do?" And then she hollers to her students, "Flip it!"

A young man who looks about 15 mutters, "I'm confused." She responds in a loud voice, "Where did I lose you?" She walks over to his table and works with him one-on-one and then asks him to explain the solution to the class. She encourages him: "Talk louder cause you know what you're talkin about." He sits up and starts talking, but then stops and shakes his head in confusion. As he struggles, an older student, Amir, shares his approach with him: "This is how I caught onto it hella quick. Take y^4, if you say something positive to someone you're like bringin em up, makin em feel better, but if you say somethin negative, you bringin em down. So, to make y^4 negative, you gotta bring it down. Say something positive and raise it up. Ya feel me?" The teacher grins and faces her class: "Amir has just Omegasized these fractions!"

Class continues and after 2 hours the teacher informs the students that their "homework is due Thursday." Ms. Estell, another Omega teacher, walks to the front of the room. She tells the students they have a break but need to be back in their seats in 10 minutes for writing class.

During the break, I look around the room. The "Commandments of the Hood" are listed on the right side of the board. These rules (e.g., "Thou shall get thy money on") describe the mentality of the street that can—most often will—get people killed and/or incarcerated. Juxtaposed with these negatives are pictures of heroes and sheroes such as Martin Luther King, Langston Hughes, Harriet Tubman, Frederick Douglass, Malcolm X, and Gandhi. On a separate wall is a typed list of Omega college graduates.

When the class is resettled, Ms. Estell tells them to "Write about a time you felt obligated to do something you really didn't want to do. What was it? Who was involved or encouraged you to do it? What was the result?" After 15 minutes of writing time, she tells the students to put their pencils down, and says everyone needs to read what they wrote. She emphasizes that the students cannot tell each other what they wrote, but must read from their papers verbatim. This resembles Victor's writing exercises as well—writing as a tool for healing and community building.

A young man raises his hand to read: "I feel obligated to be the father in the house because my dad was never around." A teenage girl goes next: "I feel obligated to take AP Biology." Another student reads, "I felt obligated to shoot dude that put his hands on my sister." The range of responses to this question is striking. Although the students are all African-American and live in relatively similar neighborhoods in San Francisco, the ways they feel obligated range dramatically. It seems that the purpose of this exercise is for the students to voice their dilemmas as well as listen to each other. This process creates a sense of camaraderie among students who have vastly different lifestyles.

Following this exercise, Ms. Estell plays various video clips from *New Jack City, Sugar Hill Gang, Straight Outta Brooklyn*, and *Juice*. In these movies she highlights scenes in which the main characters are pressured by their "homies" to rob, steal, and kill. After the discussion about peer pressure and "fearship versus friendship," we have a 5-minute break. When we resume, we are told the family meeting will start.

I get up to stretch and I see Jack coming into the building. I walk over to him and say hi. He introduces me to an African-American woman: "This is my daughter Sharee." A number of people start coming into the building; they head straight to the multi-purpose room for the family meeting.

Now, the room is packed to capacity with over 50 people. Not a seat is empty and many people are standing. Dr. Marshall starts off the meeting by encouraging everyone to come in and find a place to sit. "Don't stand outside. If this was church you'd find your way in." Marshall tells us about the training institute and turns to the group of visitors: "A lot of you been asking to meet Jack, so here he is." Jack steps to the front of the room as if entering the pulpit.

"Welcome everybody. I know there's some out-of-town people here that been doing this Omega thing for a few days. Really it's an *Each One Teach One* philosophy and this work never stops . . . this work takes commitment. Freedom is a commitment! Gotta work for it all the time cause Satan workin all the time. We gotta be seen, be heard. What we know, we owe. We gotta empower the youngsters cause we're not gonna last forever. We're an extended family, that's how we see this. Many kids don't have a family base. We understand the roots, understand the role of a father so we play the role, but it's not a play, it's a real role."

Almost everyone present, including the participants in the training institute, is African-American. All of us have our eyes locked on Jack. His voice thunders through the room. "Never give up on anybody. Keep it real in the communication. Able to reach thousands of people—it's real." He repeats, "What you know, you owe. Never forget the roots of the extended family from the youngest to the oldest. This is genocide! We're fighting a war! You got to be committed to something. The Bay is in a state of genocide! Evil forces well and alive. Gotta fight this by any means necessary."

He continues: "Rise up and teach the young by example the best we know how. Young African-American males today are more likely to go to the state pen than Penn State. The media gotta plan. We're on a mission to awake young princes and princesses. Awake them to be a better father than they had. And then the daughters got to be better than their mama. Always gettin a little better each n every time. Never stop. Never stop. Doesn't mean can't take time out. You owe it to yourself to take care of yourself but never forget the struggle. Part of the problem is the commitment. If you're not committed you won't be effective. If you're not really committed, really though," he pounds his fist forcefully onto his chest, "you're foolin yourself! Check yourself or wreck yourself!"

Jack then turns to face the visitors. Staring at them he asks, "What's up with your anger? What's up with you?" Nobody says anything. I think about Dereca and her similar (yet softer) advice that teachers need to be honest and vulnerable in order to genuinely connect with youth. Jack, however, continues on his rampage: "Take what a youth did personal. Got your feelings hurt cause a youth doesn't like you. Don't you know you're a healer! You're a teacher! Get your feelings hurt and give up on a youth n get burned out, givin up on folks, jus givin up. So many times the youth we work with come back to juvi. Keep it real with em, don't tell em what they wanna hear, tell em the truth. You don't ever give up on anybody!"

Jack explains that sometimes it takes a person 40 years to turn their life around, so we can never give up because "God given us miracles, Allah given us miracles, every single minute." Jack proclaims that real teachers will "empower them to reach out. Empower them to take over our places. But don't patronize em. Don't baby em. Look at em eyeball-to-eyeball and listen to the youngsters. Listen to their heart. Listen to their heartbeat. Cause nobody listen in the house. Nobody listen in the school. Nobody listen in the church. You might think in church somebody would listen but someone's always standin over them talking at them. Nobody listen to them on the corner . . . I'm probably the oldest person in this room and I'm still learnin everyday about life from 15- and 16-year-olds."

Jack concludes, "We're comin together and doin this extended family. We got the strength of the motherland leadin us. Tell the truth cause the truth really will set you free . . . this is jus what it is. This is the solution right here. All the politicians, police, n preachers try to figure out something that they really don't wanna know about. The fact is, we're all spiritually connected." Jack takes his first pause in his harangue. He breathes deep and with confidence attests, "This is the solution. Pack your bags n lets fly. I'm out." With that, Jack walks out of the room.

Dr. Marshall steps to the front and in a calm monotone starts explaining that "We've been doing these meetings since 1987 and uh, Jack is the fire." Marshall talks for a while about the program and then brings to the front several young people who are visiting from college. He asks them to talk about their experiences.

Driving home, I think about Jack's sermon. Even though he told me that he is not a preacher, I swear I went to church tonight. I wonder how the visitors received his message. Was he too hardcore? I recorded his talk verbatim because he was in the zone; he was repetitive and passionate, and that is Jack. I appreciate Jack's obsessive fervor because it does take his level of commitment to address the crisis on these streets. But I am not convinced that his lecture was effective. Tonight's talk felt a bit self-righteous and condescending, though I am sure that Jack does not care if he came off that way—yet I do.

I do not doubt that Jack's the best because everyone I talk to tells me that he is. I do, however, want to get underneath his messianic persona. It has to be more complicated than just being a miracle worker. With these questions, I read a few essays that his students wrote about him and speak directly with a young man he helped. I learn that Jack is rare; however, his students believe that some aspects of his approach are valid for *all* educators. I turn to their voices now.

Tough Love

Jack has an unruly style and is missing teeth; he has a raspy voice and a lingering cough. Still, I see people rush to give him a hug, line up to talk with him, and sit crying in his arms. Some of these people are lifers at San Quentin State Penitentiary, some are grandmothers, and some are 14-year-olds at juvenile hall. But all of them, young and old, call him dad.

This is because "he gives all his heart," says one of his students, and "most of his money" to young people who are locked up. I am told Jack buys them "underwear, smell-goods [deodorant], clothes, toothpaste, everything." When they get out, Jack tries to help them get a job and encourages them to speak at YGC. As a result, he is the closest thing many of these teenagers have to a father. One student, who is currently locked up for the nineteenth time, tells me, "Jack's my father, for-real for-real. He knows my family and all about my life." Another echoes this: "The only person visitin me in CYA [California Youth Authority] was Jack. He's the only person in the world I trust. I don't even trust my family but I trust him . . . that man's my dad."

The notion of Jack as "father" is paramount. The entire March 2001 edition of *YO! Youth Outlook*[5] is dedicated to Jack. The heading on the magazine reads, "You Make Us Feel Loved, Jack—Father's Day Meditations on the Father of Juvenile Hall." In the introduction, the students write, "Jacqua works 24/7 as a youth counselor at the hall and on the street—leading discussion groups by night, doing one-on-one counseling by day. Jacqua acts variously as court-room advocate, disciplinarian, spiritual advisor and teacher. Most importantly, he helps each kid find a reason to get up in the morning. For this, dozens of young people look upon Jack as the father they may never have had." A number of young people wrote essays about Jack and I quote two of them here.

Ladie Terry explains the way Jack supported her: "When Jack realized that I was in desperate need of money, he went out of his way to help me find a job, then hired me himself as a peer counselor for juveniles who were freshly out of lock-up . . . He sacrificed his time for me and made me feel important. When I was in an awful car accident, Jack visited me in the hospital . . . when I was discharged . . . Jack stopped what he was doing to get me to the house safely. He checked on me every week, either by phone or in person. He made sure I had twenty dollars in my pocket because he knew I couldn't work, and he constantly told me to be strong. When I needed to talk, cry or be angry, Jack was there. I don't know how he did it and helped others at the same time, but Jack was always loyal to me." She concludes that Jack taught her "love is something you do, not just something you say."

When Shahim El-Arkbark was incarcerated at YGC he did not want any-thing to do with white people, including Jack. Yet today he calls Jack his friend and teacher. He explains, "I first met Jack through a friend here at Juvenile Hall. We were sitting in the program area and my friend said to me, 'This is Jack. Now tell him all that ol' Black Power you be talkin' . . . I'd always thought, the white man is my enemy, [but] I don't think anyone could talk with Jack Jacqua for five minutes and not feel the great spiritual power that he possesses. After becoming the man's friend and student, I can't leave his side."

These young people discuss the reasons why Jack is effective. The themes that come out of the article are informative: Jack makes the students feel loved, he is constantly there when they need him, he helps them get jobs, and he has a spiritual presence that makes them believe in themselves. This notion is reinforced during a conversation I have with one of his students, Kareem.

Kareem explains that Jack gave him a sense of empowerment: "Jack has this amazing thing which is picking people out at the end of meetings" at

YGC. When Kareem was locked up, Jack would often look over at him and say, "He looks like he wants to speak." Though Kareem was shy, he wanted to talk and somehow Jack picked up on that and every week challenged Kareem: "Say something, speak from your heart, whether it's just to say hey, I'm still here." Kareem developed his speaking skills so much that, upon his release, he represented the Omega Boys Club in a meeting with Congresswoman Nancy Pelosi in Washington, DC. Significantly, Jack urged Kareem to speak and be a leader amongst his peers. Jack never stereotyped Kareem, never had low expectations of him. This was drastically different from the teachers Kareem encountered at school.

When Kareem was young, he was placed into special education for having severe learning disabilities. Experts in the school system diagnosed him as handicapped, saying he was incapable and stupid, and needed Ritalin. When he was 15, this medication stopped his heart and he almost died. His foster father encouraged him to remain in special education so he could receive additional money each month from the state. "I was told by everyone I knew that I was not special. Then I came to Omega and was told, 'who are you *not* to be special?'"

Through the Omega Boys Club, Kareem realized that he had never been retarded, but merely lacked a desire to learn. Now, he wants to return to the schools he attended so he can tell them: "Look what you said I couldn't do. You need to maybe question your methods now because I've basically just shattered everything that you've written off about me!" Kareem was born inside the penitentiary, identified as slow, and, against these odds, recently graduated from the University of Memphis. He has returned to San Francisco to work at the Omega Boys Club. I try to get Kareem to help me understand Jack's role in his development.

When Kareem first met Jack in 1998 he was impressed because he "knew the slang, he knew the lingo . . . and he further let me know that he cared." Kareem grins as he tells me Jack would say things like, "What's crackin, man?" Kareem would think, "What does *he* know about what's crackin?" Then he nods emphatically, "He knows about what's crackin!"

Kareem explains that out of all the adults at Omega, in the beginning, he clung to Jack. On Tuesday nights at the family meeting, Jack would bring Kareem sandwiches and "that probably was all I had to eat that entire day" because "back then times was hard." Jack cared for him unconditionally and for Kareem that was shocking. However, Jack was *never* easy on him.

Kareem believes Jack is effective because he has a "hardcore" approach. He says, Jack will "give you a checkup from the neck-up." In these moments, Jack can be very harsh. Kareem imitates Jack: "What the hell are you doin? What the fuck is goin on?" When Kareem set goals for himself but did not follow through, Jack would get furious and would never accept Kareem's excuses. He shakes his head, smiles, and says that Jack always gives "tough love." According to Kareem, this means that he will not baby anyone, but instead "gets you to a place where you can do it for yourself." Kareem clarifies with a metaphor: "It's like he'll take you as a tweety bird to get you to see that you're an eagle and that you can spread your wings and fly on your own." Kareem concludes that Jack's ability to empower others is "what makes him amazing."

I tell Kareem that I recognize Jack gets remarkable results, but I want to discover how this happens. "It's the realness," he answers, but I ask for clarification. "He knows young people. He sympathizes with young people. He walks with young people." Kareem leans in and shares: "That's how Jesus was. He walked with the people, he talked with the people, he struggled with the people, he knew the concerns and the pain. That is the type of example that Jack is followin." Kareem is very clear: "in order to do this work you have to be in there with them, you have to know the thinking, you have to know that you're not better but you know better."

The reason for Jack's success is simple: teach by example. Jack taught Kareem to "stay dedicated, committed" and always be of "service" in response to the needs of the oppressed. Kareem learned these lessons by watching Jack: "He is non-stop. He's passionate about it and when you're passionate about it, you don't complain, you don't get tired. You don't throw your hands up when it's real and it's inside." Then Kareem starts laughing, adding that Jack told him teaching consciousness is like selling a vacuum cleaner: "You don't want to give too much information. Just tell em the truth about it and don't force it on em." I nod, but I have more questions.

I prod Kareem about Jack's role as a white man in this struggle for Black liberation. I think my question offends him because he gets very stern: "Who is he *not* to know how we think and talk? There are not many Jacks in the world so you have to know him to love him. You have to understand, once you know him, you don't see a white man." I nod. "You see a man," he states, "doin the work of humanity!"

Kareem is not the only person to tell me Jack transcends his race, nor is he the first person to compare Jack to Jesus Christ. Countless people shared these same sentiments with me. Aunty Marsha, for instance, urged me to understand: "He walks by your side just like the Lord. If you fall down and you can't walk he'll carry you the rest of the way over the finish line." Recently someone asked Marsha about Jack's nationality and she replied: "If Jesus came back, would they ask what color he is? If he is doing God's work, his race does not matter."

At first, the idea that Jack's race is irrelevant made me uneasy. But in every encounter I have had with Jack, his spirit seems so genuine and his approach is so street-tough that I have been surprised. The people he works with—hardcore, thugged-out brothers and sisters who do not even like white people—testify to his greatness. Whenever I see these interactions, I am awestruck. It is undeniable: people throughout the neighborhood love Jack. When he walks down Third Street in Hunters Point, folks on the street corner stop whatever they are doing to give Jack respect. Even in prisons, his presence is remarkable. "He is the only person I know," explains one colleague, "who can and does walk through the yard at San Quentin State Penitentiary completely alone." When Jack stands with his African-American comrades, he seems to be one of them. This is the topic of our second interview.

The Spirit

In our second conversation, I want to get a clearer understanding of Jack's story. What made this white man a radical freedom fighter? But during our interview Jack does not share many details about his upbringing. To get a complete history, I have to rely on his words along with other sources.

Jack grew up in Los Angeles and his father was a Hollywood agent. He enlisted in the army after graduating from UCLA. After the army, he became an organizer. "I've had quite a history of being a social activist and I was actually a union organizer for organized labor in Los Angeles for several years n went through some major events with AFL-CIO as a youngster." But, he continues, "I left the union because they were thinking that I was bringing too many angry Black men into the union." Then, when the Watts riots occurred, Jack was "that white man that let Black people in the house to make sure that they were protected and safe," explains Kareem. At some point after this, Jack went to seminary and studied to be a minister. When Jack was in his twenties, he moved to the Bay Area and gravitated to the "scene of the late '60s in Berkeley." He associated with Glide Memorial Church in San Francisco, a "church of liberation," which feeds 3,000 people per day. Jack explains that at the crux of everything he does is a longstanding commitment to "social change."

I ask Jack if any particular incident crystallized his commitment to the struggle. "No," he responds. He leans back in his chair and folds his arms. "I just think it's part of one's understanding of life. Whenever a person figures it out, some people don't figure it out till later on. I figured it out at a younger age." I prod him to describe how he figured it out. His answer is abrupt: "I don't like that question."

Recognizing Jack's unwillingness to talk about himself, I ask about race in general. In this line of work, does a person's race matter? He shakes his head. After all his years in the field, he believes "it's the spirit" of the person that makes the difference. "Anybody can do this work. Anybody can be a soldier for change. Anybody can be a revolutionary." I nod. "If you've got the right spirit and keep stuff real, it doesn't make any difference who you are—color, gender—it doesn't make any difference."

Perhaps this is counterintuitive. "Some folks say that if it's a young Black male in their twenties (just using that as an example), they're felt more by youngsters. I think it depends on the individual. In some cases that's correct, that's true." But "certain middle-class college-oriented Black students seem to think that in order to get a foothold in this business of change that we're talking about, that somehow they feel because they happen to be African-American, the youngsters will pay more heed to their message." Jack is to the point: "In reality, I've never really seen that." Most important is "the message, the spirit, the walk."

Jack does not care who gives this message; it could come, for instance, from the Nation of Islam. For Jack, the point is that the teaching must include a critical analysis of the system: "It's listening to a message of somebody who's been to jail and truthfully has understood how America and its social system and the inequality and there's no justice. Youngsters are ready for folks like that." The youth Jack works with already feel the oppression of this society. Naturally, they are intrigued by topics—rooted in social justice—that relate to their circumstances and force them to think critically about the system.

Jack is an ally of the oppressed. He reveals that since "I happen to under-stand" oppression, "I can be understood." Jack says his alliance with the struggles of African-Americans allows him to communicate effectively with them. And his connection is not to African-Americans in general, but to Black people in San Francisco in particular. He explains, "It's not enough to be down for the cause; you've got to be down for a particular community. If you're just committed to the cause or youth in general, you won't be able to make a steady impact over time. It's not enough to be a good teacher and skip around from job to job. You got to get some roots somewhere so you can make a real impact." I am reminded of the ways people describe Jack as an institution in Hunters Point. Since Jack knows generations of African-Americans in San Francisco, he is able to reach and teach them. In other words, because of his close association with a particular group and location, his activism is not futile or idealistic; it is rooted to sustainable change. At this moment, I realize Jack embodies a *pedagogy of commitment*.

In many ways, it seems Jack has proven himself as a genuine partner of the oppressed. In these years of service, he has gained a unique perspective. As he puts it, "God has given me that honor to feel and understand the word *oppression*. However, nobody can feel another person, really. They can only feel themselves. They walk in their own shoes. Live in their own skin." Jack understands that he is not able to have someone else's experiences, but he is able to recognize the system of which he is part. "You can feel the society, you can feel the racism, you can feel the classism." I completely agree.

Unfortunately, Jack's perspective is rare. I have always wondered how the topic of racism can evade white people when we are the ones who created it and perpetuate it. And how can people feel detached from classism when we are all integral parts of the economic (dis)order? I realize that privilege gives people the mirage of irresponsibility, but all forms of oppression are intercon-nected. Thus, Jack's position in the struggle for equity is logical and valid.

Jack has accomplished what few people, let alone a white man, dare to undertake. And his status in the community is phenomenal. A youth tells me, "Jack has one heck of a reputation." And Jack is so popular that "it takes an hour" to walk two blocks, says Aunty Marsha. She tells me that, when Jack comes by the projects, teenagers always approach him: "Hey, Jack, how ya doin? Jack, my court date's coming up. Jack, would you come to court with me? Jack this. Jack that." Though Jack will receive a barrage of requests, the youth know that if he promises something, he will make it happen. Jack is extremely reliable. This status reaches from the streets into the courtroom. He is well known among judges and public defenders—often they will seek his advice about a young person on trial.

Jack teaches four different classes a week in the county jail, and twice a week at the Youth Guidance Center. He visits inmates at San Quentin on the weekends, is the spiritual advisor for *The Beat Within*,[6] has an office in the Public Defender's Office, and also works with Omega at Downtown High School and Everett Middle School. Additionally, "I'm in court every morning." Jack's schedule is so intense that Aunty Marsha wonders "if he sleeps in that little room at juvenile hall, that room he call an office."

On most Saturday nights Jack is in juvenile hall talking with his students. He does not do this because of some grave responsibility, but because it makes him happy. "I'm not interested in having too many conversations on a social level with adults. I haven't for many, many years . . . I'm not interested in the bourgeois culture like that. I'd rather just go up and listen" to the youth inside the hall. "It gives me some inner peace and hopefully by them listening to me, that creates some peace inside of them." In Jack's perspective, healing is a reciprocal act. So is teaching. Jack is a student of the teenagers he works with. "They've taught me how to live, how to survive, how to deal with my anger, how to deal with my pain." Echoing the other community-based educators, he says, "I learn every day from youngsters."

Jack describes these young people as "hungry. More innocent than they appear. Full of pain. Very angry. Basically very little hope." This form of despair comes in all shades and economic backgrounds, but Jack is clear that "in this land" African-American "brothers" and "sisters" are "just trying to survive in a very classist culture and a very classist society in an extremely classist city of San Francisco." Given these structural constraints, the goal is "all about empowerment. It's all about change." Jack wants his students to "take over their life. Take over their community. Self-determination." He is clear: "I don't hold hands. It's to empower people to take over their own life. Like I always say, I never go after anybody . . . Call me if you need me. But I'm not holding your hand. Because if you've been trained right, if you've been coached right, then you need to be able to do right. If you need another lesson or if something goes wrong, you misjudge a situation, call me." Though Jack is with young people every step of the way, his perspective is tough: he wants them to be independent and self-sufficient. Kareem described this as being developed into an eagle.

Although this transformation occurs because of Jack, it also has a lot to do with how he organizes the Omega classes at juvenile hall. Jack explains, "If indeed it's correct that peers maybe listen to other peers more than anybody, then we actually go even a step further." Jack explains that they rely on "peers that are in custody, but who have some knowledge and who we believe are on the right track for this particular moment" to reach out and teach each other. The result: young people learn to be leaders. "They get a real sense for the first time of being a real leader." This reminds me of the way Jack asked Lee to say the prayer at the end of the evening. Jack says, "There's some real leadership and some real peer counseling that's really being taught."

As an organization, the Omega Boys Club is forthright in its goal: it wants young people to go to college. Jack does not necessarily consider this success. "It's okay to go to school and it's a big celebration when certain people go to college and many stories that are amazing that occur and happen, and that's all good. But what you know, you owe. You can't forget where you came from." The most critical part, at least for Jack, is that the students have consciousness and a commitment to the struggle. "The bottom line is taking over self, being who you are and understanding you're a strong African queen, a strong African king." Furthermore, Jack wants them to "fight the power by your footsteps, not just by your mouthpiece. It's your actions that count." This type of success is deeply connected to activism. "And that's where education comes in," he continues. Jack "learned a lot from the Black Panther struggle" and recommends "young social activists study the rise and fall of the Black Panther Party. We're tryin to empower people to do *that* work. But do it real." Here Jack reminds me of Rudy's insistence on keepin things real. I also think back to Marsha's insistence that Jack only deals with real people. This is because, Jack continues, "youngsters know who's real . . . They know which adult's real or fake. I don't have any time for fake folks. I'm lookin for real folks and that's what these youngsters are lookin for."

I ask Jack what types of young people he likes to work with. A teenager he saw yesterday "was really angry when he came into court for a detention hearing. I like to see kids angry . . . that's the type of kid who I want to go at because that's the one that's got emotion flowing. He hasn't given up. He's fightin somethin. That's the one I want to go to, straight up, eyeball-to-eyeball: What's up man? What you angry for? Tell me. Talk to me . . . I'll bet he'll tell me *ain't nobody going at me like that*" because "adults don't do that."

For Jack, redemption is by any means necessary. He does not pay attention to politics or rules. For instance, "When I go into schools, I do a prayer . . . I never thought that I would say that Moral Majority family value, but that's real too . . . You don't have to put a name on it and quote some book. Just say a prayer . . . and there's something wrong when you can't do that." In fact, one of the primary ways Jack reaches youth is through prayer. He finds that calling forth the higher power creates unity among the students; it is almost a form of communion within juvenile hall or even in a high school classroom. Jack believes prayer takes the message from the head to the heart. He understands that he is "supposed to be" teaching and counseling inside prisons because "certain people on this spiritual level are waiting, not for me, but for the message." Jack's spirituality is essential to his success.

I experience the immense power of Jack's spirit the second time I attend a family meeting at the Omega Boys Club center. The following lines come from my field notes.

> Thirty of us sit, dispersed throughout the multi-purpose room. A child sits next to his father. Three teenage women huddle together. A man in the corner of the room, who was shot multiple times, is now in a wheelchair. The participants talk about the trauma, drama, and nihilism that consumes the street and say that they have come here tonight by bus, car, and foot, to connect with each other in the spirit of Omega.
>
> A newcomer, Paul, is 14 years old and admits to the group that after seeing all his "older homies killed" he does not "expect to live too long." He tells us that most Black men will not survive past the age of 19. This fact, coupled with his life experiences, has convinced him that he must prepare to die. His candid nonchalant attitude stirs the room.
>
> Participants recount that they have often felt the same way. Everyone tries to convey to Paul that his life is important and has great value. Ms. Estell steps in and says that tonight's meeting is just for him. She continues, "we love you enough to use tonight's meeting to try and help you. Paul, you can step into a room with people who do not know you and be shown love, support, and care." Following this, Marshall brings the meeting to a close and tells us it is time for the evening's prayer. Kareem yells out into the hall, "Jack, time for prayer!" Seconds later, Jack appears.
>
> We stand in a circle, holding hands. Jack starts, "It's not so much what is said, but what is felt." His tone is commanding, "We rebuke hopelessness!" He repeats even louder, "We rebuke hopelessness!" I have never heard Jack talk with this much force. He is clear, articulate, and demanding. As he speaks, I can feel the pulses in the hands I hold. Honestly, I feel as though he is casting out demons with his every word. I feel what he is saying much more than I hear it and his prayer overwhelms me.
>
> I do not know how these words sound, or how they will be received by the secular formats of schooling, but I am recording my experience; it is highly spiritual, transformative, and empowering. This is what everyone is talking about when they speak of Jack's spiritual transcendence.

Saving Lives

On a Wednesday night in May of 2006, Cowboy, Dr. Harry, Randy, Jack, and I walk slowly toward the B-1 unit at juvenile hall. Cowboy is a former Black Panther, Dr. Harry is an affiliate of Omega, and Randy was just released from San Quentin Penitentiary. The silence between us is eerie and I do not know what is going on. Jack says to all of us that "We have a lot to talk about tonight."

Two groups of youth sit waiting for us in the program area of B-1. The B-1 unit is for first-time offenders; these youth are young (some only 10 years old), and they are all wearing white sweatshirts. There are also a dozen older youth from B-4; as usual, they have on their green sweatshirts. As is customary, we go around to each table and check in with the students, but Jack cuts this short. He goes to the center of the circle and starts talking about Marcus.

Jack tells us that Marcus was murdered last night. Many of the youth look enraged; this is someone they knew. In the next hour the youth talk about him: the intelligent, articulate, good-looking 17-year-old with "all the potential in the world." In January he was shot but survived; in April he was shot again and lived. Marcus' mother was saving money to move out of the projects. Before the first shooting, Marcus moved in with his grandparents in Suisun City in an attempt to stay out of the crossfire in his neighborhood. But when his grandparents became ill, he was forced to return to the war zone. "It's a war," one of the students says, and "you don't have to be in a gang to be a target."[7]

Jack tells the students to keep talking but "I don't want you to speak from the neck up." He places his open hand on the center of his chest. "Speak from here and be deep with it. Keep it real." A student addresses his peers: "Jack always askin me why I'm so stressed. I couldn't figure it out; then I started thinkin about how my mom has been in and out of jail my whole life. My dad was locked up for 3 years." This young man is trying to piece together the reason for his pain in an attempt to heal and assemble a future for himself. Another youth raises his hand. In a nasal tone he imitates his teacher at YGC: "One point if I say your hair is nice, five points if you stay awake." He shifts his tone and asks, "Are we just caged animals that can't do better? Don't know no better? That teacher thinks so low of us, think we ain't smart, buncha monkeys!" Heads nod.

Jack steps in. "I was on the phone with Marcus just hours before he was killed." Jack was urging Marcus to come to the family meeting. Jack shakes his head, "I was trying to save his life." Then he advises the teenagers, "Read the Bible: B.I.B.L.E.—cause it stands for Basic Instruction Before Leaving Earth. Or read the Qur'an if it'll help ya." As mentioned earlier, Jack believes politics cannot solve the problems in the hood, but spirituality might.

A month later, I am back at the hall. It is June 19, 2006—Juneteenth. Although today commemorates the physical freedom of African-Americans, Jack still sees the need to fight for their liberation. According to Jack, this struggle includes people "behind the wall" who are victims to the latest form of slavery: the prison industrial complex.

I arrive to the hall a bit early so I meander in the parking lot. A new silver sign, placed on the front of the building, reads "Juvenile Justice Center." Although it is evening, the sky is still blue. It is absolutely beautiful outside. But inside YGC—rain or shine—it always looks the same. The young men and women inside these walls do not see the light of day; their sky is the ceiling. I am reminded of this as I listen to one of the guest speakers later on that night.

Toward the end of the evening Jack turns to an African-American woman who came to visit: "Do you want to talk?" She nods. "There was once a farmer," she tells the youth in a graceful tone, "who placed a number of mosquitoes in a box and put some holes in the lid so they could breathe." She smiles and takes a deep breath before continuing. "In the first week the mosquitoes were jumping so high that they kept hitting the lid. By the second week, they learned not to jump so high. The farmer noticed this so he took the lid off." She looks around the room and asks, "Do you know what happened?" She tells us that the "mosquitoes did not even realize the lid was no longer there because they had been conditioned to believe that if they jumped too high, they would be hurt. Even when the lid was off and they could leave the box and become free, they stayed in the box because they were no longer able to perceive freedom."

Jack goes to the center of the circle and says: "Look into the mirror at four in the morning, when it's just you and God." He raises his hand and clenches his fist: "Look in the mirror, ask yourself the tough questions, and tell yourself the truth . . . Get your fears out there where you can deal with them. Deal with your pain. Deal with your anger. Take off that mask you're all wearing!"

Jack goes on to talk about the tough persona and turf drama. Jack declares, "Fuck Hunters Point!" He shouts, "If anybody asks you what turf you come from, tell them Africa!" He pauses and his voice calms: "If we unite we could have our own schools. We could build up our own businesses. It wouldn't matter how many prisons they built, cause we wouldn't be in em. I really believe that if we unite, stop fighting over crumbs, we really could do anything." With that, he utters, "Amen."

6

WHAT DOES (NOT) WORK

Dereca, Rudy, Victor, and Jack are determined to work with the marginalized students who are disregarded by schools and society. Amidst gunshots and dysfunctional family situations, these four community-based educators demonstrate that personal agency and collective action are always within reach. Scid, a student in Leadership Excellence (LE), had dropped out of high school and seemed content to spend his time selling dope, doing time, and dodging bullets. Thanks to LE, Scid discovered he was not a thug, but a king, not a drug dealer, but an academic. Other students I introduced throughout the portraits also changed their lives. Evangela was the first in her family to graduate from high school. Cloteal went from dropping out of school to dropping back in with intensity—becoming valedictorian despite (and she would say because of) the tragedies in her life. Kareem went from being in special education and prison, to being a college graduate. These first-hand testimonies of success are meant to stop you in your tracks, as each of these students defies the stereotype. Fortunately, their stories are not unique. Within Leadership Excellence (LE), United Playaz (UP), the Youth Task Force (YTF), and the Omega Boys Club, countless young people find a home: a place of solace at the intersection of the streets and school.

When Hope Disappears

Although these educators each exemplify success, they are not miracle workers and they face many challenges. Clearly, many students do not make a positive turnaround. For every story of a Scid, Evangela, Cloteal, or Kareem succeeding against the odds, we hear of someone else who continues to live a destructive lifestyle.

It is an ongoing challenge for these educators to create a genuine bond with each young person in their organization. Though they all emphasize relationships as key to their success, they cannot always sustain those connections. They recognize that their particular style might alienate some students while it can engage others. Jack's tough love approach probably would not have worked with Salim, the young man who nearly beat his teacher to death. In fact, Jack's tactics might have even angered Salim further. Salim needed Victor's soft style and found comfort in the YTF. Similarly, Rudy's hardcore street demeanor makes him unapproachable for some students and teachers at Balboa High School. Meanwhile, Dereca and Victor sometimes do not come across as "street" enough to their students who romanticize the thug life. So, not surprisingly, no one-size approach fits all students, and it is always a setback when an educator cannot help a young person. Yet, for all of the educators, the ultimate failure—quite literally—is to see a young person in their program murdered. This does happen: at UP an entire wall is filled with photos of deceased teenagers. So, after decades of doing this work, all Jack really wants is for his students to stay alive and free.

Another difficulty for these educators, though less extreme than keeping students alive, is engaging parents. Dereca has a parent on her board of directors, but I saw very little parent involvement in any of the four programs. Rudy hosts a cookout for mothers whose children have died, but it is not explicitly for UP families. In fact, I rarely saw any of the students' guardians, grandparents, or parents at an event. Since UP calls itself a family, it would seem that each teenager's own family members would have a stronger presence within the group, but this was not the case. Victor experiences very little parent involvement because his students are often separated from their families and live at group homes or in foster care. On one occasion, I attended a family food night for YTF members in which students' relatives participated in a wraparound services therapy model that appeared quite innovative. But, during all my time with them, I believe this activity only took place once. I heard Jack mention his students' grandmothers but I never saw them at juvenile hall—though students' families did attend the annual Omega Kwanzaa celebration in the neighborhood.

Though parent participation was not a strong part of these programs, I never heard the young people's families mentioned in a demeaning or degrading way. This is in stark contrast to a recent encounter I had with a superintendent. After reviewing his district's suspension data, we discussed areas for reform. To each suggestion I made, he seemed to have a similar response: it is not the school's fault that the parents are not raising their kids right. This type of rationale, even when based on facts, undermines the powerful role families can play to improve education (Brown, 2011; Fabricant, 2010; Henderson, Mapp, Johnson, & Davies, 2006).

Nevertheless, it is quite interesting that none of the educators spoke of parent engagement as a tool for effectively reaching and teaching marginalized students. Perhaps this remains a challenge for them since many of these young people have no stable family unit. Given that research suggests parent involvement is "one of the most powerful mechanisms to improving learning" (Weiss, as cited in Wilson, 2008, p. 26), what happens when a student like Kareem has a parent in prison? Quite simply: educators must seek out other ways to help these students achieve academically. The community-based educators become preoccupied with creating a family ethos *within* their programs so students have a system of support.

I also noted other, more personal, challenges. Rudy encourages his students to attend college but he never did; he lives with this obvious discrepancy between what he wants for UP youth and what he wants for himself. Also, having a notorious pimp—Fillmore Slim—speak to the youth could present a dangerous example. Slim decries pimping, but it did make him rich and famous. At best, having him speak can deter students from that lifestyle. At worst, it can send a mixed message and glorify pimping. Another challenge I noted is that Rudy and Victor do not sternly enforce high expectations; instead, they encourage unconditional love. Here, Dereca and Jack might challenge them.

Dereca has personal experiences with street life, but she sees it as part of her past. She is not active on street corners like Rudy and Jack, and to some students her approach can seem a bit condescending. Victor does not have street experience and at times he can come across as a bit of a new age hippie. This intimate approach works well with the small number of students within the YTF, but I wonder if he would be as effective with a larger group. Also, I wonder whether teenagers sometimes take advantage of Victor's flexibility. Finally, Jack emphasizes knowledge of self to understand one's calling, but he is vague about how this relates to himself. He does not talk about his background and seems detached from his own story, though he lectures about the African motherland.

Overall, then, I did see double standards, inconsistencies, and flaws, but this is hardly surprising. Under the microscope of research, both the glory and the mess of this kind of work become clearer. In fact, discrepancies make each educator more genuine and valid, especially when we think about how to replicate and transfer their lessons. In the next section I describe four key approaches that together can constitute a model, and then 10 tools for anyone interested in being part of the solution in the lives of urban youth.

Cultivating Resistance

Dereca, Rudy, Victor, and Jack break the cycle of social reproduction in the lives of their students by fostering *social resistance*. To accomplish this, they rely on four key pedagogies. Stated briefly, Dereca has a *pedagogy of communication*.

She enjoys dialogue and is a gifted speaker. Whether she is working one-on-one with a student or addressing nearly 100 youth, she creates space for honest and critical discussion. She does this by being vulnerable about her own life and is not afraid to raise controversial topics. As a result, in Dereca's class, students want to talk. Rudy creates a *pedagogy of community* in the way he lives his life and directs UP. In this community, people of all ages are involved, but the young people are the leaders. He is the ear hustler, advocate, and inspiration. His street style shows high-risk youth that it is okay to embrace the hood as long as they do so to uplift the people.

Victor embodies a *pedagogy of compassion*. His mystical orientation allows him to connect with young people who have life experiences different from his own. He approaches them with a full heart, soft eyes, and open ears. And then, he asks introspective questions and encourages them to tell their stories, speak their pain, and heal. The youth become spokespeople, leaders, and agents of change. Finally, Jack shows a *pedagogy of commitment*. For decades he has taught young people who are on street corners, in prisons, and inside schools. His duty is unstoppable: Black liberation through mental and spiritual emancipation. This is Jack's life, his calling, and his mission. Although many of us cannot replicate his constant dedication, he teaches—through his actions—that, if educators and organizers show enough commitment, no child will be left behind.

I highlighted each person's primary pedagogy in the portraits, but they all use all of them to varying degrees. Dereca is not the only educator in the group who emphasizes dialogue; it is also critical for Victor and Jack. Although Rudy has the strongest community connection, they all know about their students' neighborhoods and they all try to create a sense of camaraderie within their programs. Compassion, in the form of nonjudgmental love, is a common attribute. For Dereca, Rudy, and Jack, this love is tough, no nonsense; for Victor, however, it is very empathetic. Each educator is committed, so this quality applies to them all, but Jack has been doing this work the longest and his work ethic operates nonstop. Thus, although each educator has a primary approach, they are not exclusive; rather, all four are common to successful praxis.

In combination, the approaches of *communication, community, compassion,* and *commitment* demonstrate a relational style of teaching that cuts straight to the very definition of pedagogy: the art and science of teaching. Dereca, Rudy, Victor, and Jack emphasize teaching as art, not merely science; education as verb, not simply noun; and learning as emotional, not just cognitive. At the very center, they all personify the belief that education is foremost an act of love. This finding echoes the work of Lynch, Baker, and Lyons (2009). Though their research was not on schools or educators per se, their concept of "nurturing capital" helps describe what I found within the community-based organizations. According to these scholars, social change is based upon acts of love and solidarity, which "involves active support for others, not just passive empathy" (p. 1). Caring, in this milieu, embodies a reciprocal and relational act(ion) in which everyone involved is transformed through a humanizing process of respect (see also Lawrence-Lightfoot, 1999). Thus, the ways the community-based educators are able to cultivate resistance among youth—vis-à-vis love—is situated within a larger framework of equality.

Although love is a central, transformative force, they do use other tactics. It is interesting to note that Jack and Rudy know each other (when Rudy was an unruly youngster, Jack worked at his middle school) but none of the others have ever met. Yet their strategies resound in unison as ways to redirect the trajectory of *at-risk* youth into *at-promise* individuals (Weiner, 2006).

They share 10 values, which become methods for unlocking young people's potential.

1. *A Calling—this is not a job, but a way of life.*

    Dereca, Rudy, Victor, and Jack feel called to work with marginalized students; they describe it as an honor and a privilege. Their outlook on young people is asset-based and positive—and this constantly comes through in their pedagogies. These educators are excited, passionate, and committed beyond the job because they believe in the teenagers in their care.

2. *Family—generated through love that is tough, real, nuanced, and consistent.*

    These educators and the youth do not describe an organization, but believe they are part of a family. Their settings feel like home; they treat the young people as if they are their own children. Therefore graduation is a misnomer, since, unlike school, almost everyone stays connected, as multiple generations of students in an expanding community. For this type of cohesiveness to be real, the educators demonstrate that they love their students unconditionally, are always listening, and, as a result, have genuine relationships with them. Also, they always share meals with the teenagers; food is integral to any setting, and so is music.

3. *Listening—"ear hustlin" is keen listening in which every word, pause, and inference has meaning.*

    These educators emphasize the importance of listening deeply to young people. They listen to show they care and their listening helps them gauge the interests and motivations of the young people they are trying to help. It is the first and most critical step in the communication process, allowing honest dialogue to ensue and learning to thrive.

4. *High Expectations—young people are capable and brilliant . . . just misled.*

    These educators see youth as having great potential to succeed in any chosen area, including academics. They refuse to accept a dumbed-down curriculum, finding it oppressive. They do not dismiss troubled youth as being intellectually inferior or incapable, but just the opposite. When given a chance, these teenagers often show extraordinary leadership skills. In these programs, each person is seen in a positive light—and the programs' language, expectations, philosophies, and strategies emphasize this.

5. *Reciprocal Teaching—learning is multi-faceted and multi-directional because power is collective.*

   The community-based educators are, in their own way, teachers; this is simple enough. But what makes them good teachers is more complex. They take on this role by constantly being students of their students—and they constantly improve their lessons based on the needs of the youth. Instead of being the "all-knowing" authoritarian-style teacher, these educators demonstrate the benefits of student-centered instruction.

6. *Relevant Curriculum—learning is alive and based on reality.*

   These educators create curricula based on their students' immediate needs and interests. Doing this can take the form of discussing the latest video game or rap song, or even a recent murder. The educators then relate this personal context to larger issues of social justice.

7. *Teaching for Social Justice—sharing knowledge and tools to dismantle oppressive systems.*

   These educators exemplify *conscientization*: developing a consciousness to transform reality (Freire, 1970). The reason this learning paradigm is so effective is that many troubled youth already feel the impact of oppression. And, because of this, many of them are already rebels, just rebels without a cause. These educators make use of relevant topics (e.g., police brutality, gentrification, gang violence) to redirect their students. Dealing with these issues can inspire agency and motivate interest because these topics often resonate with real-life experiences. Furthermore, social justice learning gives teenagers a critical lens that is empowering; they are able to deconstruct injustices and recognize their abilities. Often, the outcome of this process is youth leadership: the students become rebels with a cause.

8. *Youth Empowerment—learning tangible lessons in personal and communal transformation.*

   These educators declare that a positive direction is possible for all disenfranchised urban students; they have the innate ability to save themselves. What they need, however, is to understand that they have a choice. More than just proclaiming high expectations for urban youth, these educators help them define positive, concrete goals. Self-fulfillment can take the form of academic excellence, social activism, public speaking, and more, but, whichever the domain, the educators encourage students to aim toward real accomplishment, which often happens as the young people turn their lives around in remarkable ways.

9. *Peer-to-Peer Learning—youth can be the greatest teachers and leaders of one another.*

   These educators learn from their students; clear reciprocity exists between teacher and student. By extension, the students also learn from and direct each other. Dereca encourages her students to speak, debate, and think critically. Allowing them to talk to one another is a form of peer-to-peer education in her classroom. For Rudy, this learning takes the form of leadership development through volunteer work and organizing. Victor encourages his students to share their stories with one another so they develop camaraderie and community. Jack's peer-to-peer education takes place inside juvenile hall, where he directs youth to talk to each other about their current state of recovery.

10. *Be Real—do you and do not front.*

Effectiveness is deeply personal and it is important, even encouraged, to have different styles. Victor's manner is clearly the softest, but he succeeds. He proves that we must find our own niche. Jack's philosophy is similar to the other educators', but he is unique because he is a white man who fights vehemently for African-Americans. He shows that white people can be allies of the oppressed as long as they have genuine commitment *with* the people. Rudy's approach is the most street tough. He is a powerful reminder of the expertise that comes with personal experience. Dereca is the only African-American in this study and the only woman. As a wife, mother, and head of LE, she has a distinctive personality that often translates into hectic juggling. She complicates the nonstop commitment that Jack and Rudy personify when they proclaim that this is their life. Dereca succeeds with urban students, but also prioritizes the needs of her own children. Further, Dereca and Jack both work primarily with African-American youth whereas Rudy and Victor serve multi-racial constituencies. Thus, the varying personalities and institutional contexts reinforce the need for strategies based upon our own characteristics and settings.

Altogether, these 10 attributes of effectiveness can serve as measures to reflect on and gauge our own practices as well as the mission and policies of any youth-serving system. Moreover, the ingredients that facilitated students' transformation inside the community-based organizations can influence any one person's relationship with a troubled teenager—and might even help improve the entire culture of a school.

But this is not a magic formula; it is a process. The educators declare that they feel called to work with youth; their teaching is based on activism and social justice. Consequently, the young people can sense the educators' realness and describe them as genuine, excited, and passionate. The educators in turn make a conscious effort to be humble, loving listeners. As a result, the students often feel special, wanted, and supported irrespective of the way they look or act. Encouragement is offered whole-heartedly without demeaning students or trying to force them to meet inappropriate standards. This positive approach also allows students to find natural roles with respect to their

peers, so individual talents for leadership emerge. Feeling increased competence, the young people begin to hold themselves up to higher expectations,
and are no longer complacent about failure. On the contrary, they have been
sparked: they believe they are capable of success, both academically and as
spokespeople for their programs and neighborhoods. Altogether, this is how
the community-based educators reach their students, and this is what they are
able to teach them.

Significantly, the common practices I discovered in the community resonate with the literature on urban education. In particular, Chenoweth (2009),
Dance (2002), and Delpit (1995) insist that urban teachers foster caring relationships with their students, learn about their students' lives outside school,
and maintain high expectations. Wolk (1998) demonstrates the viability of
classrooms that are dialogic and revolve around peer-to-peer (democratic)
teaching and learning. Ladson-Billings (1994) emphasizes the importance of
culturally relevant teaching. A decade later Ginwright (2004, 2009) is updating
this conversation: he holds that culturally relevant teaching must include contemporary realities. For many urban students, this includes issues of violence,
poverty, and racism. In order for these teenagers to succeed academically,
various scholars (Duncan-Andrade, 2010; Fine & Weis, 2003; Ginwright et
al., 2006) suggest, students must become activists within their schools and
neighborhoods. Influential education theorists (e.g., Apple, 1995; Dewey,
1938; Giroux, 1989, 2001) agree: education must be linked to empowerment.
This testament of education for empowerment is compelling, but is it realistic?
And, given the current constraints facing schools (high-stakes testing, teacher
recruitment and retention, funding, etc.), is it even a possibility?

Finding answers to these very questions is the focus of the next chapter, in
which I shift my gaze to analyze the schoolhouse and schools of education.

7

COMMUNITY-BASED URBAN EDUCATION

All across our country, we can find high-poverty high-achieving schools (Carter, 2000; Chenoweth, 2009). These "pockets of hope" (de los Reyes & Gozemba, 2002) come in many forms, but there are simply not enough of them. Despite school restructuring and a myriad of reform efforts, the failure rate of students, disproportionately low-income students of color, continues to rise (Anyon, 2005; Kozol, 1994; Oakes & Lipton, 2007; Orfield, 2004; Orfield & Kornhaber, 2001). In far too many places, teachers are not equipped to deal with the challenges of this generation; high-risk youth fall through the cracks, drop out, or are pushed out, leaving their futures dim and their choices narrow. But there is hope; despite restrictive mandates, several researchers confirm that supportive student–teacher relationships can alter a teenager's life trajectory (e.g., Conchas, 2001; Darling-Hammond, 1999; Lee, 1999; Michie, 2004). This is powerful. Classrooms can be one of the safety nets that can keep students alive and learning. In fact, the average child spends approximately 16,380 hours in school, assuming 12 years of 180 7-hour days. Some students spend more hours with their teachers than with their parents. So, given that about a third of a child's development happens in the school-house, what are the most effective tactics teachers can use to support student achievement?

The four community-based educators offer suggestions to teachers, but they are not in any form of scripted curriculum, proven method, or quick fix. As a general principle, they show that learning is a process, not a desti-nation. Accordingly, each person in this study demonstrates great flexibility and adaptability, emphasizing the importance of "reinventing" at each stage to implement an authentic emancipatory education (Darder, 2002; Freire, 1997; Mayo, 2004; McLaren, 2000).

More specifically, Dereca, Rudy, Victor, and Jack also have their own experiences with schools, which influence the particular advice they have for teachers. When Dereca first walked into McClymonds High School, she was disgusted by the low expectations. She understands that many factors are involved, but certainly teachers' attitudes, and their willingness to accept dumbed-down curricula, hinder achievement. Dereca urges classroom teachers to get to know each student so that they are able to have valid expectations. One of her suggestions to make this happen: go outside on the first day of school and get to know the people in your class.

Rudy offers a different angle, emphasizing that educators need culturally relevant lessons that deal with oppression and resistance alongside community partnerships in order to reach every student. Victor shares additional advice: philosophical questions about life have a role to play in the education of troubled youth. He suggests that deep, theoretical inquiries encourage students to consider their habits and actions. And Jack believes that urban educators, who might work in neighborhoods wrought by violence and turmoil, must be committed beyond the job. Like Dereca, he urges teachers to have high expectations, but adds that they must be consistent. In terms of curriculum, Jack wants teenagers to learn about their own story, in contrast to a Eurocentric his-story, so that students gain a sense of personal and collective responsibility (e.g., Hilliard, 1998; Zinn, 1995). As he often says, "the more you know, the more you owe."

Though these community-based educators have insightful comments for classroom teachers and viable ideas because of their rapport with youth, traditional school systems can present very different challenges. Mainstream educators must deal with limitations that these four avoid by operating programs that complement secondary schools. Dereca, for example, allocates time and funding for "youth development hours" for a 2-hour sit-down between each instructor and student. A little math shows that this may not be feasible in most schools, given current class sizes. For the most part, these educators can deliver a high degree of attention to each young person in a way that no teacher can hope to do in an overcrowded and underfunded classroom. Thus, some of what is so special about these educators will be challenging to implement in normal classroom settings.

Other practices can also be a bit contentious. These educators advocate that teachers listen to their students, but confidentiality can only go so far because teachers are mandated reporters. And prayer becomes complicated inside schools. Jack, Rudy, and Victor all make God explicit within their pedagogy. However, given the legal division between church and state, spiritual zeal would not be allowed in most classrooms, though it seems it could be helpful. A third issue is language; the words used in the neighborhood setting embrace who these young people are and the environments they live in. This communication strategy is critical and the students in these four programs do not have to code switch. However, in regular classes, African American Vernacular English (Ebonics), for example, is not accepted, and students cannot use it on the CAHSEE, California's high school exit examination. In other instances, the use of profanity is against California Education Code. And, in many schools, certain "urban" attire is prohibited—no sagging pants, no doo-rags—a rule that further scrutinizes and penalizes particular students. Therefore, many stylistic elements in the community-based organizations will not find a natural home in the current school climate.

Notwithstanding these restrictions, my findings dare those of us in formal educational settings to critique the codes of conduct that we sometimes (blindly) follow. Regardless of the latest rule or the newest policy, we must continue to ask ourselves: *What do children really need? What works and why?* And then, considering the 10 attributes of effectiveness and the educators' candid recommendations for teachers, we have to be bold and brave enough to meet students where they are, even if they are in a place that makes us uncomfortable. In the next section, I suggest programmatic and personal layers of engagement that can aid in the process of utilizing a community-based approach to schooling.

Layers of Community Engagement

At the classroom level, the community-based educators propose that teachers need bold attitudes and an encompassing vision to integrate students into the learning process in innovative ways. Many researchers have observed that, in the words of Lois Weiner (1999), "students bring behaviors grounded in their lives outside school into classrooms" (p. 80). The special case of the four educators is that there is no *outside the classroom* because the environment is the learning context; students' lives are the content. Therefore, we need to get to know our students. Here are some basic questions for teachers:

1. What neighborhoods do your students come from? How familiar are you with these areas? Where are your students' favorite local spots to eat, hang out, and shop? Have you been to any of these places?
2. What do you believe, fundamentally and universally, about *all* children? What do you believe, fundamentally and universally, about *all* students?
3. How would you describe your most difficult students? What are their dreams and aspirations? What are their lives like outside school? How are these students similar to and different from you? What have they taught you recently? What have you taught them? How do you know?

For urban high school teachers, in particular, students' external reality must shape the internal function of classrooms. This is integral to success but, again, it is only a piece of the puzzle.

In the larger school system, the dilemmas in urban education reinforce the need for cooperation because it is unrealistic to think that teachers alone can effectively meet the needs of every student. Now, more than ever, partnerships are pivotal to the academic and long-term wellbeing of students, especially those who are likely to drop out of school. Education, in the broad sense, must include innovative alliances—from social services to youth development initiatives to employment programs—that pull resources and people together in a *wraparound empowerment model*. The schoolhouse can actually serve as the hub of such activities (Anyon, 2005; Bryk, Sebring, Allensworth, Luppescu, & Easton, 2010; Warren, 2005).

Community–school partnerships can improve student achievement, at both the macro level of school structure and function, and the micro level of classroom culture and content. Building on this premise, let me suggest some additional guiding questions that teachers, staff, and school administrators can ask in order to increase their network of support:

1. What youth-serving agencies already exist in your school's neighborhood(s)?
2. What adults do the students identify as effective both in and out of school?
3. Where do families and children go to hang out and/or worship?
4. Are there any community-based educators in your area that you can bring into the school as guest speakers, instructional aids, or service providers?

Though these are just initial questions, they can lead to important collaborative initiatives that dramatically improve student achievement (Noguera, 2003).

From the community-based perspective, there are clear ways we can solve the crisis in urban education. However, to really have a sustained impact, we need a renewed commitment from institutions of higher education to help recruit and retain effective teachers. Credential programs, for instance, can engage with youth-serving organizations in new ways. Morva McDonald and her colleagues at the University of Washington offer a unique and exciting teacher training program that places pre-service teachers in community-based organizations. They found that participating in these settings helped prospective educators better understand children's lives outside school, which altered the traditional classroom relationship because they situated children as highly capable within their own context. They conclude: "The ability of teachers to see and understand children as competent individuals with knowledge and expertise, potentially enables them to reach into and across difference in ways that are central to their ability to provide high quality learning opportunities to all students" (McDonald et al., 2010, p. 47). As this example demonstrates, many kinds of links can be made between community-based organizations and teacher training programs. This union can also be forged in the recruitment of future teachers.

A small case in point: When I first started working at UC Davis, I developed an applied research program that fused together the best practices I found during my research and the specific context of local needs. UC Davis is surrounded by urban, rural, and suburban neighborhoods, and in each of these settings the achievement gaps and dropout rates are visible and discouraging. Since literacy is the gateway to academic success in all content areas, I relied on my partnership with Youth Speaks, Inc. to start a program called Sacramento Area Youth Speaks (SAYS). However, SAYS quickly adjusted from the traditional spoken word performance poetry model because of our position within the university, our unique partnerships with school districts, and our unremitting pledge to support youth voices for social change.

One of the special markers of SAYS is the training of poet-mentor educators (PMEs).[1] These 15 adults are all people of color,[1] and they range in age from 18 to 46. They represent a unique mix of nontraditional educators, community activists, hip-hop MCs, and spoken-word artists. The majority of them grew up in the Sacramento region and attended schools in the area. Each cohort of PMEs goes through a 6-week intensive training program in three core areas: critical pedagogy, curriculum development, and artistic expression. We then place the PMEs inside classrooms in residencies in which they act as partners with teachers. The PMEs have a unique rapport with students and their newfound passion for teaching is inspirational. Now, all they need is further certification. Just recently, a teacher told us this: "We need a revolution in education, and I believe that your poets might be the catalysts to get the ball rolling . . . The way I see it, poets could be encouraged to pursue a career as a teacher . . . There is a void in education, and I believe your program could fill a great portion of that. Keep up the great work, and thank you for the opportunity to participate in such an amazing program" (Jonathan Young, English language arts teacher). The PMEs signify the possible future of teacher education. But this is not about poetry, per se. Rather, it is about partnerships with a purpose. For where are our upcoming instructors? They are already in the neighborhood. Some of them can be found working in community-based organizations or after-school programs, or they might even be the big homie on the block. Wherever they are, what we need is to create bridges between credential programs and the communities that surround high-need schools so we can recruit a new generation of *community-based teachers*.

As a prime example of this on a large scale, the Grow Your Own teacher initiative (GYO) in Illinois represents a significant shift in recruiting and retaining teachers of color (Skinner, Garreton, & Schultz, 2011). For several years the Logan Square Neighborhood Association empowered mostly Latina mothers to work at their children's schools. The mothers soon realized they had key insights into teaching and learning. This impetus served as the catalyst for a unique partnership between colleges of education, community-based organizations, and public schools. "The promise of GYO as a national reform model lies in the possibilities that arise when the intimate community knowledge of the CBOs [community-based organizations] and their expertise in organizing for change is combined with the professional, pedagogical expertise of the COEs [colleges of education]" (Gillette, 2011, p. 149). After receiving ample legislative support and funding, GYO is poised to produce 1,000 diverse, community-based, certified teachers committed to teaching in low-income schools by 2016. As alternative credential programs such as Teach for America and Project Pipeline continue to privatize and monopolize the market, GYO symbolizes a wake-up call to schools of education—a real way to develop, nurture, and grow grassroots teachers en masse.

Even though public schools, in many ways, are fatally flawed, education remains our civil right. Some might say it is our last civil right, so we must demand that it is useful. As we define the usefulness of schooling in the twenty-first century, I can hear Yusef's warning that I placed at the beginning of the book: as long as young people's rage and pain is met with silence and fear, nothing will change. To assure that we advance these community-based strategies for *all* young people, we will need to come face to face with ourselves.

Liberating Our Selves

A high-quality education is one of the most valuable assets we can offer students. Therefore, it is a profession that demands the utmost creativity, thorough examination, and applied knowledge. Unfortunately, many credential programs and professional development activities do not meet this standard (Bennett, McWhorter, & Kuykendall, 2006). After a decade of NCLB, we have a dropout crisis in every major city; internationally, we are falling further and further behind on all academic indices (e.g., Darling-Hammond, 1997, 2010; Noguera, 2011). Although many advocates of education reform proclaim that they want the same things (e.g., to close the achievement gap, to increase literacy rates), there is less agreement about *how* we are going to do it. Firing teachers and closing schools is not the answer—but teaching for social justice might be.

Teachers should not be blamed for the educational catastrophe because inequality in this country is institutionalized. However, if we want teachers to be able to intentionally disrupt this pattern, they have to understand it. Providing educators with an understanding of the historical context of public education is a vital starting point. Education has been used as a tool for liberation among African-Americans in the South (Anderson, 1988; Perry, Steele, & Hilliard, 2003), and as a strategy for conceptual incarceration and extinction against Native people (Adams, 1995); tracking and compulsory education have also been designed as economic ploys to divide the general public (Angus & Mirel, 1999; Coleman, 1966; Oakes, 1985; Tyack & Hansot, 1992). Thus, these contradictory uses of schooling help inform, if not explain, our current complex situation.

As educators become more aware and critical, they are more likely to notice and disrupt inequalities within their classrooms and schools. Therefore, training teachers for social justice is one way to begin resisting the "ideology and practices of cultural domination and exploitation that permeate institutional structures in this society, including its schools" (Mahiri, 1998a, p. 3). This form of activism does not disregard the need for subject matter expertise. However, we desperately need to be both conscious and standards-based: mindful of the injustices and committed to help urban students excel scholastically (e.g., Duncan-Andrade & Morrell, 2008; Oakes & Lipton, 2007).

As much as teacher empowerment is political, it is also personal. Because of the nature of our profession it is critical that we courageously engage in deeper levels of introspection. In other words, since learning is relational, we must remember that we are not teaching *content*; we are teaching *people*. Therefore, the identity and diversity of our students (linguistic, cultural, economic, social, ethnic, etc.) has everything to do with who we are and our ability to engage them effectively.

Equity starts with autobiography. If we are to interact successfully with young people who are often different from us, we must actively reflect on our own stories, biases, and assumptions. (The same is true of programs for those working in health, law enforcement, and every other field addressing urban youth.) According to Dereca, Rudy, Victor, and Jack, anyone can work with low-income youth of color *regardless* of their race, class, or gender. This is probably good news for many white people, in particular. However, it is not quite that straightforward (Bradley, 1978; Frankenberg, 1993; Leonardo, 2004, 2009; Warren, 2010; Welsing, 1991). In order to be effective, we cannot simply deny our identities: to consider even a slight possibility that we can be color-blind in a racialized society is like claiming a fish in an aquarium might not be wet. It is what it is—we are all wet—so let's deal with ourselves with integrity. Being cognizant that who we are—based on racism, classism, and sexism—has shaped our experiences makes us more transparent and authentic: real. Good teaching demands introspection, personal critique, and vulnerability (Ballenger, 1999; Darder, 2002). By validating our experiences we can, in turn, begin to validate the lives of our students. This type of introspection is not easy, but it is necessary.

When I reflected on the strategies that Dereca, Rudy, Victor, and Jack use, alongside my own racial identity and experiences in the classroom, I realized I was not the equitable teacher I thought I was. Even the simplest finding in this study—the role of love—needs to be unpacked at the personal level if it is to have any traction.

Through this research, I learned first-hand that some of the most important aspects of a good education are not based on a budget line item, but in fact can be measured only by the size of our hearts. Here I clearly remember Dereca's teaching: the reason students at Freedom School make enormous strides in reading is not because of a special literacy program or intervention; no, the students love reading *because* we love them. Yet love, in and of itself, can be misleading.

I think many of the young people I have worked with over the years would describe me as loving. But something was different about the ways these four educators loved their students. I started to speculate: *in the classroom, was my conceptualization of love actually undermining certain young people's potential?*

I have experienced something very dangerous while engaging in urban school reform. At times when I would hear about a student's trauma or conduct a home visit, I would be so horrified by the child's circumstance that I was impressed that they had the willpower to simply get up each morning and survive. And, sometimes without realizing it, I would stop pushing them to thrive. Unfortunately, I am not alone in giving in to this predicament—I witness it in too many classrooms that serve low-income students of color.

As a white woman, I will never know what it means to be a person of color. But that does not mean I will not try to see the world through my students' eyes. Herein lies the crucial problem. I used to pride myself on the rapport I had with young people; I felt they could tell me *anything* going on in their lives and I would be the down teacher who tried to empathize with their woes. And then, at certain moments my kindness turned into pity, either consciously or unconsciously. I started to feel sorry for some of my urban students and then I became afraid to really challenge them. Essentially, my love became a form of coddling—a dangerous doorway into lowered expectations and complacency. Jack, an older white man, refuses to hear excuses. He showed me that pain, predicaments, and circumstances cannot and will not predict a child's future.

Many high-risk young people are living through nightmares, but that never means we should help them give up on their dreams. In fact, it is precisely why we need to support them to strive farther and harder. In other words, their grind needs to be daring, different, and full of determination. And then, when a student acts as if it is a miracle that they are the first person in their family to graduate from high school, we need to provide them with tangible steps into college and viable careers.

There can be no equity in education as long as low expectations remain rampant in urban schools. Recently, this message hit home again. I was driving a student home from a meeting at a high school in South Sacramento, and she pointed out the apartment complex where her mother lives, just blocks from the school. But we were not stopping there, because Miya was recently placed into foster care. We crossed the causeway and pulled up to a subdivision of houses far removed from her Valley High neighborhood. As she was getting out of the car, I asked about her homework. She said matter-of-factly that she is not given homework assignments. I challenged her: was she trying to get out of doing assignments? After further discussion and investigation, I discovered that she was placed in back-to-back electives because her teachers and school counselor were concerned about her stress level and did not want to burden her with coursework at this difficult time in her life. "But what about your future?" I exclaimed. Again, she answered matter-of-factly: "They do not want Black kids to be successful." Her rationale came directly out of her experiences in school. Unfortunately, without an adult advocating on her behalf, she will probably remain trapped in a series of inadequate courses that do not prepare her for, or give her access to, higher education. This is harmful and a travesty—and a call to action.

We have all heard of the social psychological phenomenon called the bystander effect: people do not offer to help in an emergency if other people are present. Ironically, the greater the number of bystanders, the less likely it is that any one of them will help (Darley & Latané, 1968; Hudson & Bruckman, 2004). This comes to mind when I think about Miya's situation and the numbers of adults who could lend a helping hand and disrupt the academic injustice, but instead look away. I am not speaking out of judgment, but about the next steps we must take so that every child's brilliance comes to fruition.

I Am Brilliant, and I'm Hood

I wonder if Kenny, who I introduced in the preface, would have gone to college if he had worked with Dereca, Rudy, Victor, or Jack. When he was in high school, he desperately needed a mentor and program that would help him navigate between the streets and school. The issue was never simply his dedication to education, or his willpower. College is a dream deferred when you start planning your funeral at age 10. Dance (2002) echoes this sentiment: "these students live in their neighborhoods and not in their schools," so "they must make surviving the streets a priority" (p. 67). It is clear that, unless we develop effective models to bridge students' upbringing to their uprising, we will lose to prison and/or death more students than we win to college and careers. Students should not have to choose between home and school, the block and class, swag and squaredom, community-based educator and teacher—for these choices will, overwhelmingly, not weigh in our favor. At best, we will help a few escape their circumstances. At worst, we will witness a generation of joblessness, hopelessness, and genocide.

These four educators tap into the genius and resistance among students left behind by an education system that is not willing or prepared to meet them on their own turf. Amidst funeral caskets, drug addiction, and penitentiary visiting hours, these students still hold an earnest desire for transformation. OG Jack put it simply: "Miracles happen every day." I rest assured that, with the right tools, change is foreseeable.

The nontraditional educators in this book can be found on street corners and inside schools but, quite significantly, their lessons accept—rather than deny, punish, or demonize—who their students are and where they come from. They see hardships and battle scars as part of a student's strength. Victor put it beautifully: he told me that his students are "the true leaders" because they have "been to the depths of the ocean . . . seen things that most people haven't seen . . . going through things that most people will never wish upon anyone and they're still survivin and for them to see and think in a different way just a little bit . . . they are changing the world." Guiding students to tap into their power as leaders is powerful. In the oasis of programs such as UP or the encompassing love of the YTF, students are elevated. But I have worried that this is a set-up. What happens when a student leaves the nurturing environment of a program only to go back into a classroom setting that demeans them? The stark contrast could be devastating, even destructive. And what do we do when a young community organizer still cannot read? How do we help students excel as activists *and* scholars? Protesters *and* professionals? Who is responsible for making this link? We all are.

Dereca, Rudy, Victor, and Jack fortified my conviction that children such as Miya and Kenny, and countless others, have tremendous potential if they are given an environment that will cultivate excellence and develop lifelong success. For this to occur en masse, we must think critically about the training and support afforded to teachers. We must help one another honestly confront issues of diversity, expectations, and equity with personal resolve; otherwise our reforms will remain as they are: piecemeal, obscure, and relatively ineffective.

8

GRINDIN FOR ALL WE GOT FROM THE BOTTOM TO THE TOP

Schools and community-based organizations are under severe attack through bureaucratic regulations and financial cutbacks. Whereas teachers deliberate about how to teach to state-mandated tests, community educators are often concerned with meeting quotas and yielding measurable outcomes for their funders. In both situations, countless people succeed despite the challenges. And, even with all of the crises, some at-risk and high-risk youth excel. Educators working within and beyond the walls of schools deal intimately with today's youth and form an important bridge in their development. Moreover, the nontraditional community-based settings provide new insights into pedagogical principles and can offer fresh approaches for anyone working with marginalized youth.

Even though the nontraditional educators in this study are not perfect, they do succeed overall. Significantly, they teach students whom many of us would see as failures. Clearly, when given a new and appropriate environment, many young people do change for the better. If this is happening, is it possible that problem students are not necessarily *the* problem? In fact, could it be that these students are the solution, while we adults employ tactics and policies that cultivate trouble? I am thinking of such practices as demeaning expectations, deficit-based instruction, metal detectors at school entrances, and giving suspensions for minor infractions. But I am not pointing fingers. My focus—like those of these four educators—is to save lives and improve our collective future. Given this, my findings underscore the need for education policymakers to heed four paramount and immediate concerns.

1. *Notice the Urgency:* Throughout this book I have emphasized the urgency of the crisis in urban education and the emergency of youth violence.

I do not suggest more conferences and increased bureaucracy; rather, I call for immediate solutions. Even as rates of violent crime have dropped around the country, many areas are experiencing an increase in youth violence—especially among youth of color in both rural and urban areas. The Violence Policy Center (2011) reported that homicide, and particularly gun homicide, continues to be one of the most pressing public health concerns in California among youth and young adults aged 10 to 24. Community-based programs can offer important alternatives for young people caught in the crossfire of turf wars. Schools can serve as safe havens, but must also become inspiring learning environments.

2. *Support Education and Leave No Child Behind (Bars):* As a society, we must critically challenge the current policy that promotes prisons over schools. In California, for instance, the prison industrial complex and the education system both receive substantial funding from the state's general fund. In 1995 there was nearly a dollar-for-dollar tradeoff between education and incarceration: schools lost $2.5 billion while the prison budget increased by $2.6 billion. This trend has only worsened over the last decade. An article in the *New York Times* (Steinhauer, 2007) reported that California lawmakers approved the largest single prison construction project in the nation's history, at $8.3 billion. Meanwhile, funding for public education continues to drop. The tradeoff between prisons and schools is important for many reasons, but is especially critical because they target the same citizenry: young adults. Thus, the fiscal tradeoffs between these two departments can be the measure of a state's hope for its future (Critical Resistance Project, 2011; Dorfman & Schiraldi, 2001; Gilmore, 2007a,b).

Instead of being a beacon for equality and justice, the very Constitution is being used as a tool to oppress. The Thirteenth Amendment abolishes slavery "except as a punishment for crime." Several researchers (Alexander, 2010; Lichtenstein, 1996a,b; Mancini, 1996) have found that inmates are being treated like legalized slaves. For example, the Louisiana State Penitentiary (commonly called Angola), the largest maximum-security prison in the United States, operates as a working farm. Warden Burl Cain once said that the key to running a peaceful maximum security prison is "to keep the inmates working all day so they're tired at night" (James, 2010). Ridgeway (2009) called Angola "an 18,000-acre complex that still resembles the slave plantation it once was."

Why does this matter to our work here? Because the path to prison often starts inside schools (Chidren's Defense Fund, 2007; Winn, 2011; Winn & Behizadeh, 2011). The school-to-prison pipeline must be disrupted immediately; these students, in particular, are being forced to stay behind. I agree with Ferguson (2001) and others (e.g., Meiners, 2007; Ogletree, 2010; Rios, 2011) that punitive measures, tighter discipline, greater surveillance, and more prisons are deterring human potential and posterity.

3. *Reconsider the Special Education Business:* Although we clearly need to support education, it is also vital to promote learning that is engaging, relevant, and challenging. Often, this does not occur in special education. True, some young people are severely handicapped and need additional services inside schools, but special education disproportionately focuses on males of color who are labeled as having attention deficit hyperactivity disorder (commonly called ADHD or ADD). Often these young people are receiving an inadequate education. Thus, we must re-evaluate the special education business because of its racist trends and its remedial curricula.

4. *Connect Schools with Communities:* Racialized poverty should not determine a child's access to a high-quality education. Here's a radical idea: equal funding for equal schooling. Among U.S. school districts, annual funding per pupil ranges from less than $4,000 to more than $15,000 (Biddle & Berliner, 2002; Lipman, 2011). This is a crime. Furthermore, in order to generate equitable outcomes, we must establish baseline services. This is hardly rocket science: children will not do as well in school if they are hungry, have toothaches, or need glasses. Therefore, in addition to appropriate classroom content, we desperately need funding for full-service community schools to revitalize neighborhoods, address the opportunity gaps, and provide real access to prosperity (Bryk et al., 2010; Noguera, 2003; Warren, 2005).

These brief points indicate some of the basic directions implied by my findings; we must work to find ways to support all students and fulfill the promise of equal education. For policymakers, in particular, I have tried to bring the struggles and humanity of marginalized youth into public awareness in order to spark a national conversation and a renewed commitment to the young people trying to survive on the streets, and to elucidate the plight of community-based educators and classroom teachers on the front lines who are saving lives and, inevitably, improving society for us all.

Let me also emphasize that it is people who make policies; it is people who make up "the system" that is blatantly critiqued in this study. People operate the current educational system and, consciously or unconsciously, stifle the opportunities of so many young people, especially those of color in the inner city. At the same time, the very same people who perpetuate the oppressive system can—and must—decide to change it. We must all heed the urgent call to do public education differently.

The quest is to make equitable neighborhoods and humane schools. However, to make real change, we must be willing to take risks because our children are at risk. We can do this, but we will forge these new paths only by walking them (Bell, Gaventa, & Peters, 1990). It is the spirit of activism that all jobs hold meaning and all positions—from the practitioner to the parent to the professor to the policymaker—can represent opportunities for greater awareness and social change. Regardless of where we live or work, whether we feel discouraged or optimistic, may we continue to combine our efforts and push onward. The world is so interconnected that the flapping of a butterfly's wings can cause a hurricane. Let us not forget that sometimes even the smallest acts seed the best improvements.

School Is My Hustle

I know that in every profession unsung heroes and sheroes struggle to make the world a better place and already employ the tactics exemplified by Dereca, Rudy, Victor, and Jack. In this study I was able to examine in depth only four such adults, though I realize that there are countless extraordinary teachers and administrators, as well as many more astounding community-based educators, who use these good practices daily, in their work with young people.

Naturally, I had to leave many subjects untouched, but I worked diligently to show—rather than tell—the keys to their success. To some readers, the portraits might have felt cathartic; to others, these educators' fervor might seem overwhelming. And I suspect many readers experienced both reactions, even momentarily. Whatever the response, I trust you are still present in the participatory nature of portraiture that permitted me to ask you the following three questions at the beginning of this journey.

1. How do I do *my* work?
2. What do I *believe* about today's students, teachers, and schools?
3. Do the community-based educators use any strategies that might affect *my* perception of and relationship with disenfranchised youth?

The four nontraditional urban educators in the San Francisco Bay Area have a particular vantage point that can inform solutions to the crisis in urban education. As beacons of hope, they illuminate ways we can help students to be both street smart *and* school smart. But this is not to imply that *their* praxis should fit us all. We can modify—or ignore—the strategies as we see fit based upon our experiences. Rather, the underlying message is to get involved and get real about who young people are and what they actually need.

As I ponder the above three questions, I recognize the ways this research process has affected my own life. When I began my quest for best practices, I did not know where this investigation would take me. All I knew was that I had an insatiable desire to understand how to work effectively with students who were often deemed troublemakers, hoodlums, and the like. This curiosity stemmed from my challenges in the classroom, my desperate desire to make a difference, and my steadfast belief that all children are capable of greatness, in school and beyond. And, though it might sound selfish, I just wanted tools that I could use to become a better teacher. After years of investigating, I found them—and part of me simply wanted to superimpose Dereca, Rudy, Victor, and Jack onto my own work. But that would be disingenuous for anyone seeking a true liberatory praxis.

The lessons I learned from the community-based educators helped me see young people in a renewed light. This revelation hit home just the other day. A vice principal at a local school sent me the following email about one of her most difficult students:

> Today our girl Jelintha had a rough day . . . At the end of our conversation she said she created a poem this morning as a result of her challenges:
>
> It's the pain behind her smile
> And the smile that hides the pain
> A lost girl in a cold world
> Her tears are invisible in the rain
> She runs and runs
> But couldn't find an open door
> She wants to cry it to the world
> But instead she cries to her book!
> . . . Yeah, never in life would she ever thought to speak her life
>   on the mic,
> So if it wasn't for SAYS,
> The only door open would be suicide.
> So thanks SAYS for letting me speak my pain
> Y'all eyes was the only one who saw my tears that were once
>   invisible in the rain.

Jelintha's words bring a shiver to my soul: she, like too many others, is crying out to be seen and heard. Dereca, Rudy, Victor, and Jack have demonstrated what is under the "tough fronts" (Dance, 2002), and I encourage everyone to look anew at our "problem" students. However, simply recognizing a child's pain will not remedy the ills that face this generation. We must also connect them with opportunities to shine. As sacred caretakers, healers, and educators, our responsibility is great. If we do not raise the bar of expectations, it is likely that these very same students will end up behind bars.

Guided by the wisdom of the community-based educators, I now recognize that school must become "the hustle" in urban education. When school is the hustle, the walls of the classroom become transparent and the drive for achievement is personal, communal, nonstop, and emancipatory. Here is one example. When Adrian first started coming to SAYS meetings in the ninth grade, he wowed us with his rap skills. When we brought him back to his junior high school for a hip-hop literacy assembly, the teachers and administrators were awestruck by his talents; they never knew about his passion to write and spit (recite) spoken word. But within our program we have been able to encourage his voice and develop his consciousness. Adrian is now in eleventh grade at Grant High School in North Sacramento. I was at Grant doing classroom observations and ran into him as he was rushing to his next class. I asked about his grades: he said he was on the honor roll. Then I inquired about his next course; he said advanced placement statistics. "It's like that now!" I exclaimed. He grinned: "You taught me that school is *my* hustle." With that, he turned to walk away, his pants sagging and his backpack heavy, ready to make education his own. The youth of today are ready for empowerment. But are we?

The Struggle Continues

To close on a reflective note, much has happened since I first began interviewing the four educators almost a decade ago. I have shared chapters of the book with all of them as well as their staff, and I have given the typical research presentations to colleagues and graduate students. The positive response has been overwhelming. This feedback has come from individuals who personally know the four educators, and from people far removed from any youth development work. However, everyone has expressed their gratitude for the educators' passion, bravery, and commitment. Alongside the applause, audience members have asked me some critical and important questions. I find two of them particularly striking.

1. Is the benchmark of effectiveness—illuminated by the educators in this study—simply unattainable for the rest of us?
2. Is the success of their organizations based solely on one person's bold personality or are there larger support systems that institutionalize change? In other words, will the programs still be effective whether or not a particular educator is at the helm?

To answer the first question: No, we can all be effective. I definitely did not intend the portraits to make these people feel out of reach. Rather, I tried to describe in detail particular tactics that worked for specific individuals. To clarify, I do not endorse a list of useful practices as some sort of "checklist for transformation"; doing so would undermine the reflective nature of this work.

And to answer the second question: No one person can shoulder the weight of the world. Although it was not my main research focus, within each community-based organization I noted systems of shared leadership. This type of extended family organizational structure insures that no program depends exclusively on one person. For example, now that United Playaz has expanded to multiple school sites, it is impossible for Rudy to be at every location. He has had to train others—often former students—to take on his position. And, a couple years ago, Dereca stepped down as executive director for Leadership Excellence, though she continues to play an important role. The organization continues to excel because of its mission, strategic plan, and alliances throughout Oakland. In sum, personality is part of the key to effectiveness, but it is hardly the entire story.

Moving forward, these important questions from audience members over the years also reveal the need for further research. This book focused exclusively on community-based educators, but I see much more to explore. For example, because of a generous Improving Teacher Quality grant from the California Post-Secondary Education Commission, I am currently investigating the pedagogical effects on teachers of placing poet-mentor educators into their middle and high school classrooms. In addition, further studies are required on effective community–school partnerships, as only a few exist now. Another element still missing is the perspectives of students; I am particularly interested in examining the ways that people who have dropped out conceptualize school reform. There is also an urgent need for research that analyzes the educational experiences of people inside detention facilities. Given how widely incarceration is expanding throughout the country, it is vital that we understand successful models for rehabilitation, such as the "Missouri Miracle" of systemic juvenile justice reform (Edelman, 2010). Obviously, my curiosity and passion persist. I remain committed to use research to advance equity. In this vein, I urge us to think critically about the types of questions we ask that will inevitably inform our answers to authentic school change. As I ponder ways to help schools, the following questions continue to arise:

1. What does student-centered instruction look like in an era of high-stakes testing? What are effective pedagogical strategies across disparate content areas? And how do the common core standards shift this terrain for both teachers and principals?
2. What does it take to create high-poverty high-achieving schools? What are the benchmarks of success and how do we get there?
3. In what ways can principals redefine their role as instructional allies to teachers? How can schools of education help facilitate this process?

Even though various stakeholders are already addressing the above topics (e.g., Anyon, 2005; Carter, 2005; Darling-Hammond, 2005; Elmore, 2000), I would urge more of us to heed the call for *engaged activist scholarship* (Apple, 2010; Barker, 2004; Gilmore, 2008; Stoecker, 2009; Sudbury & Okazawa-Rey, 2008). At its best, research can help us analyze areas of injustice, find tools for effectiveness, and propel innovation in the field.

Yet research and ideals alone will *never* be enough. This is a call to arms. Arms that care, reach out, and restore basic principles of our common humanity. Although reading the word and the world serves as a critical foundation, our future is dependent upon our actions (Bell et al., 1990). Alas, it saddens me to report that, while I was writing the final pages of this book, I lost another student and friend, Diezal Boss, on February 1, 2011. Diezal was a father and entrepreneur; I called him Teddy Bear because of his large size, large heart, and sheer innocence. But kindness is not a form of armor. Gunshots are relentless. They break through bones and cascade into hearts, and shatter homes every hour of every day in this country. When I feel my hope withering into the sound of sirens and breathless silence, I turn to schools because they are filled with possibility. I walk the hallways, visit classrooms, and hang out during lunchtime. Every time I talk to kids, my energy is restored.

As we each continue our work in the coming days and years, I beg that you never give up on social justice, on schools, or on one another. And, by all means, never give up on learning to liberate. For if education cannot spark the heart and mind to improve our world, what can?

APPENDIX A

Terminology

Since *high-risk* youth and *urban* schools are loaded terms and often conjure up particular images and assumptions, it is important to take a step back from this language and ask: What do *at-risk* and *high-risk* really mean? Who are we talking about? Are these just code words for "our" masked racism about "others"? Furthermore, what does an urban school look like? Is it Lowell High School or Thurgood Marshall in San Francisco, or both?[1] Is Pittsburg High School, located in a Bay Area suburb, considered urban because it serves low-income students of color? What dynamics of particular neighborhoods make them urban?

Indeed, the word *urban* "is less likely to be employed as a geographic concept used to define and describe physical locations than as a social or cultural construct" (Noguera, 2003, p. 23). Since the term does not necessarily demarcate a particular location, its meaning is more complex. Developing this point and tackling the ambiguity of urban schools, Lois Weiner (2000) suggests these public schools are best understood on a continuum of traits. Drawing on the work of other researchers, she identifies five main characteristics: (1) the size and cultural diversity of the student population; (2) the percentage of students from cultural and linguistic groups whose model of schooling is different from, or in conflict with, that of the dominant culture; (3) the centralization of the decision-making process within a large bureaucracy that is politically isolated from communities; (4) the extent to which decisions about teaching and learning are affected by chronic underfunding; and (5) the extent to which students are classified based on standardized measures of "intelligence." These five qualities are helpful because they provide a particular picture of the urban school landscape (p. 370). The descriptors are relatively negative and underscore the deficit model that many people draw on when thinking about urban schools, urban communities, and urban youth.

In the literature, youth with an at-risk status are characterized as living in impoverished, inner-city neighborhoods where they encounter multiple stressors (physical, psychological, economic, and social) that make them more likely to drop out of school, use drugs, engage in violence, and become incarcerated (Aronowitz, 2005; Brendtro, Brokenleg, & Bockern, 1990; Erikson, 1968; Garbarino, 1999). High-risk youth are already identified as being out of school, engaged in high-risk behaviors, and/or involved with the criminal (in)justice system (Pittman, Irby, & Ferber, 1999). Although these definitions are helpful as indicators about the stressors facing particular youth, they are also dangerous because they negatively categorize and label young people. Ray Rist's (1970) study is apropos here. He analyzed the way teachers use derogatory labels, and how these descriptors perpetuate inequality. Rist's findings demonstrate that harmful descriptors, such as *at-risk*, can actually encourage negative behavior. Other research (e.g., Ferguson, 2001) also emphasizes this point. So the language we use to describe young people is important.

The community-based educators and teenagers in this book do not use or support words such as *at-risk* and *high-risk*. As one young woman told me, everyone her age is at-risk. On the other hand, she is "goin through it." She used this term to emphasize her struggles. It is significant that many researchers do not use terms such as "at-promise" (Weiner, 2006), or even "misled," like one of the community-based educators in this book. The term *misled*, for instance, removes the onus of responsibility from the teenagers and places it on adults, society, and the system. Nevertheless, although words carry weight, I used the terms *high-risk, marginalized, misled,* and *disenfranchised* interchangeably throughout the book—though none of these simple phrases gives due attention to the diversity of experiences among today's urban students.

APPENDIX B

Methods and Validity

Research Questions

My research scrutinized the strategies employed by a select group of community-based educators. To learn about the best practices of these educators, I investigated three main research questions.

1. What are each community-based educator's philosophies and strategies for working with high-risk youth?
2. How do personal experiences and institutional contexts shape and influence the ways these educators engage youth?
3. In what ways, if at all, can the lessons derived from the work of these educators inform the practices and pedagogy of high school teachers in low-income urban communities?

To answer these research questions, I turned to portraiture.

Portraiture

To begin my investigation, I sought a methodology that encourages respectful reciprocity between myself, as researcher, and my participants. Portraiture was a natural fit, but it demanded a unique level of intimacy. For instance, to develop the aesthetic whole of each portrait, I had to remain cognizant of central elements, including *voice*, *context*, *emergent themes*, and the *complex relationship* that develops out of the intensity of the research process (Behar, 1996; Lawrence-Lightfoot & Davis, 1997; Davis, 1996).

Accommodating a wide range of investigative techniques, portraiture anticipates that participants and researcher engage in a co-construction of the narrative. Because the researcher does not preconceive ideas, it is possible to uncover a clearer appreciation for each participant's unique reality, as well as the contradictions that often come hand-in-hand with those realities. In this interactive process, the researcher is not an abstract entity removed from the findings, but instead an active participant throughout the data collection stage. The researcher's voice is integral to the multi-dimensional story that emerges—and integral in a way that amplifies the experience and perspective of each participant without obscuring or filtering their voice. This humanistic approach does not restrict data to a predetermined set of measurable factors, but instead allows the human experience to unfold, as it will. Thus portraiture forces the researcher to be inquisitive and self-reflective as a way to bring the story to light (Lawrence-Lightfoot & Davis, 1997, pp. 148–9).

Therefore I am part of this account, not removed from it. From my perch of human-as-instrument, my goal as portraitist was to discover the universal within the particular and to communicate that in recognizable terms (Lawrence-Lightfoot, 1983; Maxwell, 1996; Glesne, 1999). When doing portraiture, then, I must take a stance that is simultaneously inside and outside the moment. That is, while documenting conversations and taking in the subtle nuances of meaning and implication—and details such as the color of the walls—I am also thinking about who I am. This encourages a free association of the five senses, heart, and soul, in fluid qualitative description and does not seek to isolate conditions to make them duplicable. As such, it is a practice of emancipation, unfolding in the form of human archaeology (Lawrence-Lightfoot & Davis, 1997, p. 139).

Along this journey, I would often think about how much I'd come to love the educators in this book. When I described this development, my colleagues always seemed taken aback, as if I should have more restraint. I tried to rationalize (to others and to myself) that this love grew out of my passionate curiosity coupled with the intimate inquiry process of portraiture—and that it would not undermine the research, but add to its depth. Yet in the dark of night, I always wondered if I was doing something wrong, or even shameful, because I wasn't detached from the work.

After one of my all-night sessions analyzing data, I picked up Lawrence-Lightfoot's (1994) *I've Known Rivers* in a sleepless daze. As dusk melted into dawn, I sat on my living room floor enraptured by her opening words: "For a portraitist to see her subject clearly, she must fall in love" (p. xv). This single statement not only helped me justify my process as a qualitative researcher, but pierced through my data to its core. As I observed the community-based educators, I was constantly inspired and challenged by love. This love rarely flowed in one direction from the educators to the youth (though it often started out that way); but resembled more of a loving relationship (not unlike all relationships from marriage to friendship) that are hard work, multifaceted, and glorious all at the same time. In my qualitative quest for answers, love was active in the dialectic between me and my participants and me and my data. To authentically discover the story, I had to submit to this emotion on multiple levels; essentially, I sought to become an active listener ("ear hustler") to the very heartbeat and pulse of this work. My findings blossomed from the soul in order to take root in mind, body, and eventually upon the page.

Access into the Community-Based Organizations

From the onset, I was guided by the possibility that alternative modes of instruction can enrich the understanding of high school teachers. Since the teacher-like position of the educators was an overarching theme, I sought individuals who work directly with youth and are considered successful, particularly with misled youth. I chose to examine the experiences of four community-based educators; this number is small enough to allow in-depth treatment, but large enough to compare diverse, individual perspectives.

Once I identified whom I wanted to participate in my study, I had to gain access. Two of the educators said they have consistently rejected research studies because they did not trust them and because they did not want to subject the youth or themselves to an "investigation." But they agreed, telling me, with a hint of trepidation, they believed I would act with integrity and honesty.

Distinctions between the Community-Based Organizations

My selection process identified educators who, in my estimation and that of knowledgeable researchers and colleagues, had proven their capacity to move youth toward positive goals. As it happened, the selection process yielded satisfactory variation in terms of educators and types of programs they operate. Two programs (Leadership Excellence and the Omega Boys Club) say forthrightly that they will never apply for federal funding. On the other hand, the Youth Task Force is affiliated with the San Francisco Department of Public Health, and United Playaz, which recently established itself as a nonprofit organization, acquires grants from the government. Many other similarities and differences exist among these programs. The largest program, the Omega Boys Club, serves hundreds of students and the smallest group, the Youth Task Force, serves eight youth on average. However, no matter how large or small, these programs overwhelmingly serve teenagers of color from low-income backgrounds. Divided almost equally by gender, the youth range in age from 12 to 24. At the start of data collection, the community-based educators ranged in age from 24 to 68. Three are people of color (one is African-American and two are Filipino) and one is white; three are men and one is a woman. Three of the organizations work within schools and one does not.

These attributes provide a preliminary snapshot of the similarities and dif- ferences between the respective organizations. Notwithstanding these facts, it is the community-based educators' pedagogy, not necessarily their programs, that is the focus of my work. Although I consider the institutional context of each participant, I do so only enough to let me clarify how (s)he is effective.

Methods of Data Collection and Analysis

My data collection process involved the community-based educators, their colleagues, and youth participants at each site. In addition to observing partici- pants and asking youth to fill out questionnaires, I conducted several in-depth interviews. Though the educators were my primary focus, I used insights from others to triangulate the various emerging themes. The methods of portrai- ture include observational work, thematic in-depth interviews, and document analysis (Davis, 1996; Lawrence-Lightfoot & Davis, 1997; LeCompte, 1993), all of which I employed in creating the final portraits.

Participant observation was a critical component of my data collection. Researchers use it to "understand the research setting, its participants, and their behavior" (Glesne, 1999, p. 45). Observing the community-based educa- tors in action allowed me to "draw inferences about someone's meaning and perspective" that I could not "obtain by relying exclusively on interview data" (Maxwell, 1996, p. 76). Accordingly, I observed each program for a minimum of 30 hours, attending weekly meetings, activities, and community events, to get a clearer picture of the multiple facets of the work. In my field notes I documented the educator's actions in context, the educator–youth relations, and how each educator's pedagogy aligns with their espoused beliefs and goals. These notes also provided me with data on the general ambiance, which is a hallmark of portraiture.

In order to strengthen my analysis, I asked youth participants in each organization to complete an anonymous questionnaire (taking about 30 min- utes) to probe how they experience the program and whether or not they find it beneficial. At each program I also selected one to four teenagers to engage in a 60- to 90-minute interview. I used a semi-structured, open-ended interview format. The interviews all focused on the students' perspectives, experiences, and general feelings toward the group and the educator (a copy of the ques- tionnaire is available in Appendix D).

I also interviewed one to two colleagues of each educator, which allowed me to explore their impressions about how the educator works with and relates to youth. Specifically, I asked for examples of effectiveness and areas for improvement.

The community-based educators were interviewed in greater depth in four semi-structured, open-ended, 90-minute sessions.[1] The interviews were accumulative; each built upon previous themes. This made the process more interactive and allowed me to clarify issues as they arose. These conversations focused on biographical information and professional experiences, as well as strategies and reflections about teaching high-risk students.

In addition to participant observation, the questionnaire, and the interviews, I gathered documents such as curriculum materials, newspaper articles, video documentaries, funding reports, and meeting notes from each participating organization. Collectively, these diverse data sources allowed me to create the thick description (Geertz, 1974) necessary to properly contextualize their practices within the aesthetic whole of each portrait.

Portraiture provides a descriptive narrative to communicate essential findings. However, this does not imply that the researcher is subjective. Drawing mainly from grounded theory (Miles & Huberman, 1994; Strauss & Corbin, 1998; Tuckman, 1999) to construct the portrait of each educator, I applied a systematic approach to analyze the data collected. First, I coded all the data using both open and theoretical codes as a way to trace themes related to my research topic. This process also helped me develop further analytic questions (Emerson, Fretz, & Shaw, 1995; Strauss, 1987). In addition, memos, which included crafted profiles and narrative summaries (Glesne, 1999), pushed me to categorize salient attributes as they emerged (Seidman, 1998). This combination of various types of data, combined with particular analytic strategies, allowed me to answer my research questions.

More specifically, first I highlighted the prominent philosophy and strategy of each community-based educator (my first question) in all the material. I then sifted this information to note discrepancies and parallels with actual observations, colleague interviews, and insights from the youth. Simultaneously, I examined the personal background of each educator (my second question) as it bears on daily operations and activities: how they relate to youth, what language they use, and so forth. This provided a biographical backdrop to their present-day work with students.

My first two research questions dealt with the interplay between abstract philosophy and strategy, and each educator's institutional context and life history. To answer my third question (what can inform teacher pedagogy) I used a three-pronged approach. First, and most directly, I asked each educator what types of advice (s)he has for traditional teachers. Second, I constructed matrices to cross-reference theoretical concepts about effective teaching with emergent topics from my data. Third, I compared and contrasted the four educators in order to identify elements that are transferable to urban schools. As I used these various analytical strategies, my findings emerged.

Validity

Maxwell (1996) defines validity as "the correctness or credibility of a description, conclusion, explanation, interpretation, or other sort of account" (p. 87).

To enhance the validity of my findings, I compared multiple data sources for consistency and contradictions. By triangulating my information sources, I could probably (though not certainly) notice and tease out aberrations.

My own personal preferences, consciously and unconsciously, entered into data selections and perhaps affect the general outcome. However, a significant strength of portraiture is the author's inclusion in the final description. Prejudices might be revealed in a way that does not diminish the empathetic understanding communicated to the reader or alter the results. Still, I acknowledge that working toward the aesthetic goal of portraiture does not relieve me of the responsibility to address potential problems. Accordingly, I employed several strategies to address researcher bias and reactivity.

To ensure descriptive validity, I tape-recorded and transcribed all interviews verbatim, including words such as "um . . ." and "you know." I processed all my field notes within 1 week of observation and created initial open-coding along with journal entries (Emerson et al., 1995; Maxwell, 1996). These journal entries were ethnographic tools that helped me document my emotions as I became part of the group under study (Kleinman & Copp, 1993). I also used these memos to document how I was interacting with the participants. At all times I tried to be cognizant that portraiture is a process of co-construction in which teller and listener create meaning collaboratively (Lawrence-Lightfoot & Davis, 1997; Riessman, 2002).

To ensure interpretive validity, I systematically emphasized evidence in my analytic memos and narrative summaries by citing participants' own words and documenting transcript page numbers to connect my interpretations back to the data. I examined discrepant data against my working observations to assess whether or not I should modify my developing sketches and consider alternative explanations (Lawrence-Lightfoot & Davis, 1997).

As further assurance of validity, the educators are all identified by their real names along with the programs they direct. I also asked each of them to review all of their interview transcripts. These member checks (Maxwell, 1996) allowed us to clarify and expand upon any issues raised. Also, each educator reviewed his or her final portrait to insure accuracy. Although I asked them to respect my analysis, their feedback was a critical, and necessary, part of this investigation.

Finally, at each stage of data collection and analysis, I solicited regular feedback from my study group. These colleagues are skilled researchers who are not intimately connected to the data. Their alternative interpretations and constant feedback strengthened the accuracy of my findings (Glesne, 1999; Luttrell, 2000).

APPENDIX C

Participant-Observer or Observing Participant?

Collecting data is not straightforward and in a number of instances I felt confused about my position as participant-observer. I think it important to share some of these difficult moments because they are integral to my data collection process, and perhaps will clarify my role.

In the case of Rudy and United Playaz, at least two dilemmas surfaced. At a *Books Not Bars*[1] rally, Rudy called us to the stage: "UP front and center!" Like all the UP members, I was wearing my black-and-white UP shirt; it definitely looked as if I was part of the group. However, when Rudy summoned us to the front, I stood on the sidelines watching the young people speak about "education not incarceration." I assumed nobody would notice my absence, but I was wrong. Afterwards, a few students came up to me and, with a hint of disgust, asked why I did not go up with them to the stage. They concluded, "You should have been up there!" Taken aback, I told them that I was shy, but that was just my way of deflecting the truth.

The truth is, I almost went. As soon as I heard the call for UP members, my first thought was *that's me*. But my second thought was that somehow I would be overstepping a boundary in my responsibilities as a researcher. I vacillated about my role and convinced myself that I should simply observe. When the students noticed that I had stayed behind and then approached me, I felt disappointed in myself. Despite their upset, their reaction made me feel even more a part of the group. I made a conscious decision: never again would I choose to be an outsider.

On a second instance I might have stepped too far from my research role with UP. Rudy and I talked at length about UP becoming its own nonprofit because, quite frankly, I thought his parent organization was taking advantage of him. He confessed that he wanted to be independent, but did not know how to make the move. I connected him with a phenomenal grant writer who became so impressed with UP that she quit her full-time job in order to work for Rudy. Becoming a nonprofit has proven worthwhile; UP's budget has expanded and the number of young people served in the last couple of years has grown exponentially.

While collecting data on Dereca and Leadership Excellence, I initially tiptoed around my participation. Because I am white, I was concerned that my presence would be intrusive since LE is exclusively African-American. As much as possible, I tried to hide my notebook until I was back in my car recording the day's events. Dereca kept telling me I had a "pass" and was welcome at every event, notebook in hand. Eventually her insistence forced me to let my guard down. After that, I was able to laugh along with the students and easily express my point of view when asked. I am convinced that her insistence inevitably led me to have a more authentic understanding of her work.

When I went to see Victor and the Youth Task Force, I was immediately an active member of the group. Since Victor included me in the circle of conversation from the outset, I never had the option of being an onlooker. Because of this level of involvement, I got to interact with and know the students very quickly. Within weeks, they had my phone number and would invite me to events, from baby showers to conferences. At one meeting, I asked Cloteal if I could tape record her as she read her poem to the group. She responded, "Hell nah!" Then, after a moment of silence, she looked straight into my eyes and said I could record her—but *only* because "I got love for you Vajra." Although the methodology of portraiture assumes an embedded observer, this level of participation might call into question my impartiality and objectivity. As I experienced with Cloteal, the degree of trust between us allowed me to note what otherwise might have been denied. Building authentic relationships with the community-based educators and their students was a significant part of collecting reliable and honest information.

Jack and the Omega Boys Club presented special challenges for me. I tried to build trust with everyone concerned, as I did with the other educators, but conducting research was difficult on several levels. First, the environment of juvenile hall was not a relaxed one in which everyone could get to know each other. Second, it never felt appropriate to take notes during these classes at juvenile hall. So after each gathering I would sit in my car (usually until 10:30 or 11:00 p.m.) writing down, in as much detail as possible, everything that had happened. Third, Jack and his crew are very skeptical of newcomers. To this day, I do not feel like a bona fide Omega participant.

I must also accept some responsibility for this unwelcoming attitude, I think. If I had been able to attend more classes regularly, both inside juvenile hall and at the Omega recreation center, I could possibly have changed my relationship to Jack and his comrades. As it was, I observed only two family meetings, one math class, and one writing session at the center. My participation at juvenile hall lasted over a year but it was sporadic. I told Jack that I was juggling a difficult personal schedule (with no evening childcare, for instance) but he acted as if this was just an excuse. I believe that he takes me to be uncommitted as a result. Although Jack might question my intentions, I have remained undaunted in my mission to uncover best practices. And my research had to include Jack and the Omega Boys Club because I wanted the best of the best. Aspects of Jack's personality may be hard to deal with, but his reputation, his commitment to youth, and his results are unassailable. I do not think I could have done justice to this study without him.

APPENDIX D

Interview Protocols and Youth Questionnaire

Community-Based Educator Interview Protocol

Greetings and thank you so much for taking time out of your busy schedule to speak with me. I have been looking forward to having the opportunity to get to know you better and the work that you do with young people. I want to remind you that you can tell me you don't want to answer any question you don't feel like answering, and you can stop the interview at any point. I'd like to tape record the interview. Is that okay? You can tell me to turn off the recorder at any point, if you want. If, after the interview is over, you want to withdraw from the study, I'll destroy your information.

Do you have any questions?

Are you ready to begin?

Program

1. What is the name of your program?
2. Where did the name come from?
3. What is the program's mission?
4. Are there any requirements for being a participant in the program?
5. How long have you worked with the program?
6. What is your background and/or specific qualifications?
7. How large is the staff that supports the day-to-day operations of the program?
8. Where do you get your funding?
9. What's a typical day/meeting like?
10. How do youth, if at all, complete/graduate from the program?

The Youth

11. Please tell me about the youth you serve.
12. How would you characterize the youth you work with?
13. What are some of the greatest challenges that the youth face?
14. How do you respond to these needs?
15. How often do the youth meet?
16. What types of activities do the youth participate in? Why?
17. What is the role of youth in your program?
    Probe: leadership roles

Adult's Role

18. You mentioned the program's mission. I am curious: how would you describe your personal mission?
19. Why do you do this work?
    Probe: What happened? Personal awakening? Belief/behavior shift?
20. What experiences shaped these personal goals/beliefs?
21. What is your greatest challenge?
22. What prepared you for this work?
23. What is your role in the lives of these youth?
24. What do you try and teach the youth?
25. What do you want for them?
    Probe: goals, accomplishments
26. What do you expect from the youth?
27. How do you deal with youth who are working below their potential?
28. How do you recruit youth for the program? Or, how do youth come to participate in the program?
29. How do you keep youth engaged in the program?
30. How, and in what ways, do you connect with the youths' cultures?
31. In what ways do you try to create a sense of family/community within the program?

Beyond the Program's Walls

32. What is your program's role in the community? Can you give some specific examples?
33. What is your program's role in schools? Again, can you please give some examples?
34. How do you, if at all, incorporate elements of youth culture into your program? Why do you do this?

35. How do you feel that the youth you work with are viewed by teachers, and society at large? How do you see this affecting their behavior? Levels of achievement?
36. What comments would you make to conventional teachers concerning the needs of students similar to yours?

Adult's Background/Narrative

37. What is your full name?
38. What does it mean? Where is it from?
39. Where did you grow up?
    Probe: family background, personal experiences . . .
40. Thinking back, tell me about your experiences in school?
41. How do your experiences, if at all, affect/shape how you run the program?
42. Whose shoulders do you stand on? What people influence/inspire the work that you do?
43. Think of a particular youth in your program . . . In 10 years, what do you see them doing?

Advice

44. What advice do you have for teachers working with at-risk youth?
45. How can adults working with youth connect? . . . communicate? . . . support their education and achievement?

School

46. What do you consider to be the purpose of school?
47. In what ways, if at all, do you encourage/support youth to be successful in school?
48. Do you have allies within the school? If so, who are they?

Youth Interview Protocol

Thank you so much for taking the time to talk with me and tell me about yourself. I really appreciate your willingness to be a part of my study. This interview will take no more than 30 minutes. I'm going to ask you questions related to your participation in <Program Name>. I want to remind you that all your answers will be confidential. Only I will know what you said, so you can be honest. If you don't want to answer a question, just let me know. There are no right or wrong answers—I want to learn what you think.

I'd like to tape record the interview so that I can remember what you say, if that's okay with you. You can pick a code name so that I do not use your real name in any part of my data collection.

Before you start, please read and sign the form I handed out, so I know that everyone is participating voluntarily. Do you have any questions? Is it okay for us to start?

Date: _____

Time Starting: _____

Time Stopping: _____

Location: _____

Student Name: _____

Code Name (if applicable): _____

Background

1. How old are you?
2. What grade are you in?
3. What school do you attend?
4. What kind of music do you like?
5. Who are some of your favorite artists? Why do you like them?
6. How would your friends describe you?

Program

7. In the survey you talked about . . . ?
8. How long have you been participating in <Program Name>?
9. Why do you participate in <Program Name>?
10. How would you describe the director?
11. Do you consider the program successful? Why? Please give specific examples.
12. What is the best part of <Program Name>?
13. Is there anything that you don't like about the program? Explain.
14. How is this program similar to and/or different than other programs you've participated in?
15. How is this program similar to and/or different from school?
16. How are the adults in this program similar to and/or different from your teachers?
17. Has <Program Name> worked on or participated in any projects in the community? If so, what?
18. Do you feel that <Program Name> is making a difference in your life? How so?

19. Do you think that <Program Name> is making a difference for others? The community? Please explain . . .
20. What would you improve about <Program Name>?
21. What is school like for you?
     Probes: Do you look forward to coming to school? Explain.
22. What's your favorite class? Why?
23. What kinds of grades do you make in school? What's your GPA?
24. Do you believe it is important to do well in school? Why?
25. Describe your favorite teacher.
     Probes: What makes a good teacher?
26. Describe your least favorite teacher.
     Probes: What makes a bad teacher?
27. How would you describe your behavior in classes?
28. How would you describe your behavior in <Program Name>?
29. How would you describe your relationship with adults in your school?
     Probes: Teachers, Administrators, Counselors
30. How would you describe your relationship with adults in <Program Name>?
31. Do you feel like you can be yourself at school? Why?
32. Do you feel like you can be yourself at <Program Name>? Why?
33. What do you think is the purpose of school?
34. What do you think is the purpose of <Program Name>?
35. What do you need from school?
36. What do you need from <Program Name>?
37. Would your family or friends consider you to be a successful person? Why?
38. What are some of your goals in life? Is school helping you reach them? Is <Program Name>?

Closing

39. Is there anything else that you would like to add?
40. Do you have any questions for me?

Colleague Interview Protocol

Date: _____

Time Starting: _____

Time Stopping: _____

Location: _____

Name: _____

Code Name (if applicable): _____

Script:

Greetings and thank you so much for taking time out of your busy schedule to speak with me. I want to remind you that you can tell me you don't want to answer any question you don't feel like answering, and you can stop the interview at any point. I'd like to tape record the interview. Is that okay? You can tell me to turn off the recorder at any point, if you want. If, after the interview is over, you want to withdraw from the study, I'll destroy your information.

Do you have any questions?

Are you ready to begin?

1. How long have you worked with the program?
2. What is your background and/or specific qualifications?
3. What's a typical day/meeting like?
4. Do you consider the program successful? Why? Please give specific examples.
5. What are some areas for improvement?
6. Describe the <Program Director>.
7. Do you think <Program Director> successfully engages youth? If so, why and in what ways? What makes him/her successful?
8. How could <Program Director> better serve the youth?
9. Any final remarks?
10. Is there anything you'd like to ask me?

Abbreviated Sample of UNITED PLAYAZ Questionnaire

Greetings and thank you so much for taking the time to complete this questionnaire. I want to learn about you and your experiences in *United Playaz*. Your answers will be kept confidential because I am the only person who will have access to the information you choose to share. Please take your time to respond to every question to the best of your ability. There are no right or wrong answers; just keep it real and be honest!

At the end of this questionnaire, you will be asked whether or not you would like to continue to participate in this study. If you think that you would like to be part of a short interview and/or a group discussion with your peers, please enter your contact information in the space provided. However, your answers to the questionnaire will remain confidential. Thank you.

The following questions are about your participation in UP.

(please circle *one response* for each statement)

		NO!!!	no	Not really	Kind of	yes	YES!!!
1.	I look forward to coming to United Playaz.	1	2	3	4	5	6
2.	An important part of United Playaz is taking action in the community to create positive change.	1	2	3	4	5	6
3.	In United Playaz, I feel like others really get to know me.	1	2	3	4	5	6
4.	United Playaz is relevant to my life and needs.	1	2	3	4	5	6
5.	I wish there were more programs like this.	1	2	3	4	5	6
6.	Youth and adults work together to make decisions in United Playaz.	1	2	3	4	5	6
7.	United Playaz is really diverse.	1	2	3	4	5	6
8.	I feel challenged to push myself in United Playaz.	1	2	3	4	5	6
9.	The larger community sees United Playaz as important.	1	2	3	4	5	6
10.	In United Playaz, I learn about ways that youth can take action in the community.	1	2	3	4	5	6
11.	Other participants in United Playaz acknowledge my identity and cultural background in a positive way.	1	2	3	4	5	6
12.	United Playaz materials are available in the language that I speak at home.	1	2	3	4	5	6
13.	I feel prepared to talk with other people about my experiences in United Playaz.	1	2	3	4	5	6
14.	United Playaz challenges me.	1	2	3	4	5	6

		NO!!!	no	Not really	Kind of	yes	YES!!!
15.	Adult staff make sure there are leadership roles for youth in United Playaz (i.e., planning activities, facilitating meetings, etc.).	1	2	3	4	5	6
16.	Information in *school* is relevant to my life.	1	2	3	4	5	6
17.	Information at United Playaz is relevant to my life.	1	2	3	4	5	6
18.	I wish *school* was more like United Playaz.	1	2	3	4	5	6
19.	I would be comfortable asking Rudy for help in an emergency.	1	2	3	4	5	6
20.	I would be comfortable asking a teacher for help in an emergency.	1	2	3	4	5	6
21.	Because of United Playaz, I am more committed to doing well in school.	1	2	3	4	5	6
22.	My program makes me feel better about school.	1	2	3	4	5	6

23. What are 3 words that describe United Playaz?
24. Where would you be and where would your life be headed if you were not part of United Playaz?
25. If you could change or improve one thing about UP, what would it be and why?
26. What is Rudy's role in United Playaz?
27. What is Rudy's role in your life?
28. What are 3 words you would use to describe Rudy?
29. How is Rudy similar to and/or different from other adults in your life? Please explain.
30. If you could change or improve one thing about the way that Rudy works with you/UP what would it be? Explain.
31. Is there a particular moment or event that stands out in your mind when you think about United Playaz?
32. Why are you part of United Playaz?
33. What are 3 words that describe your school?

Anything Else You Wanna Tell Me . . . _____

_____

_____

_____

_____

Your Information (please check one answer for each question)

How long have you been involved with United Playaz?
- ❑ Less than 6 months
- ❑ 7 months to 1 year
- ❑ 1 to 2 years
- ❑ Over 2 years

In the past 4 weeks (1 month), about how often have you participated in program activities?
- ❑ Not at all
- ❑ Once or twice a month
- ❑ About once a week
- ❑ More than once a week

When you have participated in program activities, how long did you usually stay?
- ❑ Did not attend
- ❑ Less than 1 hour
- ❑ 1 hour to 2 hours
- ❑ More than 2 hours

What is your gender?   ❑ Female ❑ Male ❑ Decline to state

How old are you?   _____ years old

What is your neighborhood and zip code?   Neighborhood: _____
Zip Code: _____

What is the *primary* language spoken by your family/guardian(s)?   _____

How would you describe your ethnicity, race, and/or cultural background?

- ❑ African-American/Black
- ❑ Asian/Pacific Islander
- ❑ Middle Eastern/Arab
- ❑ Chicana/o, Latina/o, Caribbean
- ❑ Multi-ethnic/-racial:

_____

- ❑ Native/Indigenous
- ❑ white/European
- ❑ Ethnicity/cultural background not listed above:

_____

- ❑ Decline to state.

Thank you very much for completing this questionnaire!

✂CUT————————DETACH————DETACH————————CUT✂

Would you be willing to participate in a short interview (about an hour)? ____ yes ____ no

Would you be willing to participate in a group discussion with other UP members? ____ yes ____ no

If you answered yes to either question, please provide the following information:

Name: _____

Age: ____

Phone/Cell Number: _____

Email: _____

APPENDIX E

Website and Contact Information for the Community-Based Educators

1. Dereca Blackmon and Leadership Excellence

http://leadershipexcellence.org/
1629 Telegraph 5th Floor, Oakland, CA 94612
(510) 267-9770 ext 14
Dereca Blackmon: dereca@gmail.com

2. Rudy Corpuz, Jr., and United Playaz

http://www.unitedplayaz.org/
1038 Howard Street, San Francisco, CA 94103
(888) ZPLAYAZ/(415) 863-9883
Rudy Corpuz: rudy@unitedplayaz.org

3. Victor Damian and the Youth Task Force

http://www.sfdph.org/dph/comupg/oservices/mentalHlth/CBHS/
CBHSadvComm.asp
1305 Evans Ave., San Francisco, CA 94124
(415) 920-7715
Victor Damian: victor.damian@sfdph.org
http://thoughtmovement.wordpress.com/

4. Jack Jacqua and the Omega Boys Club

http://www.street-soldiers.org/
1060 Tennessee Street, San Francisco, CA 94107
(415) 826-8664

NOTES

1 Introduction

1 And just as I wrote the word "generation" I received another call: my former student and friend, Jason Reddic (J-Redd), was shot and passed away on the evening of his 28th birthday (Salonga, 2010).

2 As I elicited the names of community-based educators, I purposefully did not define success. Rather, I followed Lawrence-Lightfoot's lead: "Not only do portraits seek to capture the origins and expressions of goodness, they are also concerned with documenting how the subjects or actors in the setting define goodness" (Lawrence-Lightfoot & Davis, 1997, p. 9). I presumed that success meant different things for different programs—from consistently keeping troubled youth out of jail to procuring four-year scholarships to college for needy teenagers. Thus, I remained open to interpreting *their* understanding of success.

3 The educators are all identified by their real name along with the program they direct. Students were given the option to remain anonymous, but the majority felt that changing their names would be an injustice in and of itself. Thus, like other researchers who use portraiture, I chose to keep identities unobstructed. Lawrence-Lightfoot (1983) writes:

> Throughout the text I use the real names of the high schools I studied and the real names of their headmasters and principals . . . The decision to use the high schools' and leaders' real names . . . reflected the school people's generosity and confidence, my wish to publicly applaud their efforts, and my decision to portray the settings in vivid, exacting detail. (pp. 21–22)

2 Dereca Blackmon

1 The Center for Young Women's Development (CYWD) organizes young women in San Francisco who are severely marginalized—those in the street economies and the juvenile justice system—to design and deliver peer-to-peer education and support.

2 *Sankofa*, by Haile Gerima (1993), is a vivid account of the slave system—describing both the brutality of oppression and the fight for liberation.
3 An associate degree is an academic degree usually awarded by community colleges upon completion of a course of study generally lasting 2 years.
4 McClymonds High School is a public high school in the West Oakland neighborhood.

3 Rudy Corpuz, Jr.

1 The ball brought together people from across the city—"from the Tenderloin to the Mission to the Point to the Swamp"—and many of the "dudes there had beef. When they seen each other there," Rudy said, they told him, "we're not even goin to go there today." This was monumental. "For that one day there was no killings. I can't speak for the next day but at least for that one day we came together."
2 The Vice Lords is the oldest and second-largest street gang in Chicago. They began some time in 1958, as a youth gang in the Illinois State Training School for Boys. In the late 1960s they legally incorporated their group into a forceful community-based organization that fought for people's rights (Dawley, 1992).
3 http://dbacon.igc.org.
4 Rudy recommends that teachers address, for instance, issues of police brutality. This is something he also tries to deal with. Evangela told me that her and her friends are afraid of cops because they are the biggest gang around. Rudy wanted Evangela and other UP members to have an opportunity to voice their concerns. He brought them to a town hall meeting and from this encounter Evangela realized that "all police are not bad but it's them certain ones that make everybody look bad." In order to improve the relationship between youth and the police, the officers agreed to provide UP participants with rides to an upcoming event. On the day of the field trip, the police called and canceled.
5 *San Francisco Chronicle*, August 26, 2007.

5 Jack Jacqua

1 All the quotes from Dr. Marshall are from his *Street Soldier* (1996).
2 These statements come from an Omega Boys pamphlet.
3 The Potrero Hill Neighborhood House, called the NABE, is a community center that serves the Potrero Hill, Mission, Visitation Valley, and Bayview Hunters Point neighborhoods. Programs range from a Head Start preschool to the Experiment in Diversity (EID). EID enrolls youth aged 14 to 18 who are considered "hard to serve" because they are in the juvenile justice system and/or have dropped out of school. This particular initiative takes youth off the streets and engages them in activities in which they learn new values of community responsibility and accountability. The Omega Boys Club started at the NABE and Jack still has a strong presence there.
4 The IEP, or Individualized Education Plan, is a written document that is developed for each public school child who is eligible for special education. By federal law, a multidisciplinary team must determine that (1) the child has a disability and (2) the child requires special education and related services in order to benefit from the general education program.
5 *YO! Youth Outlook* is an award-winning literary journal of youth life in the Bay Area. It chronicles the world through the eyes and voices of young people between the ages of 14 and 25. *YO!* has a national distribution of 25,000 magazines printed monthly.
6 *The Beat Within* is a journal of young people's poetry, artwork, and essays. It was founded in 1996 when a social worker inside YGC realized that there was no

vehicle for the voices of incarcerated youth. He decided to provide that vehicle, and *The Beat* was born. *The Beat* has grown to about 100 pages a week of writing from the 40-plus juvenile hall units in the Bay Area.

7 For more on innocent victims of street violence, see Rich (2009).

7 Community-Based Urban Education

1 They are seven African-American men, four African-American women, two bi-racial women (African-American/white; African-American/Latina), one bi-racial man (Blaxican), and one Filipino man.

Appendix A

1 Lowell is rated among the top 10 public schools in California and admits students based on special admission requirements such as standardized test scores and GPA. The school disproportionately serves Chinese-American students. Thurgood Marshall high school in the Bayview district in San Francisco enrolls over 1,000 students; its mission is to increase the academic achievement of students of color.

Appendix B

1 The exception is Jack Jacqua. He was interviewed twice.

Appendix C

1 *Books Not Bars* is a component of the Ella Baker Center in Oakland, CA. *Books Not Bars* fights to redirect California's resources away from youth incarceration and toward youth opportunities. Currently, it is trying to close California's youth prisons and replace them with rehabilitation centers and community-based programs.

BIBLIOGRAPHY

Adams, D. (1995). *Education for extinction: American Indians and the boarding school experience 1875–1928*. Lawrence: University Press of Kansas.

Adams, F. (1975). *Unearthing seeds of fire: The idea of highlander*. Winston-Salem, NC: John Blair.

Alexander, M. (2010). *The new Jim Crow: Mass incarceration in the age of colorblindness*. New York: New Press.

Anderson, E. (1994). The code of the streets. *Atlantic Monthly, 273*(5), 80–94.

Anderson, J. D. (1988). *The education of blacks in the south, 1860–1935*. Chapel Hill: University of North Carolina Press.

Anderson, M., Kaufman, J., Simon, T., Barrios, L., Paulozzi, L., Ryan, G., et al. (2001). School-associated violent deaths in the United States, 1994–1999. *Journal of the American Medical Association, 286*, 2695–2702.

Angus, D., & Mirel, J. (1999). *The failed promise of the American high school 1890–1995*. New York: Teachers College Press.

Anyon, J. (2005). *Radical possibilities*. New York: Routledge.

Apple, M. W. (1995). *Education and power*. London: Routledge.

Apple, M. W. (2004). *Ideology and curriculum* (3rd edn.). New York: Routledge.

Apple, M. W. (2006). *Educating the "right" way: Markets, standards, God, and inequality*. New York: Routledge Falmer.

Apple, M. W. (Ed.) (2010). *Global crises, social justice, and education*. New York: Routledge Falmer.

Apple, M. W. (2011, February). Grading Obama's education policy. *The Progressive, 25*(2), 368–382.

Aronowitz, T. (2005). The role of "envisioning the future" in the development of resilience among at-risk youth. *Public Health Nursing, 22*(3), 200–208.

Aronowitz, S., & Giroux, H. (1993). *Education still under siege*. Westport, CT: Bergin and Garvey.

Ballenger, C. (1999). *Teaching other people's children: Literacy and learning in a bilingual classroom*. New York: Teachers College Press.

Barker, D. (2004). The scholarship of engagement: A taxonomy of five emerging practices. *Journal of Higher Education Outreach & Engagement, 9*(2), 123–137.

Behar, R. (1996). *The vulnerable observer: Anthropology that breaks your heart.* Boston: Beacon Press.

Bell, B., Gaventa, J., & Peters, J. (Eds.). (1990). *We make the road by walking: Myles Horton and Paulo Freire (conversations on education & social change).* Philadelphia, PA: Temple University Press.

Bennett, C., McWhorter, L., & Kuykendall, J. (2006, Fall). Will I ever teach? Latino and African American students' perspectives on PRAXIS I. *American Educational Research Journal, 43*(3), 531–575.

Biddle, B. J., & Berliner, D. C. (2002). Unequal school funding in the United States. *Educational Leadership, 59*(8), 48–59.

Blum, R., & Rinehart, P. (1999). *Reducing the risk: Connections that make a difference in the lives of youth.* Minneapolis: University of Minnesota.

Bordieu, P., & Passeron, J. C. (1977). *Reproduction in education, society and culture.* Beverly Hills: Sage.

Bowles, S., & Gintis, H. (1976). *Schooling in capitalist America: Educational reform and the contradictions of economic life.* New York: Basic Books.

Bradley, M. (1978). *The iceman inheritance: Prehistoric sources of western man's racism, sexism and aggression.* New York: Kayode Publications.

Brendtro, L., Brokenleg, M., & Bockern, S. (1990). *Reclaiming youth at risk: Our hope for the future.* Bloomington, IN: Solution Tree Press.

Breslau, J. (2010, March). Health in childhood and adolescence and high school dropout. *California Dropout Research Project Report (#17).* Retrieved October 2010 from http://cdrp.ucsb.edu/dropouts/pubs_reports.htm.

Breslau, N., Davis, G., & Peterson, E. (1991). Traumatic events and posttraumatic stress disorder in an urban population of young adults. *General Psychiatry, 48*(3), 216–222.

Brofenbrenner, U. (1979). *The ecology of human development.* Cambridge, MA: Harvard University Press.

Brown, J. (2011). Parents building communities in schools. In E. A. Skinner, M. T. Garreton, & B. D. Schultz (Eds.), *Grow your own teachers: Grassroots change for teacher education* (pp. 49–60). New York: Teachers College Press.

Bryk, A. S., Sebring, P. B., Allensworth, E., Luppescu, S., & Easton, J. Q. (2010). *Organizing schools for improvement: Lessons from Chicago.* Chicago: University of Chicago Press.

California Dropout Research Project (2009, April 9). *Dropout crisis contributes to substantial economic losses in California cities.* Retrieved October 2010 from http://www.cdrp.ucsb.edu/pr7.pdf.

Carter, M. (2005). Helping African American males reach their academic potential. In T. Hatch, D. Ahmed, A. Lieberman, D. Faigenbaum, M. E. White, & D. H. Pointer Mace (Eds.), *Going public with our teaching: An anthology of practice* (pp. 189–209). New York: Teachers College Press.

Carter, S. C. (2000). *No excuses: Lessons from 21 high performing, high poverty schools.* Washington, DC: Heritage Foundation.

Catalano, R., Berglund, L., Ryan, J., Lonczak, H., and Hawkins, J. (1999). *Positive youth development in the United States: Research findings on evaluations of positive youth development programs.* Washington, DC: Office of the Assistant Secretary for Planning and Evaluation, US Department of Health and Human Services.

CDC (Centers for Disease Control and Prevention) (n.d.a) *Web-based Injury Statistics Query and Reporting System (WISQARS)*. Retrieved December 30, 2010, from http://www.cdc.gov/injury/wisqars.

CDC (n.d.b) *Web-based Injury Statistics Query and Reporting System (WISQARS)*. Retrieved December 30, 2010, from http://www.cdc.gov/violenceprevention/pdf/YV-DataSheet-a.pdf.

Chatmon, T. (2007, April). Interrogating classroom relationships and events: Using portraiture and critical race theory in education research. *Educational Researcher, 36*(3), 156–162.

Chenoweth, K. (2009). *How it's being done: Urgent lessons from unexpected schools.* Cambridge, MA: Harvard Education Press.

Children's Defense Fund. (2007). *America's cradle to prison pipeline.* Retrieved March 2010 from http://www.childrensdefense.org/PageServer?pagename=c2pp_report2007.

Coleman, J. S. (1966). Equality and educational opportunity: Summary report. *United States Office of Education & National Center for Education Statistics.* Washington, DC: U.S. Dept. of Health Education and Welfare Office of Education.

Conchas, G. Q. (2001). Structuring failure and success: Understanding the variability in Latino school engagement. *Harvard Educational Review, 71*(3), 475–504.

Connell, J. P., & Gambone, M. A. (1998). *Youth development in community settings: A community action framework.* Working paper. Philadelphia, PA: Institute for Research and Reform in Education and Youth Development Strategies.

Cooley-Strickland, M., Quille, T. J., Griffin, R. S., Stuart, E. A., Bradshaw, C. P., & Furr-Holden, D. (2009, May 27). Community violence and youth: Affect, behavior, substance use, and academics. *Clinical Child Family Psychological Review, 12,* 127–166.

Critical Resistance Project. (2011). *Organizational website.* Retrieved April 2011 from http://www.criticaltesistance.org.

Dance, L. J. (2002). *Tough fronts: The impact of street culture on schooling.* London: Routledge.

Darder, A. (2002). *Reinventing Paulo Freire: A pedagogy of love.* Cambridge, MA: Westview Press.

Darder, A., Baltodano, M., & Torres, R. (Eds.). (2003). *The critical pedagogy reader.* New York: Routledge Falmer.

Darley, J. M. & Latané, B. (1968). Bystander intervention in emergencies: Diffusion of responsibility. *Journal of Personality and Social Psychology, 8,* 377–383.

Darling-Hammond, L. (1997). *Doing what matters most: Investing in quality teaching.* New York: The National Commission on Teaching and America's Future.

Darling-Hammond, L. (1999, December). *Teacher quality and student achievement: A review of state policy evidence.* Seattle, WA: Center for the Study of Teaching and Policy, University of Washington.

Darling-Hammond, L. (2005). *A good teacher in every classroom: Preparing the highly qualified teachers our children deserve.* Indianapolis, IN: Jossey-Bass.

Darling-Hammond, L. (2006). *Powerful teacher education: Lessons from exemplary programs.* San Francisco: Jossey-Bass.

Darling-Hammond, L. (2010). *The flat world & education: How American's commitment to equity will determine our future.* New York: Teachers College Press.

Davis, J. (Ed.). (1996). *Safe havens: Portraits of art centers.* Cambridge, MA: Harvard Project Zero, Harvard University Graduate School of Education.

Dawley, D. (1992). *A nation of lords: The autobiography of the vice lords.* Prospect Heights, IL: Waveland Press.

de los Reyes, E., & Gozemba, P. (2002). *Pockets of hope: How students and teachers change the world.* Westport, CT: Bergin and Garvey.

Delpit, L. (1995). *Other people's children: Cultural conflict in the classroom.* New York: New Press.

Dewey, J. (1916). *Democracy and education.* New York: Macmillan.

Dewey, J. (1938). *Experience and education.* New York: Macmillan.

Dimitriadis, G. (2001). *Performing identity/performing culture: Hip-hop as text, pedagogy, and lived practice, vol. 1.* New York: Peter Lang.

Dorfman, L., & Schiraldi, V. (2001). *Off balance: Youth, race & crime in the news.* Retrieved January 2011 from http://www.justicepolicy.org/research/2060.

Duncan-Andrade, J. (2004). Toward teacher development for the urban in urban teaching. *Teacher Education, 15*(4), 339–350.

Duncan-Andrade, J. (2009). Note to educators: Hope required when growing roses in concrete. *Harvard Education Review, 79*(2), 181–194.

Duncan-Andrade, J. (2010). *What a coach can teach a teacher.* New York: Peter Lang.

Duncan-Andrade, J., & Morrell, E. (2008). *The art of critical pedagogy: Possibilities for moving from theory to practice in urban schools.* New York: Peter Lang.

Eccles, J., & Gootman, J. (Eds.). (2001). *Community programs to promote youth development.* Washington, DC: National Academy Press.

Edelman, M. (2010). *Missouri's "miracle" is a model for juvenile justice reform.* Retrieved March 20, 2010, from http://news.change.org/stories/missouri-miracle-is-a-model-for-juvenile-justice-reform.

Elmore, R. (2000). *Building a new structure for school leadership.* Washington: Albert Shanker Institute.

Emerson, R. M., Fretz, R. I., & Shaw, L. L. (1995). *Writing ethnographic fieldnotes.* Chicago: Chicago University Press.

Erikson, E. (1968). *Identity, youth, and crisis.* New York: Norton.

Espinosa, H. (2006). The crusader: Rudy Corpuz and his fight to end youth violence. *Manila Bulletin USA, 14*(9), 5–7.

Fabricant, M. (2010). *Organizing for educational justice: The campaign for public school reform in the south Bronx.* Minneapolis: University of Minnesota Press.

Fanon, F. (1976). *The wretched of the earth.* New York: Grove Press.

Ferguson, A. (2001). *Bad boys: Public school in the making of Black masculinity.* Ann Arbor: University of Michigan Press.

Fine, M. (1991). *Framing dropouts: Notes on the politics of an urban public high school.* Albany, NY: SUNY Press.

Fine, M., & Weis, L. (2003). *Silenced voices and extraordinary conversations: Re-imagining schools.* New York: Teachers College Press.

Fisher, M. (2007). "Every city has soldiers": The role of intergenerational relationships in participatory literacy communities. *Research in the Teaching of English, 42*(2), 139–162.

Fisher, M. (2008). *Black literate lives: Historical and contemporary perspectives.* New York: Routledge.

Fordham, S., & Ogbu, J. (1986). Black students' school success: Coping with the burden of "acting white." *Urban Review, 18*(3), 1–31.

Forman, M. (2002). *The hood comes first: Race, space & place in rap & hip-hop.* Hanover, NH: Wesleyan University Press.

Frankenberg, R. (1993). *White women/race matters: The social construction of whiteness.* Minneapolis: University of Minnesota Press.

Freire, P. (1970). *Pedagogy of the oppressed.* New York: Continuum.

Freire, P. (1995). *Pedagogy of hope.* New York: Continuum.

Freire, P. (1997). *Pedagogy of the heart.* New York: Continuum.

Freire, P. (1998). *Teachers as cultural workers.* Boulder, CO: Westview.

Freire, P. (2000). *Pedagogy of freedom.* Lanham, MD: Rowman & Litttlefield.

Freire, P., & Freire, A. (1997). *Pedagogy of the heart.* New York: Continuum.

Freire, P., & Macedo, D. (1987). *Literacy: Reading the word and the world.* Westport, CT: Bergin and Garvey.

Gambone, M. A., & Arbreton, A. J. A. (1997). *Safe havens: The contributions of youth organizations to healthy adolescent development.* Philadelphia, PA: Public/Private Ventures.

Garbarino, J. (1999). *Raising children in a socially toxic environment.* San Francisco, CA: Jossey-Bass.

Geertz, C. (1974). From the native's point of view: On the nature of anthropological understanding. *Bulletin of the American Academy of Arts and Sciences, 28,* 221–237.

Gersh, D. (1987). The corporate elite and the introduction of IQ testing in American public schools. In M. Schwartz (Ed.), *The structure of power in America* (pp. 163–183). New York: Holmes and Meier.

Gillette, M. (2011). Doing it better together: The challenges and the promise of community-based teacher education. In E. Skinner, M. T. Garreton, & B. D. Schultz (Eds.), *Grow your own teachers: Grassroots change for teacher education* (pp. 146–162). New York: Teachers College Press.

Gilmore, R. W. (2007a). *Golden gulag: Prisons surplus, crisis, and opposition in globalizing California.* Berkeley: University of California Press.

Gilmore, R. W. (2007b). In the shadow of the state. In Incite! Women of Color Against Violence (Eds.), *The revolution will not be funded: Beyond the non-profit industrial complex* (pp. 41–52). Cambridge, MA: South End Press.

Gilmore, R. W. (2008). Forgotten places and the seeds of grassroots planning. In C. R. Hale (Ed.), *Engaging contradictions: Theory, politics, methods of activist scholarship* (pp. 31–61). Berkeley: University of California Press.

Ginwright, S. (2004). *Black in school: Afrocentric reform, urban youth, and the promise of hip-hop culture.* New York: Teachers College Press.

Ginwright, S. (2009). *Black youth rising: Activism and radical healing in urban America.* New York: Teachers College Press.

Ginwright, S., Noguera, P., & Cammarota, J. (Eds.). (2006). *Beyond resistance! Youth activism and community change.* New York: Routledge.

Giroux, H. (1989). *Popular culture: Schooling and everyday life.* New York: Bergin and Garvey.

Giroux, H. (1997). *Pedagogy and the politics of hope: Theory, culture, and schooling.* Boulder, CO: Westview.

Giroux, H. (2001). *Theory and resistance in education: Towards a pedagogy for the opposition* (revised and expanded ed.). Westport, CT: Bergin & Garvey.

Glesne, C. (1999). *Becoming qualitative researchers.* New York: Longman.

Gramsci, A. (1971). *Selections from the prison notebooks.* New York: International.

Hall, S. (1998). Notes on deconstructing the popular. In J. Storey (Ed.), *Cultural theory and popular culture: A reader.* Athens, GA: University of Georgia Press.

Haycock, K. (1998). Good teaching matters: How well-qualified teachers can close the gap. *Thinking K–16, 3,* 3–14.

Heath, S. (1983). *Ways with words.* Cambridge: Cambridge University Press.

Heath, S. (1999). Rethinking youth transitions. *Human Development, 42*(6), 376–386.

Heath, S., & McLaughlin, M. (Eds.). (1993). *Identity & inner-city youth: Beyond ethnicity and gender.* New York: Teachers College.

Heath, S., & McLaughlin, M. (1996). The best of both worlds: Connecting schools and community youth organizations for all-day, all-year learning. In J. Cibulka & W. Kritek (Eds.), *Coordination among schools, families, and communities: Prospects for educational reform* (pp. 69–94). Albany, NY: State University of New York Press.

Hebdige, D. (1979). *Subculture: The meaning of style.* London: Routledge.

Henderson, A., Mapp, K., Johnson, V., & Davies, D. (2006) *Beyond the bake sale.* New York: New Press.

Hilliard, A. (1998). *SBA: The reawakening of the African mind.* Gainesville, FL: Makare.

Hinsdale, M., Lewis, H., and Waller, S. (1995). *It comes from the people: Community development and local theology.* Philadelphia, PA: Temple University Press.

hooks, b. (1994). *Teaching to transgress: Education as the practice of freedom.* New York: Routledge.

Hudson, J. M., & Bruckman, A. S. (2004). The bystander effect: A lens for understanding patterns of participation. *Journal of the Learning Sciences, 13*(2), 165–195.

James, E. (2010, March 10). 37 years of solitary confinement: The Angola three. *The Guardian.* Retrieved February 2011 from http://www.guardian.co.uk/society/2010/mar/10/erwin-james-angola-three.

Justice Policy Institute. (2000). *The punishing decade: Prison and jail estimates at the millennium.* Report. Washington, DC: Justice Policy Institute.

Kleinman, S., & Copp, M. A. (1993). *Emotions and fieldwork.* Newbury Park, CA: Sage Publications.

Kozol, J. (1991). *Savage inequalities.* New York: Crown.

Kozol, J. (1994). The new untouchables. In J. Kretovics and E. Nussel (Eds.), *Transforming urban education* (pp. 75–78). Needham Heights, MA: Allyn and Bacon.

Kozol, J. (2005). *The shame of a nation.* New York: Crown.

Ladson-Billings, G. (1994). *The dreamkeepers: Successful teachers of African American children.* San Francisco: Jossey-Bass.

Ladson-Billings, G. (1995). But that's just good teaching! The case for culturally relevant pedagogy. *Theory into Practice, 34*(3), 195–202.

Lawrence-Lightfoot, S. (1983). *The good high school.* New York: Basic Books.

Lawrence-Lightfoot, S. (1994). *I've known rivers: Lives of loss and liberation.* Reading, MA: Addison-Wesley.

Lawrence-Lightfoot, S. (1999). *Respect: An exploration.* Cambridge, MA: Perseus Books.

Lawrence-Lightfoot, S., & Davis, J. (1997). *The art and science of portraiture.* San Francisco: Jossey-Bass.

LeCompte, M. (1993). *Ethnography and qualitative design in educational research* (2nd edn.). New York: Academic Press.

Lee, P. W. (1999). In their own voices: An ethnographic study of low-achieving students within the context of school reform. *Urban Education, 34*(2), 214–244.

Leonardo, Z. (2004, April). The color of supremacy: Beyond the discourse of "white privilege." *Educational Philosophy & Theory, 36*(2), 137–152.

Leonardo, Z. (2009). *Race, whiteness, and education.* New York: Routledge.

Lewis-Charp, H., Cao Yu, H., & Soukamneuth, S. (2006). Civic approaches for engaging youth in social justice. In S. Ginwright, P. Noguera, & J. Cammarota (Eds.), *Beyond resistance* (pp. 21–36). New York: Routledge.

Lichtenstein, A. (1996a). *Twice the work of free labor: The political economy of convict labor in the new south.* London: Verso.

Lichtenstein, A. (1996b). Good roads & chain gangs in the progressive south: "The negro convict is a slave." *Journal of Southern History, 59*(1), 85–110.

Lipman, P. (2011). *The new political economy of urban education: Neoliberalism, race, and the right to the city.* New York: Routledge.

Lortie, D. (1975). *Schoolteacher: A sociological study.* Chicago: University of Chicago Press.

Luttrell, W. (2000). "Good enough" methods for ethnographic research. *Harvard Educational Review, 70*(4), 499–534.

Lynch, K., Baker, J., & Lyons, M. (2009). *Affective equality: Love, care and injustice.* London: Palgrave Macmillan.

MacLeod, J. (1995). *Ain't no makin' it: Aspirations and attainment in a low-income neighborhood.* Boulder, CO: Westview Press.

Mahiri, J. (1998a). *Shooting for excellence: African American and youth culture in new century schools.* New York: Teachers College Press.

Mahiri, J. (1998b). Streets to schools: African American youth culture and the classroom. *Clearing House, 71*(6), 335–338.

Mahiri, J., & Conner, E. (2003). Black youth violence has a bad rap. *Journal of Social Issues, 59*(1), 121–140.

Mancini, M. (1996). *One dies, get another: Convict leasing in the American south.* Columbia: University of South Carolina Press.

Mann, H. (1848). *Twelfth annual report to the Massachusetts Board of Education.* Retrieved December 2010 from http://www.tncrimlaw.com/civil_bible/horace_mann.htm.

Marley, B. (1976). War. On *Rastaman Vibration.* Kingston, Jamaica: Island.

Marshall, J. (1996). *Street soldier: One man's struggle to save a generation one life at a time.* New York: Delacorte Press.

Maxwell, J. A. (1996). *Qualitative research design: An interactive approach.* Thousand Oaks, CA: Sage Publications.

Maykut, P., & Morehouse, R. (1994). *Beginning qualitative research: A philosophic and practical guide.* London: Routledge.

Mayo, P. (1999). *Gramsci, Freire and adult education.* London: Zed Books.

Mayo, P. (2004). *Liberating praxis: Paulo Freire's legacy for radical education and politics.* Westport, CT: Greenwood Publishing Group.

McDonald, M., Tyson, K., Brayko, K., Bowman, M., Delport, J., & Shimomura, F. (2010). Innovation and impact in teacher education: Community-based organizations as field placements for preservice teachers. *Teachers College Record, 113*(8), ID no. 16162.

McLaren, P. (2000). *Che Guevara, Paulo Freire, & the pedagogy of revolution.* Lanham, MD: Rowman & Littlefield.

McLaughlin, M. (2000). *Community counts.* Presentation for the Public Education Network. Retrieved July 2008 from http://www.publiceducation.org/pdf/Publications/support services/community counts.pdf.

McLaughlin, M., Irby, M., & Langman, J. (2001). *Urban sanctuaries: Neighborhood organizations in the lives and futures of inner-city youth.* San Francisco: Jossey-Bass.

Meiners, E. (2007). *Right to be hostile: Schools, prisons, and the making of public enemies.* New York: Routledge.

Michie, G. (1999). *Holler if you hear me: The education of a teacher & his students.* New York: Teachers College Press.

Michie, G. (2004). *See you when we get there: Teaching for change in urban schools.* New York: Teachers College Press.

Miles, M. B., & Huberman, A. M. (1994). *Qualitative data analysis.* Thousand Oaks, CA: Sage.

Miron, L., & Mickey L. (1998). Student voice as agency: Resistance and accommodation in inner-city schools. *Anthropology and Education Quarterly, 29*(2), 189–213.

Moll, L. C., Amati, C., Neff, D., & Gonzalez, N. (1992). Funds of knowledge for teaching: Using a qualitative approach to connect homes and classrooms. *Theory into Practice, 31*(1), 132–141.

National Commission for Teaching and America's Future. (2003). *No dream denied: A pledge to America's children.* Washington, DC: Author.

Nocera, J. (1990, Sept./Oct.). How the middle class has helped ruin the public schools. *Washington Weekly.*

Noguera, P. (2003). *City schools and the American dream.* New York: Teachers College Press.

Nogeura, P. (2008). *The trouble with Black boys . . . and other reflections on race, equity, and the future of public education.* San Francisco: Jossey-Bass.

Noguera, P. (2011, February 2). The race to the top. *Motion Magazine.* Retrieved April 2011 from http://www.inmotionmagazine.com/erll/pn-racetop.html.

Noguera, P., & Akom, A. (2000, June 25). Disparities demystified. *The Nation, 270*(22), 29–31.

Oakes, J. (1985). *Keeping track: How schools structure inequality.* Hew Haven, CT: Yale University Press.

Oakes, J. (1994). Tracking, inequality, and the rhetoric of reform: Why schools don't change. In J. Kretovics & E. Nussel (Eds.), *Transforming urban education* (pp. 146–164). Needham Heights, MA: Allyn & Bacon.

Oakes, J., & Lipton, M. (2007). *Teaching to change the world.* Boston: McGrawHill Press.

Oakes, J., Wells, A. S., Jones, M., & Datnow, A. (1997). Detracking: The social construction of ability, cultural politics, and resistance to reform. *Teachers College Record, 98*(3), 482–510.

Ogbu, J. U. (1985). A cultural ecology of competence among inner-city blacks. In M. B. Spencer, G. K. Brookings, & W. R. Allen (Eds.), *Beginnings: The social and affective development of black children* (pp. 45–66). Hillsdale, NJ: Erlbaum.

Ogletree, C. (2010). *The presumption of guilt: The arrest of Henry Louis Gates, Jr. and race, class and crime in America.* New York: Palgrave Macmillan.

Orfield, G. (Ed.). (2004). *Dropout in America: Confronting the graduation rate crisis.* Cambridge, MA: Harvard Education Press.

Orfield, G., Bachmeier, M., & James, D. (1997). *Deepening segregation in American public schools.* Cambridge, MA: Civil Rights Project, Harvard Graduate School of Education.

Orfield, G., Losen, D., Wald, J., & Swanson, C. (2004). *Losing our future: How minority youth are being left behind by the graduation crisis.* Cambridge, MA: Civil Rights Project, Harvard University Graduate School of Education.

Orfield, G., & Kornhaber, M. (Eds.). (2001). *Raising standards or raising barriers?* New York: Century Foundation Press.

Patton, M. (1990). *Qualitative evaluation and research methods* (2nd edn.). Newbury Park, CA: Sage Publications.

Payne C., & Strickland C. (2008). *Teach freedom: Education for liberation in the African-American tradition.* New York: Teachers College Press.

Perkins, W. (Ed.). (1996). *Droppin' science: Critical essays on rap music and hip-hop culture.* Philadelphia, Temple University Press.

Perry, T. (2003). Up from the parched earth: Toward a theory of African American achievement. In T. Perry, C. Steel, & A. Hilliard, III (Eds.), *Young gifted and Black: Promoting high achievement among African-American students* (pp. 1–108). Boston, MA: Beacon.

Perry, T., Steele, C., & Hilliard, A. (Eds.). (2003). *Young, gifted and Black: Promoting high achievement among African-American students.* Boston: Beacon.

Pittman, K., Irby, M., & Ferber, T. (1999). *Unfinished business: Further reflections on a decade of promoting youth.* Baltimore, MD: International Youth Foundation.

Pittman, K., & Wright, M. (1991). *Bridging the gap: A rationale for enhancing the role of community organizations in promoting youth development* (Commissioned Paper #1 for the Task Force on Youth Development and Community Programs at the Carnegie Council on Adolescent Development). Washington, DC: Center for Youth Development and Policy Research.

Plaut, S. (Ed.). (2009). *The right to literacy in secondary schools: Creating a culture of thinking.* New York: Teachers College Press.

Pollock, M. (2004). *Colormute: Race talk dilemmas in an American school.* Princeton, NJ: Princeton University Press.

Quartz, K., Olsen, B., & Duncan-Andrade, J. (2003, October). *The fragility of urban teaching: A longitudinal study of career development and activism.* Retrieved November 2008 from http://www.ucla-idea.org.

Rich, J. (2009). *Wrong place, wrong time: Trauma & violence in the lives of young black men.* Baltimore, MD: Johns Hopkins University Press.

Ridgeway, J. (2009, March 13). 36 years of solitude. *Mother Jones.* Retrieved on August 26, 2010, from http://motherjones.com/politics/2009/03/36-years-solitude.

Riessman, C. (2002). Analysis of personal narratives. In J. F. Gubrium & J. A. Holstein (Eds.), *Handbook of interview research* (pp. 695–710). Thousand Oaks, CA: Sage.

Rios, V. (2011). *Punished: Policing the lives of Black and Latino boys.* New York: New York University Press.

Rist, R. (1970) Student social class and teacher expectations: The self-fulfilling prophecy in ghetto education. *Harvard Educational Review, 40*(3), 411–451.

Roach, C., Yu, H., & Lewis-Charp, H. (2001, July/August). Race, poverty, and youth development. *Poverty & Race, 10*(4), 3–6.

Rosenthal, R., & Jacobson, L. (1968). *Pygmalion in the classroom.* New York: Holt, Rinehart & Winston.

Ross, A. and Rose, T. (Eds.). (1994). *Microphone fiends: Youth music and youth culture.* New York: Routledge.

Salonga, R. (2010, December 30). Man killed on Sycamore marks 15th homicide for year. *Contra Costa Times.* Retrieved January 2011 from http://www.antiochpoa.com/news/2010/12/30/man-killed-on-sycamore-marks-15th-homicide-for-year.html.

Scott, J. (1990). *Domination and the arts of resistance: Hidden transcripts.* New Haven, CT: Yale University Press.

Segarra, J., & Dobles, R. (Eds.). (1999). *Learning as a political act.* Cambridge, MA: Harvard Educational Review.

Seidman, I. E. (1998). *Interviewing as qualitative research: A guide for researchers in education and the social sciences*. New York: Teachers College Press.

Selassie, H. (1963, October 4). *Speech by the King of Ethiopia*. New York: United Nations.

Shor, I. (1992). *Empowering education: Critical teaching for social change*. Chicago: University of Chicago Press.

Shor, I., & Freire, P. (1987). *A pedagogy for liberation: Dialogues on transforming education*. Westport, CT: Bergin & Garvey.

Sizer, T. (1984). *Horace's compromise*. Boston: Houghton Mifflin.

Skinner, E. A., Garreton, M. T., & Schultz, B. D. (Eds.). (2011). *Grow your own teachers: Grassroots change for teacher education*. New York: Teachers College Press.

Smitherman, G. (2000). *Talkin that talk: Language, culture and education in African America*. London: Routledge.

Steinhauer, J. (2007, April 27) California to address prison overcrowding with giant building program. *New York Times*. Retrieved January 2011 from http://www.nytimes.com/2007/04/27/us/27prisons.html.

Stigler, J. W., & Hiebert, J. (1999). *The teaching gap: Best practices from the world's teachers for improving education in the classroom*. New York: Free Press.

Stoecker, R. (2009). Are we talking the walk of community-based research? *Action Research, 7*(4), 385–404.

Strauss, A. L. (1987). *Qualitative analysis for social scientists*. Cambridge: Cambridge University Press.

Strauss, A., & Corbin, J. (1998). *Basics of qualitative research: Techniques and procedures for developing grounded theory*. New York: Basic Books.

Sudbury, J., & Okazawa-Rey, M. (Eds.). (2008). *Activist scholarship: Antiracism, feminism, & social change*. Boulder, CO: Paradigm Publishers.

Swalwell, K., & Apple, M. W. (2011). Starting the wrong conversations: The public school crisis and "waiting for superman." *Educational Policy, 25*(2) 368–382.

Tucker, J. (2007, August 26). Children who survive urban warfare suffer from PTSD, too. *San Francisco Gate*. Retrieved February 2011 from http://articles.sfgate.com/2007-08-26/news/17256954_1_ptsd-war-zone-post-traumatic-stress-disorder.

Tuckman, B. (1999). *Conducting educational research* (5th edn.). Philadelphia, PA: Harcourt Brace College.

Tyack, D., & Hansot, E. (1992). *Learning together: A history of coeduction in American public schools*. New York: Russell Sage Foundation.

Vigil, J. D. (1997). Learning from gangs: The Mexican American experience. *ERIC Digest*, no. RC020943.

Violence Policy Center (2011, January). *Lost youth: A county-by-county analysis of 2009 California homicide victims ages 10 to 24*. Retrieved February 2011 from http://www.vpc.org/studies/cayouth.pdf.

Wacquant, L. (2001). The penalization of poverty and the rise of neo-liberalism. *European Journal of Criminal Policy and Research, 9*(4), 401–412.

Wacquant, L. (2008). The place of the prison in the new government of poverty. In M. L. Frampton, I. Haney Lopez, & J. Simon (Eds.), *After the war on crime: Race, democracy and a new reconstruction* (pp. 23–36). New York: New York University Press.

Warren, M. (2005). Communities and schools: A new view of urban education reform. *Harvard Educational Review, 75*(2), 133–173.

Warren, M. (2010). *Fire in the heart: How white activists embrace racial justice*. New York: Oxford University Press.

Watson, V. (2004). *It's bigger than hip-hop: Rappers educating educators about the purpose of school*. Qualifying paper, Harvard University Graduate School of Education, Cambridge, MA.

Weiner, L. (1999). *Urban teaching: The essentials*. New York: Teachers College Press.

Weiner, L. (2000). Research in the 90s: Implications for urban teacher preparation. *Review of Educational Research, 70(3)*, 369–406.

Weiner, L. (2006). *Urban teaching: The essentials*. New York: Teachers College Press.

Weis, L., & Fine, M. (Eds.). (1993). *Beyond silenced voices: Class, race, and gender in United States schools*. Albany, NY: SUNY Press.

Welsing, F. C. (1991). *The Isis papers: The keys to the colors*. Washington, DC: C.W. Publishing.

West, C. (1993). *Race matters*. Boston: Beacon Press.

Whyte, W. F. (1943). *Street corner society*. Chicago: University of Chicago Press.

Willis, P. (1977). *Learning to labor: How working class kids get working class jobs*. New York: Columbia University Press.

Wilson, D. (2008). *Family Valued*. Magazine of the Harvard Graduate School of Education, 51(2). Retrieved March 2008 from http://www.gse.harvard.edu/news_events/ed/2008/winter/features/family.html.

Winn, M. (2011). *Girl time: Literacy, justice, & the school-to-prison pipeline*. New York: Teachers College Press.

Winn, M. T., & Behizadeh, N. (2011, March). The right to be literate: Literacy, education, and the school-to-prison pipeline. *Review of Research in Education, 35*, 147–173.

Wolk, S. (1998). *A democratic classroom*. Portsmouth, NH: Heinemann Press.

Woodson, C. G. (1933). *The mis-education of the negro*. Trenton, NJ: Africa World Press.

Wortham, S. (Ed.). (2011, March). Youth cultures, language, and literacy. *Review of Research in Education, 35*, 1–243.

Yeo, F. (1997, June). Teacher preparation and inner-city schools: Sustaining educational failure. *Urban Review, 29(2)*, 127–143.

Zinn, H. (1995). *A people's history of the United States 1492–present*. New York: Harper Perennial.

INDEX